WITHDRAWN
UTSA LIBRARIES

The Liberalism-Communitarianism Debate

RENEWALS 458-4574
DATE DUE

Studies in Social and Political Philosophy
General Editor: James P. Sterba, University of Notre Dame

Social Contract Theories: Political Obligation or Anarchy?
by Vicente Medina, Seton Hall University

Collective Responsibility: Five Decades of Debate in Theoretical and Applied Ethics
edited by Larry May and Stacey Hoffman, Purdue University

Original Intent and the Constitution: A Philosophical Study
by Gregory Bassham, King's College

Patriotism, Morality, and Peace
by Stephen Nathanson, Northeastern University

The Liberalism-Communitarianism Debate
edited by C. F. Delaney, University of Notre Dame

On the Eve of the 21st Century: Perspectives of Russian and American Philosophers
edited by William C. Gay, University of North Carolina at Charlotte, and T. A. Alekseeva, Russian Academy of Sciences

Democracy and Social Injustice
by Thomas Simon, Illinois State University

Marx and Modern Political Theory
by Philip J. Kain, Santa Clara University

An Environmental Proposal for Ethics: The Principle of Integrity
by Laura Westra, University of Windsor

Critical Legal Theory and the Challenge of Feminism: A Philosophical Rewriting
by Matthew H. Kramer

Morality and Social Justice
by James P. Sterba, University of Notre Dame; Tibor Machan, Auburn University; Alison Jaggar, University of Colorado, Boulder; William Galston, White House Office of Domestic Affairs; Carol C. Gould, Stevens Institute of Technology; and Milton Fisk, Indiana University

The Liberalism-Communitarianism Debate

Liberty and Community Values

C. F. Delaney, Editor

Rowman & Littlefield Publishers, Inc.

ROWMAN & LITTLEFIELD PUBLISHERS, INC.

Published in the United States of America
by Rowman & Littlefield Publishers, Inc.
4720 Boston Way, Lanham, Maryland 20706
3 Henrietta Street
London, WC2E 8LU, England

Copyright © 1994 by Rowman & Littlefield Publishers, Inc.

All rights reserved. No part of this publication may be
reproduced, stored in a retrieval system, or transmitted
in any form or by any means, electronic, mechanical,
photocopying, recording, or otherwise, without the prior
permission of the publisher.

British Cataloging in Publication Information Available

Library of Congress Cataloging-in-Publication Data

The Liberalism-communitarianism debate / edited by C. F. Delaney.
p. cm.
1. Liberalism. 2. Community. I. Delaney, C. F. (Cornelius F.).
HM276.L4643   1994   320.5'1—dc20   93-573   CIP

ISBN 0-8476-7863-6 (cloth : alk. paper)
ISBN 0-8476-7864-4 (paper : alk. paper)

Printed in the United States of America

∞™ The paper used in this publication meets the minimum requirements of
American National Standard for Information Sciences—Permanence of
Paper for Printed Library Materials, ANSI Z39.48–1984.

Contents

Introduction		vii
1	The Privatization of Good: An Inaugural Lecture *Alasdair MacIntyre*	1
2	Liberalism and Its Critics *Jeffrey Reiman*	19
3	Moral Pluralism, Disintegration, and Liberalism *Richard F. Galvin*	39
4	Romantic Communitarianism: Blithedale Romance Versus the Custom House *Nancy Rosenblum*	57
5	Some Comparisons between Liberalism and an Eccentric Communitarianism *Thomas Moody*	91
6	The Theoretical Marginalization of the Disadvantaged: A Liberal/Communitarian Failing *Thomas W. Simon*	103
7	Rawlsian Constructivism: A Version of Liberalism *C. F. Delaney*	137

8	Should Political Philosophy Be Done Without Metaphysics? *Jean Hampton*	151
9	Liberalism and the Political Character of Political Philosophy *Paul Weithman*	189
10	A Hobbesian Foundation for Welfare Rights *Sheldon Wein*	213
11	Liberalism and a Non-Question-Begging Conception of the Good *James P. Sterba*	227
Index		245
About the Contributors		249

Introduction

C. F. Delaney

In recent years the central debate in political philosophy has been that between the liberals and the communitarians. Although admittedly these labels mask important differences, they focus attention on significant commonalities or family resemblances that can helpfully distinguish one general perspective from the other. John Rawls, Robert Nozick, and Ronald Dworkin share certain basic commitments that divide them from Alasdair MacIntyre, Charles Taylor, and Michael Sandel; and a substantial subset of these commitments on both sides can be collected under these labels.

An emphasis on the values of equality, freedom, and toleration, and a genuine openness to different models of human fulfillment characterize members of the liberal camp. These concepts undergo different modulations at the hands of individual liberal theorists, but the most fundamental division among liberals is between the utilitarians who try to defend these values instrumentally and the rights-theorists who construe them as fundamental. It is this intramural debate that was on center stage in political philosophy, but in the wake of John Rawls's *A Theory of Justice*, the battle has clearly tilted in favor of the rights-theorists. Their project has been to develop an account of individual rights that is not parasitic on any particular substantive vision of the human good but rather circumscribes a sphere of self-determination—and in some cases the necessary conditions for that self-determination—in a genuinely pluralistic society.

The new challenge to the liberal perspective comes from a tradition that does maintain that there is a single model of human fulfillment and puts considerable emphasis on shared values of community and civic virtue that it claims the liberal perspective can't underwrite.

The label "communitarianism" has come to designate this general tradition, notwithstanding the fact that some members of its pantheon resist this designation. Communitarians reject the individualism (particularly with regard to the account of the human good) that they see at the heart of the liberal tradition, arguing the case that only a theory of society that puts common goods on center stage can provide a justification or explanation of a coherent and viable social order.

Communitarians divide over the issue of the nature and extent of any society for which this kind of genuine social union is even an ideal possibility. Many think in terms of a total society whose structure is modified so that the political order embodies shared values, but there is also the more modest aspiration for a political arrangement that would foster within it small subgroups in which the goods of genuine community could be realized. This divide hinges on differing assessments of the possibilities of general political structures and the relevance of scale. The more modest regional "communitarian" aspiration can be motivated either by the belief that no modern political structure can sustain the kind of life envisioned or by the belief that matters of scale are of overriding importance. It may well be the case that the kind of community envisioned would require a level of personal communication and interaction that can extend only so far.

This characterization of the liberal-communitarian debate in terms of a sharp divide between individualism and shared values is an oversimplification of the issues actually under discussion. Each side surely accords in its view some status to the values on center stage in the other view. Liberals clearly acknowledge that some common commitments and common values are necessary for a viable society, while communitarians provide space for genuine individuality within their conception of a cohesive social order. Specifically, liberals urge a common commitment to a framework of acknowledged rights and obligations, and to the support of institutions that will foster the development of the corresponding liberal virtues. Communitarians, for their part, certainly don't have in mind a completely monolithic society where everyone has the same commitments, values, and interests all the way down. For them, there is room for a dimension of individuality within a society informed by a common conception of the good. But even given this overlay, the differences between the perspectives are deep and pervasive.

Both sides agree that human beings are intrinsically social and need the mutual supplementation and interdependencies of the social order for their genuine fulfillment. This commonly acknowledged sociality ranges all the way from the division of labor to the accomplishments of high culture, with the public and social character of language and significant action as the universal bonding agents. It is with regard to their respective visions of the *kind* of social union optimal for genuine human fulfillment that the two perspectives divide. Liberals, given their recognition of plural models of human fulfillment, underscore the value of autonomy and argue for a social union sufficiently open to allow the development of these various models and thus for a structure that provides the necessary conditions for this diverse development. In the liberal view of the social order, the right is prior to the good. This allows only for what might be called a "shallow community" since the common commitments do not permeate to the level of the total good. The communitarians, on the other hand, think that a "deep community"—that is, one informed by a common conception of the human good—is necessary for real human fulfillment. The intrinsically social character of humans cannot be realized in a fragmented society that does not institutionally manifest and foster the unique ideals of human fulfillment. Many of the dimensions of this deeper debate between the liberals and the communitarians are explored in the papers in this volume.

The first cluster of papers begins with Alasdair MacIntyre's critique of any liberal attempt to found rationally a system of moral rules independent of a rationally justified conception of the human good. This paper is followed by a series of papers directly on the debate: Reiman's and Galvin's defenses of liberalism, Rosenblum's and Moody's articulation of different kinds of communitarianism, and Simon's critique of both perspectives. The next cluster of papers deals specifically with the Rawlsian project as a version of liberalism with those of Delaney and Weithman elaborating and extending the project and that of Hampton criticizing it. The final two papers attempt to transcend features of the stalemate either by attempting nonliberal arguments for key liberal tenets (Wein) or by articulating a conception of the good on which liberals and communitarians can agree (Sterba). Sterba's concluding paper specifically addresses issues raised by MacIntyre in the first paper in the collection.

Most of the papers in this collection are previously unpublished and some of them are developed versions of papers delivered at the meeting of the Sixth International Social Philosophy Conference held at the University of Vermont. "The Privatization of Good" by Alasdair MacIntyre originally appeared in *The Review of Politics*, and is reprinted here with the permission of the publisher and the author. "Should Political Philosophy Be Done Without Metaphysics?" by Jean Hampton originally appeared in *Ethics*, and is reprinted here with the permission of The University of Chicago Press and the author. "Liberalism and Its Critics" by Jeffrey Reiman and an earlier version of "Some Comparisons between Liberalism and Eccentric Communitarianism" by Thomas Moody originally appeared in *Communitarianism, Liberalism, and Social Responsibility*, C. Peden and Y. Hudson (eds.) (Lewiston, N.Y.: The Edwin Mellen Press, 1992).

1

The Privatization of Good: An Inaugural Lecture

Alasdair MacIntyre

When in 1879 in the encyclical *Aeterni Patris* Leo XIII contrasted the moral and political philosophy of Thomas Aquinas with that of the secular liberalism of the late nineteenth century, he directed our attention to an area of conflict whose importance has not diminished in the succeeding century. Nowhere is this conflict more evident or persistent than in the radical disagreement between Aquinas and the moral philosophy of modern liberalism over the question of the relationship between how the human good is to be conceived and achieved and how those rules, obedience to which is required for morally right action, are to be formulated, understood, and justified.

For Aquinas, as for Aristotle, we can only understand the right in the light afforded by the good. The good for the members of each species is that end to which, *qua* members of that species, those members move in achieving their specific perfection. The rules for right action for rational animals are those rules intentional conformity to which is required if their specific perfection is to be achieved. The content of those rules, their exceptionless character, and their authority all derive from the end that obedience to them serves. But they are not to be understood as specifying types of actions the performance of which as a matter of merely contingent fact will bring about some particular type of end-state. They are not specifications of means *ex*-

---

Presented here is Alasdair MacIntyre's inaugural lecture as the McMahon-Hank Professor of Philosophy at the University of Notre Dame. It appeared in *The Review of Politics*, 42, no. 3 (Summer 1990); 344–61.

ternally related to an end. They are rather rules partially constitutive of a form of life, the living out of which is the peculiar function of human beings as rational animals, and the completion of which lies in that activity which is itself supreme happiness and which makes of the life of which it is the completion a happy life. So to disobey such rules in any way and to any degree is in that way and to that degree to separate oneself from one's good. And, insofar as anyone lacks knowledge of his or her true good, such a person is also deprived of the only sound reasons for right action.

This is not, of course, to imply that, either for Aristotle or for Aquinas, human beings do or are able to begin with a full-fledged knowledge of the good and from it deduce the rules of right action. Each of us learns how to articulate his or her own initial inner capacity for comprehending what the good is in the course of also learning from others about rules and about virtues, so that, through a dialectical process of questioning the ways in which rules, virtues, goods, and *the* good are interrelated, we gradually come to understand the unity of the deductive structures of practical reasoning. But what we thus come to understand is in part that, to the extent that what we take to be the case about the human good is false or confused, to that extent our understanding of the rules defining right action will also be apt to be false and confused and that, to the extent to which we ignore or put out of mind or otherwise fail to take account of the distinctive character of the human good, to that extent we shall be unable to provide an adequately determinate or authoritative formulation of those same rules. Adequate knowledge of moral rules is inseparable from and cannot be had without genuine knowledge of human good.

It follows that on any substantively Aristotelian or Thomistic view rational agreement on moral rules always presupposes rational agreement on the nature of the human good. Any political society, therefore, that possesses a shared stock of adequately determinate and rationally defensible moral rules, publicly recognized to be the rules to which characteristically and generally unproblematic appeals may be made, will, therefore, implicitly or explicitly, be committed to an adequately determinate and rationally justifiable conception of the human good. And insofar as the rational justification of particular moral stances is a feature of its public life, that conception will have had to be made explicit in a way and to a degree that will render general allegiance to that particular conception itself a matter of public concern.

This is not, of course, how things are in the contemporary advanced societies of Western modernity. What shared moral rules there are—and later I shall need to enquire how far there are in fact shared moral rules in such societies—are and cannot but be invoked and upheld independent of any corresponding shared conception of *the* human good. For as to the nature of the human good, as to whether there is indeed any such thing as the human good, disagreements are numerous and fundamental. This socially embodied divorce between rules defining right action on the one hand and conceptions of the human good on the other is one of those aspects of such societies in virtue of which they are entitled to be called liberal. For it is a central tenet of recent liberal moral and political theory that public institutions and more especially the institutions of government should be systematically neutral as between rival conceptions of what the human good is. Allegiance to any particular conception of human good ought, on this liberal view, to be a matter of private individual preference and choice, and it is contrary to rationality to require of anyone that he or she should agree with anyone else in giving his or her allegiance to some particular view.

In this respect, the status of conceptions of the human good is very different from that of moral rules. Moral rules, in this modern liberal view, prescribe those actions and those refrainings from action that any rational person may require of any other. About them, about their content, about their binding force, and presumably about the appropriate ways of responding to their breach, agreement among rational persons is therefore required. The type of agreement required about moral rules by liberals and the type of disagreement permitted and expected by those same liberals about conceptions of the good can both be characterized in terms of one and the same understanding of the relationship of freedom to reason. The autonomy of a free and rational individual, according to liberalism, is not infringed by, but requires that individual to assent to the deliverances of reason, where these are unequivocal; and so it is with assent to moral rules. But where the state of the argument is such that there are alternative and incompatible views on some matter, and rational argument currently does not, and provides no prospect of being able to, provide unequivocal support for only one set of conclusions out of those that are in contention, the autonomy of a free and rational individual can be exercised in embracing any one of the contending views. It is in the light of this contrast that concerns about elaborating, defending, and living out particular conceptions of the good are, in this type of liberal view, to be assigned to and restricted to the sphere of the private life of individuals, while concerns about obedience to what are taken to be the moral rules required of every rational person can be legitimately pursued in the public realm. So appeals to particular moral rules always provide *relevant*, although not necessarily *sufficient* grounds for advocating legislation of various kinds, while appeals to particular conceptions of the human good never do. Insofar as it is this liberal view that has been embodied in social practice in contemporary advanced societies, the good has been privatized.

There are, of course, important differences between liberal theorists in the ways in which they articulate their positions, but there is also a remarkable degree of concurrence. So Virginia Held, who expresses the contrast between the right and the good in terms of principles defining rights, asserts that, "We can agree that persons' conceptions of the good will diverge and that, although not all such conceptions will be equally admirable, persons can legitimately pursue a pluralism of admirable goals. But their recognition of principles of freedom, justice, and equality yielding a system of rights for human beings is not a matter of preference, or choice between goods. . . . That all persons ought as moral beings to adhere to principles assuring respect for rights can be asserted and defended" (*Rights and Goals* [Chicago: University of Chicago Press, 1984], 19).

Ronald Dworkin had earlier identified a distinctively liberal theory of equality as one that "supposes that political decisions must be, so far as is possible, independent of any particular conception of the good life, or of what gives value to life. Since the citizens of a society differ in their conceptions, the government does not treat them as equals if it prefers one conception to another, either because the officials believe that one is intrinsically superior, or because one is held by the more numerous or more powerful group" ("Liberalism," in *Public and Private Morality*, ed. S. Hampshire [Cambridge: Cambridge University Press, 1978], 127). And John Rawls had already gone further than either Held or Dworkin in contending not only that "agreement upon the principles of rational choice" is presupposed in arriving at principles of justice, while in the case of planning one's life in the light of some conception of the good "unanimity concerning the standards of rationality is not required," since "each person is free to plan his life as he pleases (so long as his intentions are consistent with the principles of justice)," but also that "variety in conceptions of the good is itself a good thing" (*A Theory of Justice* [Cambridge: Harvard University Press, 1971], 447–48).

Notice that for liberalism understood in this way everything turns on two contentions: first, that in the debate between particular rival and alternative conceptions of the human good, not only has none established a claim to decisive rational superiority over its rivals, but that it should not even be a matter of public, as against private interest how we ought to proceed in evaluating the rational merits of rival claims in this area; and second that rational agreement on moral rules can be—and indeed, given the liberal case, must already have been—somehow or other assured in a way that deserves to secure the consent and compliance of all rational persons, and that this agreement is available or can be made available as a key point of reference in public debate and decision-making. It is with this last claim that I am going to be first of all concerned in this lecture, for it is a claim that we have the strongest of reasons to doubt.

It is not that we do not have a variety of recommended methods for arriving at rational agreement of the kind required. It is rather that we have all too many such methods, each of them incompatible in important ways with some of the others, not only in the type of argument proposed as appropriate for settling disputes about the nature and content of moral rules, but also in the substantive conclusions arrived at about the nature and content of such rules. So we have a range of types of Kantianism, a similar range of types of utilitarianism, and of intuitionism, contractarianism, and various blends of these. And since each of these rival and competing views claims to supply the *ultimate* principles by which disputed questions in this area are to be adjudicated, we lack any further rational court of appeal, whose verdicts might settle such questions. Radical and *de facto* ineliminable disagreement confronts us.

Moreover, what these various types of philosophical theory mirror are just the types of reasoning upon which ordinary nonphilosophical reflective persons in our culture rely in their moral reasoning. Universalizability arguments, utilitarian attention to consequences, intuitionist appeals to not further to be argued for principles of duty and invocations of contractarian thoughts are as much part of the common currency of everyday practical argument as they are of the academic study of moral philosophy. So that we should expect to find the same range of disagreements at the level of everyday morality. But recently Jeffrey Stout has argued that this is in fact not the case, that disagreements do, of course, occur on some major issues, but that we have a stock of agreements embodied in what Stout calls "moral platitudes," learned as children in the nursery (*Ethics After Babel* [Boston: Beacon Press, 1988], 211). Disagreements presuppose a background of agreement, for "we are initiated into a moral consensus as very young children" (43). Such differences as there may be in modes of reasoning do not, at least on many fundamental topics, issue in significant differences in moral conclusions.

Against Stout, I want to suggest that he is indeed right in thinking that there is a consensus of platitudes in our moral culture, but that this belongs to the rhetorical surface of that culture, and not to its substance. The rhetoric of shared values is of great ideological importance, but it disguises the truth about how action is guided and directed. For what we genuinely share in the way of moral maxims, precepts, and principles is insufficiently determinate to guide action and what is sufficiently determinate to guide action is not shared. And this, after all, is what we might expect, if it were the case *both* that the variety and heterogeneity of the types of moral reasoning recognized among us issued in as wide a range of disparate normative conclusions in everyday practical life as it does in the realm of moral theory *and* that a refusal, or perhaps a failure, to allow that this is so, was a prerequisite for the effective functioning of our central political, legal, and educational institutions. I take as a test case for deciding the issue between Stout and myself, not those much debated issues such as the wrongness of abortion or the nature of a just war (by focusing on which, so Stout claims, I have in the past exaggerated the degree of conflict in our culture), but the subject matter of one of the maxims—platitudes in Stout's idiom—which constitute the moral consensus into which children are initiated, the matter of truth-telling and lying.

What is the shared maxim, so far as there is one, by which children are instructed in this area by parents, teachers, and other authoritative adults? It runs as follows: "Never tell a lie" (this first part is uttered loudly and firmly) "except when" (and here the adult voice tends to drop) and there then follows a list of exceptions of varying types ending with an "etc." We all agree on the maxim; where we disagree is first of all upon which types of exception are to be included in the appended list. Is it permissible to lie when the utterance of the truth will be discourteous? Is it permissible or perhaps obligatory to lie when an innocent human life is immediately at stake? Is it permissible to lie when a lie just *might* contribute to the future saving of such a life? Is it permissible to lie to save face? Is it permissible or even obligatory to lie to help a friend out of a difficulty? If I am, in fact, the best candidate for a job, but I will only get it if I lie, may I lie? If it will serve the national interest or if some highly placed official says that it will serve the national interest, ought I to lie? If it furthers the cause of the National Rifle Association, the

ACLU, or the Girl Scouts, should I lie? If doing my job as a journalist, a private detective, or an investigator of insurance claims involves lying, should I change my employment?

There is no socially established agreement on the answers to these questions. And both between and within different influential moral and religious traditions, Catholic, Protestant, Jewish, and secular, rival and conflicting answers are defended. But our disagreements are not confined to the question of which types of lie, if any, are permissible. For even when it is agreed by some large number of persons that a particular type of lie is impermissible, there will still be extensive disagreements as to how serious an offense it is to tell that type of lie. We disagree as to how to rank order offenses against truth-telling in terms of their gravity. But even this is not all. For we also disagree about how lies, when exposed as such, ought to be responded to by the exposed liar, by those who have been lied to, and by members of the society at large. Is it guilt or shame that the offender should feel if exposed in various types of lie, and to what degree, and what kind of subsequent conduct is to be required of the guilty or the ashamed? When, if ever, is the liar to be punished or, if not punished, reproached or shunned and by whom and for how long? From membership in what bodies should proven liars be excluded? Once again we have range of questions to which different and incompatible answers are given.

Nor is it the case that different individuals each give one clear and consistent set of answers to each of these questions, albeit disagreeing with other individuals. To some significant, even if unmeasured extent, these disagreements seem to occur within individuals, one and the same individual hovering between two or more rival opinions, inclining to one on some occasions and in some contexts, to another on others. Only thus can the inconsistency and instability of our shared public responses to lying be made fully intelligible. For what is apparently one and the same type of lie will, among the same groups of people or in the same political institution, be treated as a grave offense on some occasions, as a minor offense upon others, and upon yet others be simply ignored. In our public and political life, there are strange oscillations between wild outbursts of self-righteous indignation on the one hand and complacent silences on the other. We do know from empirical psychological research that lying is endemic in the population at large: Bella de Paulo, a psychologist at the University of Virginia, who studies lying by having her experimental subjects keep a diary of the lies they tell, has concluded that "People tell about two lies a day, or at least that is how many they will admit to"

(*New York Times*, February 12, 1985, 17). And the indeterminacy of our shared public maxims and the unpredictability of our public responses about truth-telling point to widespread uncertainties about both our own behavior and that of others.

There have been in the past and there are now rival and contending moral traditions about what a strict determinate rule about truth-telling and lying should in fact be. But these disagreements were and are rooted in more fundamental disagreements about the place and purpose of speech and writing within the kind of life that it is best for human beings to lead. The determinate character of such rules in each case arises from their relationship to and their implementation of some particular determinate conception of the good and the best. And whatever rational authority each may possess, that in virtue of which rational persons ought to treat it as binding is derived from whatever rational authority that particular conception of human good may possess.

As against Stout, therefore, and indeed against contemporary liberal theory in general, I initially conclude that a necessary precondition for a political community's possession of adequately determinate shared rationally founded moral rules is the shared possession of a rationally justifiable conception of human good. And that insofar as appeals to moral rules are to play a part in the public life of such a community, respect for and allegiance to that shared conception of the human good will have had to be institutionalized in the life of that community. On this issue, then, a Thomistic Aristotelianism is so far vindicated. Notice that it is in an important way a specifically Thomistic Aristotelianism that is thus vindicated. In what way becomes clear when we consider a rival attempt to render Aristotle's ethics of virtue relevant to the debates of contemporary moral philosophy, one undertaken in different versions by a number of thinkers who agree in recognizing the superiority of Aristotelianism to Kantianism and utilitarianism, but who aspire to do this in a way compatible with a modern liberal allegiance. It is this latter that leads them to substitute for the single and unitary, if complex, final good conceived by Aristotle, a multiplicity of goods, each *qua* good worthy of being pursued, and each, at least in certain circumstances and perhaps as such, incommensurable with the others. Which good or set of good any particular individual pursues is to be determined by that particular individual's preferences. And the choice of any one such good or set of goods will characteristically exclude the choice of certain others.

When Aristotle is thus emended, however, practical reasoning, as understood by Aristotle, ceases to yield unambiguous directives for action. For the first premise of such reasoning—often of course left tacit—is, as Aristotle remarks, of the form "Since the *telos* and the best is such and such" (*Nicomachean Ethics* vi, 1144a32–33), and where there are alternative and competing goods, each of which may equally be treated as the *telos* and the best, there will also, in particular situations, be alternative and competing practical syllogisms with alternative and competing courses of action as their conclusions. So it will be equally rational to act in any one out of a number of different and incompatible ways, and nonrational preference will have become sovereign in decision-making.

It is not then surprising that, while Aristotle found no need to discuss practical dilemmas, this kind of would-be Aristotelian characteristically finds them of notable importance in the moral life, for practical rationality thus reconceived renders systematically indeterminate what is required of us in just too many types of situation. So that if this were indeed a faithful rendering of Aristotle, Aristotelianism would afford us no resources with which to challenge the indeterminacy of public shared moral rules in contemporary culture. It is only Aristotelianism understood as specifying in adequate outline a single and unitary, albeit complex, conception of the human good, Aristotelianism, that is, understood very much as Thomists have understood it, which is capable of challenging effectively the privatization of conceptions of the good, their exclusion from the public realm, that privatization which precludes the possession of an adequately determinate, rationally justifiable morality. But this is not all that it precludes.

For there are certain issues of the moral life that cannot get raised at all in any adequately systematic way in the public realm, if appeal to conceptions of the overall human good is excluded from that realm. Consider two areas of concern often considered separately in our society: on the one hand, the horrifying infant mortality rate in the United States, one that comes close in some parts of the country to ranking it with Third World rather than other advanced countries, and on the other, the condemnation of the old in our society to boredom, nursing homes, and Alzheimer's disease. What these together represent is a distribution of resources, such that more and more has been directed to the mindless extension of the length of human life by medical science into a more and more mindless old age, while the unborn and the very young have continued to be radically deprived. And this maldistribution of resources represents an answer to a set of questions that have not yet been systematically asked, let alone answered.

Aristotle makes it clear that what the living out of the best life for human beings requires of us is not the same at every period of life; and in specifying what participation in which activities is required at each stage in the movement from early childhood to old age—in an Aristotelian view each age has its tasks and functions, including old age; no period of life is functionless—and in what the relationship between older and younger is at each stage, one would have had to have made considerable progress in specifying what the best life for human beings is. Conversely, without some determinate conception of the good and the best, it would be impossible to provide adequate answers to these questions. So answering questions in any systematic way, which could be implemented in practice, concerning the overall relationships of the very young, the adolescent, the working adult, and the old within families, parishes, schools, clinics, workplaces, and local neighborhood communities, so that we can agree in recognizing what the old owe to the young and the young to the old, is a task inseparable from that of formulating a conception of the good and the best. And when that task is one excluded from the public realm, then it will become impossible to ask and answer such questions, let alone questions about a just distribution of resources between the young and the old. The privatization of the good thus ensures not only that we are deprived of adequately determinate shared moral rules, but that central areas of moral concern cannot become the subject of anything like adequate public shared systematic discourse or enquiry.

Morality is thereby diminished in scope. And hence in part derives the sterility of much public debate, on issues that *are* admitted to the public realm, such as that of abortion. For what one holds rationally about abortion is inseparable from what one holds about the point and purpose of family life, about the place of the conception and upbringing of children in that life, and about the relationship of family ties to other social ties. To abstract the issue of abortion from these contexts is necessarily to obscure what is at issue. Moral questions treated one by one piecemeal in isolation from larger contexts of argument and of practice always begin to appear rationally unanswerable; and since, when morality is defined independent of the good, the relationships between different moral rules disappear from view, one result is that moral questions tend to be presented as a grab bag of separable, isolable, and so insoluble problems.

So we confront a situation in which there is great danger and great difficulty. The danger arises from our inhabiting a political and economic system in which a rhetoric of moral consensus masks fundamental dissensus and moral impoverishment. The difficulty arises from the fact that a standard liberal retort to the arguments that I have advanced is at first inspection highly plausible. It runs as follows:

Even if it were the case that the absence of a shared conception of the human good both rendered our shared moral rules indeterminate and impoverished the definition of our moral concerns, we could not find a remedy in the adoption of such a shared conception, for in our culture, radical disagreement about the nature of the good does seem to be ineliminable among rational persons. We need do no more than point to the range and diversity and incompatibility of widely held rival and conflicting conceptions of the good for this to be evident. But what ought we to conclude from this range and diversity and incompatibility? Is it the case that there has been somewhere or other in our past history a prolonged and systematic rational debate, whose procedures were fair and impartial, between such conceptions, whose outcome was a failure on the part of each contending party to defeat its rivals, so that by the best that which the resources of rationality can afford radical disagreement and conflict has indeed proved ineliminable? The answer to this question is "No." It is a piece of false mythology to suppose that our fundamental disagreements have either emerged from or been tested by prolonged rational debate. Even such debate as has occurred has been defective in at least three ways.

First, what has in fact taken place over the past two hundred years has been at best a series of particular and intermittent engagements of relatively sporadic and unsustained kinds in particular, local issues and problems practical or theoretical. There have been few occasions, perhaps none, in which one point of view, presenting itself systematically and as a whole, has been able to engage with its major rivals, also presented systematically and as a whole. And it is easy to understand why this should be so. The genres of debate, the institutionalizations of the expression of disagreement, either restrict it to the piecemeal treatment of isoluble issues in the more serious academic journals or to relatively brief and rhetorically insinuating treatments in other media.

Second, liberalism has played two roles in the modern world. It has been and is one of the contending parties with respect to theories of the good. But it has also by and large controlled the terms of both public and academic debate. Other points of view have generally been invited to debate with liberalism only within a framework of procedures whose presuppositions were already liberal. But, important as these two points are, they are much less crucial than a third.

Fundamental disagreement over the nature of the good is not only a matter of theoretical contention, but also and essentially of practice. It is rival conceptions of practical rationality, of the relationship of human beings to the good in their actions, of the practically embodied rules and virtues that are specific to each rival conception of the good, which are in contention. And practical claims cannot be made in exclusively theoretical ways. Certainly, the theory of practice is important, but only as in key part arising reflectively from, throwing light upon, and being vindicated or failing to be vindicated by the practice of which it is the theory. Hence, there can be no genuine abstract, merely theoretical debate between rival conceptions of the good. Such conceptions only confront one another in any decisive way, when presented within the embodied life of particular communities that exemplify each specific conception. It is in key part in the lives of families, parishes, schools, clinics, workplaces, and local neighborhood communities that any particular conception of the good achieves recognizable form.

So just as we only know what a particular conception of the good and the corresponding conceptions of virtues, intellectual and moral, and of rules really amount to when we encounter them to some significant degree embodied in the particularities of social life, so also genuine debate between rival conceptions only occurs when the actualities of one mode of social life, embodying one such conception, are matched against the actualities of its rivals. It is as it is concretely lived out that one fundamental standpoint is or is not vindicated against its rivals. And my earlier criticism of liberalism was expressed in a way that was designed to recognize this. My accusation was not or not only that liberal theory involves a fundamental indeterminateness in respect of moral rules and of impoverishment in respect of moral concerns; it was that as such theory is lived out in practice, this indeterminateness and this impoverishment are exemplified in social reality. And correlatively, if it is, as it is, a Thomistic contention that the Thomistic conception of human good can supply a more adequate determinateness in respect of rules and a more adequate specification of moral concerns, that contention too can be vindicated only insofar as it can be translated into the actualities of social life.

To say this, is not of course to deny that any particular social embodiment of any particular standpoint about the goods, virtues, and rules is always a more or less imperfect embodiment. But it is crucial to note that a central aspect of any such social embodiment is the institutionalization of standard responses to rule-breaking, whether mild or flagrant, and to what are taken to be vices and errors about the good; indeed, without such responses there can be no adequate institutionalization of rule-observance or of the recognition of virtues or goods. So what would it be for us here now to give particularized social form to a Thomistic conception of the good and of those virtues the cultivation of which and those rules the observance of which are integral to the achievement of the good thus conceived? And how would that conception, when thus socially embodied, contrast with the actualities of recent liberalism? These are large questions and here I can only gesture toward them. But even such a gesture may be worthwhile. So let me focus attention on the same two issues that I identified as relevant to the critique of liberalism: truth-telling and lying, and the relationship of the young to the old.

Aquinas, like Augustine before him and Kant after him, but unlike John Chrysostom, Benjamin Constant, and John Stuart Mill, held that lying is unconditionally and exceptionlessly prohibited. Not all lies are equally grave offenses, but all lying defects from what is required of us by the virtue of justice. If I lie to someone else, I fail to give to him or to her what is his or her due as a rational being. And since rational beings can only achieve their good and the good in and through a variety of social relationships, familial and political, informed by friendship, it follows that I both injure those relationships and put in crucial danger my relationship to the good whenever I lie. The virtue of justice and the rules of truth-telling, which partly specify that virtue, are not, of course, means external to the end toward which rational beings move; they are partially constitutive of that end. So that, if and when I lie, it is not that I have been inefficient in my choice of means to achieve my good; it is rather that I have temporarily at least put my good and the good out of mind and renounced them. And if someone lies to me, they have thereby affronted me by denying my status as a rational being, and ought to be responded to accordingly. There is no room for indeterminateness here, either in action or in response.

It is not of course possible to observe justice in speech merely by refraining from lying. No moral rule, no particular precept of the natural law, can be adequately understood in isolation from other such precepts or from that good, movement toward the achievement of which gives to obedience to such rules their point and purpose. Hence, we always need to supply a good deal more than the statement of some particular rule itself supplies in order to understand that rule. What else is it then that we need to understand, if we are to make adequately intelligible the rule that prohibits lying, and to do so in such a way as to know how to institutionalize it in our practices?

Someone would certainly not have understood that rule adequately who supposed that, while we are required to speak and write truthfully, utterance in other respects can be allowed to be whatever we want it to be. It is to the place and purpose of utterance in human life as a whole that this rule is addressed. The ethics of conversation, as understood by Aquinas, is a complex matter and there are some important aspects of it with which I shall not be concerned here. Aquinas, for example, devotes no less than eight questions of the IIa–IIae of the *Summa* to types of use of language that sin against charity and justice, characteristically, uses informed by either malice or negligence. And it is of course, in Aquinas's view, the adding of malice to lying that makes of lying a mortal sin. Nonetheless, it is lying as such that is prohibited.

Moreover, Aquinas holds that the human good cannot be achieved without games, jokes, and dramatic entertainments—even inaugural lectures perhaps—and failure either to engage in these, or to be responsive to and appreciative of others so engaging, is both vicious and sinful. So an institutionalization of any Thomistic conception of the moral and political life will have to be one that provides both for negative responses to malice and for positive responses to wit and to laughter. And once again such wit and laughter and the responses to them will, as Aquinas notes explicitly, have to be truthful. But what gives to this continuous insistence upon truthfulness its point?

A concern for truth as a standard of rectitude in life, says Aquinas, following Jerome, is a constitutive part of all the virtues. And although truthfulness is a special virtue and an aspect of the virtue of justice (*Summa Theologiae* IIa–IIae 109, 2, 3), the detail of Aquinas's discussions makes it clear that all the virtues involve truthfulness as part of their exercise. For all the virtues, moral as well as intellectual, have to be developed throughout one's entire life, and this development requires a lifelong process of learning and imparting truths, learning in which reflection upon experience needs initially to be guided by teachers who enable one to learn from experience and so, later on in one's interactions with others, to contribute to their learning as well as to one's own, and in so doing to learn from them.

So mutual relationships of teaching and learning inform all well-ordered relationships, and consistent truthfulness is therefore an essential ingredient of all such relationships. There is an informative analogy between the high value that the modern scientific community sets on truthfulness within the community of scientific enquirers, a value expressed in the penalties imposed upon those who falsify data, and the value that, in a Thomistic view, is to be set on truthfulness within any human community. For, on a Thomistic view, every human community is a community of practical enquiry, the subject matter of whose enquiry consists of everything actually and potentially relevant to the relationship of the individuals who compose it and of the community itself to its and their good. Hence, it is precisely as enquirers, as rational beings, that the truth is part of what we owe to one another. And this enquiry is lifelong, having at each particular stage of life its own peculiar tasks, tasks that involve the contribution that those at each such stage have to make both to each other and to those at other stages of life.

To spell out in full what this view of the relationships of those of different ages to each other involves would of course be an immense task, one in which Aristotle's brief but illuminating remarks on this matter would have to be developed in a way appropriate to our own very different circumstances. But for the purposes of my present argument, I need only consider two related implications of this standpoint. One is that we have to think of the old, those approaching and at retirement from earning their living, as both learners and teachers, as people who owe it to the young in a variety of ways to transmit what they have learned and are still learning. The grandparent and the great aunt and the elderly neighbor have to be once again thought of as teachers, so reconstituting one older type of family. How *are* they to do this? In part, it will be through telling stories, in part through instructing in the performance of tasks, through making the past present and restoring those various links to the past that modern social mobility and the increasing brevity of the modern attention span all too often break.

Another implication is that we have to stop thinking of teaching and learning as activities restricted to specialized, compartmentalized areas of life within schools, colleges, and universities. Of course schools, colleges, and universities have their own highly specific tasks, but these tasks need to be defined in terms of their contribution to lifelong learning and teaching, most of it carried out in nonscholastic and nonacademic contexts. We need, that is, to think of formal academic education not primarily as a preparation for something else, a life of work, that terminates when that life of work begins, but rather as itself the beginning of, and the providing of skills, virtues, and resources for, a lifelong education directed toward and informed by the achievement of the good.

We need, for example, to teach our students to read, so that they go on reading throughout their lives. We need to make such reading a way of illuminating their social relationships, so that their familial and communal lives continue to be enriched by a stock of common reading. We need to rethink the time-scale of education so that we make one of the tests of the adequacy of what we teach now the answer to the question: "What will our students be reading when they are forty, sixty, seventy-five?" and to accept that if they are not then returning to the *Republic* and the *Confessions*, to *Don Quixote* and Dostoyevsky and Borges, we will have failed as teachers.

It is within this kind of overall perspective that moral questions about truthfulness and moral questions about the relationship of the old to the young can be seen to be rationally answerable together or not at all. And this exemplifies what I have already suggested is true of moral questions in general, that we cannot expect anything but frustration from a problem-by-problem or issue-by-issue approach. To do so will be sterile just because adequately determinate moral rules can only be identified and characterized as parts of the specification of some particular overall conception of the human good and how it is to be achieved. Hence, rational debate about what our shared moral rules are to be will always inescapably be also debate about the competing claims of rival conceptions of that good.

To this claim I have added another. It is that even such debate can still be sterile, if it is restricted to competing statements and arguments at the level of a theory that isolates itself from practice. The central weaknesses of recent liberalism are, in the view that I have advanced, only to be understood in the light of those institutionalized practices of contemporary American society that give concrete and particularized expression to the present condition of liberalism. And correspondingly the strengths of an Aristotelian and Thomistic position will only become clear insofar as it too is seen to be embodied in particularized forms of practice in a variety of local modes of communal activity, in teaching and learning, in farming, in craftsmanship of various kinds. Debate and conflict as to the best forms of practice have to be debate and conflict between rival institutions and not merely between rival theories.

Not everyone who contributes to the making and sustaining of the type of practices and institutions that Aristotelianism and Thomism require will of course think of themselves as Aristotelian or Thomist. What, for example, Andrew Lytle and Wendell Berry, neither of whom thinks of himself as such, have written and done for the practices of farming and writing provide as good examples of what I am saying as any available. And to a Thomist, this should not be in the least surprising. For it is Aquinas's view that rational persons, who are able to develop their practical rationality in undistorted ways, become natural Thomists without having had to read Aquinas. But in our culture—indeed in any culture—how relatively few of such persons there are!

The argument of this lecture began from reflections on the consequences for contemporary society of the modern liberal attempt to render our public, shared morality independent of conceptions of the human good. I have tried to explain why this attempt is bound to fail, by indicating what kinds of argument would have to be developed and sustained in detail, both in theory and practice, to make an alternative view, one drawing upon Aristotle and Aquinas, rather than upon Hume and Kant and Mill, compelling. Notice, however, that the remaking and the sustaining of our own local institutions and practices, which, in the view that I have been developing, is a necessary first step in the transformation of public debate, let alone of public moral practice, are primarily activities worthwhile in themselves and immensely so, and only secondarily a means to further outcomes. As to whether we can even contrive a reopening of genuine public debate about rival conceptions of the good in contemporary America, let alone bring such a debate to an effective conclusion, the evidence, as I understand it, suggests that we ought to be as deeply pessimistic as is compatible with a belief in Divine Providence. But as to that remaking of ourselves and our own local practices and institutions through a better understanding of what it is that, in an Aristotelian and Thomistic perspective, the unity of moral theory and practice now require of us, we have as much to hope for as we have to do, and not least within the community of this university.

2

Liberalism and Its Critics

Jeffrey Reiman

The defense I shall make of liberalism is divided into three parts. In the first part, I present a version of liberal moral theory, which I call "the ideal of individual sovereignty." In the second part, I sketch a number of arguments in defense of it. In the third part, I state what I take to be the main Marxian, communitarian, and feminist objections to liberalism, and show that at least in the version that I endorse, liberalism has effective answers to those objections.

The Ideal of Individual Sovereignty

The liberalism that I shall defend is a moral conception rather than a political program, though it will have some far-reaching implications for political programs. By a moral conception, I mean a standard that distinguishes between morally right and morally wrong behaviors. But I do not mean to say that liberalism is a complete moral doctrine. It is, I believe, limited to a domain within the realm of morality, though an extremely important if not the most important domain in that realm. The domain of liberalism is what I call "the moral requirements." These are those things that human beings can rightly insist on from their fellows, even on threat of force or other unpleasant sanction.

This chapter originally appeared in *Communitarianism, Liberalism and Social Responsibility*, C. Peden and Y. Hudson, eds. Lewiston, N.Y.: Edwin Mellen Press, 1992

This delimitation of the liberal domain has several important implications: first, the test of the validity of the moral requirements is an especially hard one, since the requirements must be shown to bind individuals, so to speak, against their wills—and we shall see that liberalism has distinct advantages over other moral doctrines in passing this test. Second, since liberalism governs the moral requirements, it is not so much an alternative to the other moral ideals that are sometimes thought to compete with it—such as caring or community—as it is a kind of protective outer boundary within which those other ideals can be pursued voluntarily. The implication of this is that those who urge that liberalism be replaced with other *ideals* fail to see that liberalism already leaves room for people to follow their ideals freely—and those who would replace liberalism with other *requirements* can only mean to force people to act on ideals that they would not voluntarily pursue.

I call the version of liberalism that I shall defend, *the ideal of individual sovereignty*.[1] It holds that the only things that can rightly be required of human beings (meaning here sane adult human beings) are those forms of conduct that are necessary to maximizing the scope of everyone's freedom to control his or her life according to his or her own judgments. I do not say maximize *equal* freedom, because I think it is more important to have the most possible freedom than to have the same amount as others. Nonetheless, there is a strong tendency toward equality because the standard insists on maximum compatible freedom for everyone, thus any extension of one person's freedom that reduces another's is ruled out.

It seems to me obvious that there are some inequalities of freedom that increase the freedom of those with less freedom, such as the freedom that police have to arrest suspected wrongdoers or the freedom that judges have to interpret laws or the freedom from arrest that congresspersons have when going about their business. These inequalities will, however, be the exception. More generally, an extension of one person's freedom will mean a reduction of another's, and thus be ruled out. Thus, individual sovereignty calls for a kind of difference principle distribution of freedom that mandates that everyone should have the maximum possible equal share in freedom except when a greater-than-equal share to some will increase the freedom of the rest.[2]

That this liberal standard governs the moral requirements means that any other moral ideal must be promoted by appeal to voluntary compliance. And this, in turn, means that education of the young must, at very least, prepare them to make voluntary moral choices when they are mature enough to do so.[3] Thus, while the liberal standard applies in the first instance to sane adults, it does entail a requirement regarding the preparation of children for adulthood, and therefore a limit to their subjection to parental authority.

The ideal of individual sovereignty is logically related to what Kant calls the "universal law of justice: act externally in such a way that the free use of your will is compatible with the freedom of everyone according to a universal law"[4]—where "according to a universal law" means according to a rule that favors no one at the expense of others. What my version adds, or, I like to think, makes explicit, is that shares in freedom are to be the maximum compatible with the same for everyone else.

Within their spheres of protected freedom, individuals are held to be entitled to do what they judge they should do—where this judgment refers to the final executive judgment that precipitates the action of a rational agent. This is not primarily a moral judgment since it includes the judgment that they should do what they believe they morally should do. Within their spheres of freedom, then, sovereign individuals are entitled to act on their overall executive judgment about how to behave, and are expected to use their rational capacities to reach that judgment.

That human beings may not know what they want to do, or may not use their reason correctly to determine what they should do, or may lack the will to do what they want or should do because of fear or habit or addiction or the strength of competing desires implies that the freedom that individual sovereignty calls for is not exactly the same as the freedom from interference that liberalism commonly demands. Even John Stuart Mill holds that one might rightly block an unwitting pedestrian from going over a faulty bridge, because the pedestrian doesn't really want to be killed.[5] Liberalism doesn't simply protect one's body from interference; it protects one's capacity to act on one's real judgments. Since the pedestrian doesn't really want to or judge that he or she should fall off the bridge, his or her liberty is protected by stopping him or her. Thus, human fallibility implies that paternalistic coercion may be justified by liberalism itself.

Nonetheless, in practical terms, since the dangers of an individual mistaking what he or she truly wants or should do are likely to be matched (if not exceeded) by the danger that others will be mistaken when interposing their judgments for his or hers, paternalistic coercion is as likely (if not more so) to violate freedom as to protect it. The practical implication of this is that the actual occasions on which paternalistic coercion is clearly justified will be few and obvious; in other cases, the risk is unjustified. Moreover, the only way in which we can be sure that we have intervened to protect the true freedom of another is if he or she comes eventually to ratify our intervention. This means that any such intervention can be justified only as a short-term loan drawn against the eventual judgment of the recipient.

Thus, while the ideal of individual sovereignty is a logical descendant of Kant's principle, it is practically rather than logically related to Mill's notion that people are not to be subject to coercion except to prevent them from harming others against their wills.[6] That is, as a rule, we protect individual freedom most effectively by allowing people to reach their own decisions and act on them, and by limiting only to rare and obvious cases paternalistic interference. This, I think, is one way of seeing the difference between liberalism and libertarianism. Libertarianism's first principle of justice is noninterference; it is logically equivalent to noninterference. Liberalism's first principle is the promotion of individual sovereignty to which noninterference is a practical means rather than a logical equivalent. Consequently, liberals are willing to countenance interference that seems needed to promote individual sovereignty overall, such as prohibiting racial discrimination or taxing people to pay for public education; while such interference is ruled out for libertarians from the start.

Before I begin to defend the liberal ideal, it should be clear that the liberal doctrine I have sketched here is not equivalent to the economic liberalism that supports free enterprise economic systems and that forbids or drastically restricts the range of permissible governmental intervention in the market. This is so on the same grounds as we distinguished liberalism from libertarianism. Liberalism is not simply a prohibition on interference, and thus it is not automatically a prohibition on government intervention in economic affairs. Rather, the ideal of individual sovereignty is a standard against which economic systems are to be judged. Free enterprise economies with little or no governmental involvement will only pass muster by this standard if they yield societies in which people in fact have the maximum compatible individual freedom, and this will be an empirical matter of what actually happens in such economies compared to the alternatives.[7]

Moreover, the ideal of individual sovereignty says nothing about what people *own* beyond their bodies. Consequently, to get from the liberal principle to a system such as that of free enterprise, one needs a theory of property rights that is not in any sense logically contained in the principle itself.[8] To develop a theory of property rights compatible with the liberal principle requires testing alternative property systems by how well they realize the principle. I shall have more to say on this issue when I take up the Marxian critique of liberalism. For the moment, it suffices to say that the question of whether private ownership and free enterprise adequately meet the ideal of individual sovereignty is an open one.

Defending the Ideal of Individual Sovereignty

I want now to propose four ways of defending the ideal of individual sovereignty, which I call respectively, the "antisubjugation defense," the "respect defense," the "universal interest defense," and the "mortality defense."

The Antisubjugation Defense

The ideal of individual sovereignty applies only to moral requirements. Moral requirements spell out ways that people must act even if they are not inclined to do so, even if they do not endorse the requirement. If they depended on people wanting to or judging that they should act on them, they wouldn't be requirements. To show the validity of a moral requirement, then, we must show that they are binding on people *who disagree with them*. We must demonstrate their capacity to override the contrary judgments of their recipients. To understand what is at stake in satisfying this condition, imagine a situation in which one person asserts that another is morally required to act in some way other than the way he judges he or she should act. Unless and until we can demonstrate that the asserted requirement really should override the recipient's judgment, any case in which it does in fact override may be no more than a case of one person simply imposing her will on another—a matter of might, not right.

In short, when a person is gotten to act according to the judgment of another (about what he or she morally or otherwise should do) at the expense of his or her own judgment (about what he or she should do), one of two things has happened: either the requirer's judgment has prevailed because it should prevail, or it has prevailed because (somehow) it could prevail. If it prevailed because it could prevail not because it should, I call this *subjugation*. By "subjugation," I mean here to refer not to the motives of the people involved, but to the relationship between two wills, one of which has prevailed over another without justification. Anytime one person gets another to comply with an asserted moral requirement against his or her will, the possibility of subjugation is present. We cannot assume that some asserted moral requirements—say, turn the other cheek—are nonsubjugating on their face. Nietzsche has taught us that even the most unselfish of moral ideals might be means to subjugate others.

In light of this, a person confronted with a requirement to act contrary to the way he or she judges that he or she should act is always entitled to suspect that the requirer is attempting to subjugate him or her, that is, trying—consciously or otherwise—to get the requiree to act according to the judgment of the requirer, without justification. And, as long as that is a possibility, then the recipient of the asserted requirement is entitled to think that he or she is not really morally required to comply. It follows that to show that he or she is morally required to comply, it is necessary to refute the suspicion of subjugation. How can this be done?

It seems to me that there are only two possibilities: one would be to prove beyond a reasonable doubt that the asserted requirement is a true moral requirement. Then, the recipient is being asked to override his or her own judgment because he/she should—his or her own judgment is wrong. Now, while I have not given up on the possibility of proving some moral requirements true beyond a reasonable doubt, the prevailing view among moral philosophers is not optimistic. I shall, then, for the present, treat this option as for all intents and purposes impossible. This does not, by the way, commit us to moral agnosticism or moral skepticism. It amounts, rather, to recognizing that in the real interactions between individuals with differing moral beliefs, we are not in fact able to prove the truth of one of those beliefs in such a way as to show that the one who differs is wrong beyond a reasonable doubt. There may be, nonetheless, true moral ideals, and we may even know the truth of some or all of them, even if we cannot prove their truth beyond reasonable doubt.

The second alternative is to show that the requirement asserted is needed in order to defend people against subjugation itself. If subjugation is a possibility, then those requirements on behavior that are needed to prevent it can hardly be called subjugating. Now, since subjugation amounts to unjustified overriding of people's own judgments about how they should behave, requirements necessary to maximize each person's ability to act according to his or her own judgments are not subjugating. But these requirements are equivalent to those entailed by the ideal of individual sovereignty.

The point here is a simple one, but, I think, quite far-reaching in its implications. Any moral requirement must be a matter of right not might. To establish this, we must show—*show*, not just believe firmly—either that the requirement is true beyond a reasonable doubt, or that it is needed to restrict to a minimum the role of might in human affairs. This shows that the liberal ideal has an advantage over all others. Unless and until one of those others can be proven true beyond a reasonable doubt, only the liberal ideal can satisfactorily rebut the suspicion of subjugation. It is the only one that can withstand the charge of being might not right.[9]

The Respect Defense

The respect defense starts from the assumption that human beings are rational, where this means at least that they can generally use their brains to distinguish what is better for them to do from what is worse. Given this assumption, it seems to me that there is no way to accord special respect to human beings without according special value to human beings reaching their own judgments about how to behave. Any alternative will have to hold that what is above all important is that human beings behave in some particular way whether or not they have figured out for themselves that this is the best way to behave. But then there can be no special respect for human beings, since humans who have been drugged or hypnotized, animals that have been trained or conditioned, and robots that have been programmed so to act will have the same value. Only if there is value to the fact that individuals somehow figure out what to do, do it because they so figure, could have failed but don't, and so on, does human action warrant any special respect.

It follows that human beings will be worthy of special respect to the extent that their actions are the outcomes of their own judgments. And that, in turn, implies that a social arrangement designed to maximize the respect-worthiness of human beings will maximize the range in which individuals govern their own lives by their own judgments. It follows, then, that holding people only to the requirements entailed by the ideal of individual sovereignty maximizes the degree to which human beings are worthy of special respect.[10]

The Universal Interest Defense

Kant realized that for a person to have a duty, that person must be able to recognize it as his or her duty. Recognizing something as a duty is, as the word implies, a cognitive act. It is more than feeling something is one's duty, since a duty must be something that one can recognize as one's own even when no such feeling is present. But to recognize something as one's duty requires that one have a reason for acting on it that holds even when one feels or judges that one should act to the contrary. Moreover, since moral duties are generally held to apply to all rational human beings, if there are any moral duties, then recognizing them will require that all rational human beings have a reason for acting on them. It follows that if there are moral duties at all, they must be such that everyone at all times has a reason for acting on them.

What could such a reason be? Kant thought he found it in the categorical imperative, and, as I shall suggest later, in one version of the imperative, I think he was right. But in the commonest version, namely, the requirement of universalizability, I don't think it can give us what we need. The reason, I think, is that all that universalizability requires is sincere willingness to have others act toward me for the same reasons as those upon which I base my action toward them. If I am a masochist, then I can universalize a principle that allows me to hurt others. This, by the way, shows the general mistake of the universalizability approach. It only works if we can assume that people have the same standard motives. And that shows that it is not really universalizability as such—that is, consistency with my own motives—that makes an action morally acceptable. Rather, because my motives are expected to be the standard ones shared by others, consistency with my own, in fact, amounts to accommodation to those of others. It is this latter that is absent when the masochist universalizes his or her desire for pain and thus "justifies" his or her infliction of it on another who is not a masochist. It is the accommodation to the motives of others that morally justifies my action, and universalizability simply mimics this accommodation as long as my own motives are not too exotic.[11]

The universal reason for moral action must be a universal interest, one that all rational human beings have at all times. This interest cannot be equivalent to every individual human being's overall self-interest, since moral requirements are precisely requirements to overcome one's own self-interest. Moral requirements wouldn't have to be requirements if all they asked was fully self-interested behavior. Likewise, we cannot suppose that the universal interest is an interest in happiness, since this is equivalent to self-interest; nor is it the avoidance of suffering, since it is not always in people's interest to avoid suffering.

Is there then an interest that every rational human being has at all times that can support moral requirements? I think there is. A rational being has a continuing interest in living according to how he or she judges that he or she should. We may differ in what we judge happiness to consist in, and we may differ in the value that we judge suffering to have—what we share is the interest in being able to live according to our judgments whatever they are. Even the person who wants to have another run his or her life wants to be able to live according to his or her own judgment that that other knows best. In short, I think that any rational human being has an interest in being able to live according to his or her judgments about how to live. This is an interest that, so to speak, comes with being rational. But this is just the interest to which the ideal of individual sovereignty appeals.

Naturally, the ideal does not promote everyone's interest in acting according to his or her own judgment at the expense of everyone else's. It promotes that universal interest to the extent that it is possible for everyone to have and act on it together. Since people's ability to act according to their own judgment is vulnerable to the ability of others to block them in so acting, everyone has an interest in principles that maximize each one's ability to act according to his or her own judgments as far as this is compatible with a like ability for everyone else. Thus, everyone has an interest in the ideal of individual sovereignty. Note that I am not saying that the rules entailed by this ideal serve everyone's full self-interest—they would not be moral rules if they did. What I am saying is that such rules always serve a real and important interest that rational human beings always have.

This shows that the ideal of individual sovereignty is uniquely suited to spell out the moral requirements. Any other moral ideal may appeal to an interest that some or all people contingently have, for example, an interest in pleasure or in being charitable. But, people may not have this interest. And then there is no reason for them to act according to the ideal that corresponds to it. And no grounds for holding them required so to act, since that, as we saw, requires showing that they have a reason to so act. If the existence of such a reason is a necessary (though not sufficient) condition for holding something to be a duty, then we can say that only the ideal of individual sovereignty satisfies the necessary condition for being a universal human duty. This isn't as good as satisfying the sufficient condition; but since no other can satisfy the necessary one, it follows that if there are moral duties at all, they are equivalent to the ideal of individual sovereignty.

The Mortality Defense

The mortality defense is the most unorthodox and speculative of the four; it is, I think, ultimately the most important of all.

In his book *The View from Nowhere*, Thomas Nagel makes constructive use of the distinction between the third-person, objective viewpoint characteristic of science and the first-person, subjective viewpoint that we have because we are individual subjects.[12] This distinction between third-person observation and the sort of first-person awareness one has of oneself by virtue of being oneself, while new to Anglo-American philosophers, has been a staple of European philosophy at least since the beginning of the century when it figured in the work of Henri-Louis Bergson and Edmund Husserl. Crucial to this distinction is the notion that to really know what this subjective viewpoint is like, one must be it, or be capable of imaginatively identifying with being it. In *Being and Time*, following upon Husserl, Martin Heidegger launched a full-scale exploration of the existing subject from the standpoint of the existential awareness available to the subject by virtue of being it. On the basis of this, Heidegger maintains that as I live my life in the first-person, I find that my being is *at stake*.[13] I do not simply live out my being as if it were a blueprint or a preconceived idea in the mind of God. Rather, in the face of my mortality, my being confronts me as a task that I must take up and yet at which I can fail.

Now, I think that there is an insight here that can be separated out from the obscure language of German existentialism and that opens the road to the solution of many important problems in moral philosophy, chief among them, the fact-value problem, and with it, the factual basis of human moral equality. It also provides a plausible interpretation of Kant's notion that human beings are ends in themselves.

The point, as I see it, is that being a human subject, I confront my mortality as the very limit of myself. Dying is not something that happens to me the way the flu does. I do not persist through my dying. My dying is the end of my being at all. Mortality teaches me that I am not simply being like a chair, but that my being is a finite and one-time chance *to be*. To capture this difference, Heidegger will say that chairs and animals for that matter *are*, but humans *exist*. By putting a kind of edge on my being, mortality transforms living into living *a life*. And as that life is the sum of my being bounded on the other side by endless darkness and silence, mortality opens up for me the difference between living well and living poorly. Made aware of the fact that I have one finite chance to be in all eternity, I am confronted by the need to live a life whose worth to me somehow satisfies me that I have used my chance well.

Moreover, as I live this in the first person, it has an urgency that is missed when we think of it from the outside as a series of properties of a certain kind of being. Though I cannot here present the full argument, I contend that this opens the way toward a solution to the fact-value problem and thus a way around the naturalistic fallacy, since the fact of being a human subject entails a value commitment, namely to living a life that satisfies in the face of endless nonbeing.[14] This is what Heidegger means when he says that the being of human beings is at stake. It is what Nietzsche meant when he said in *The Gay Science*, "You must become who you are!"[15] Further, I think we find here the natural factual basis of human moral equality. However different we are, we all confront our lives as our once-in-eternity chance to live a life we can deem worthy.

If I am on the right track here, it follows that what is above all important in each person's life is not that she or he live one particular way or another, but that she or he live a life that somehow satisfies her or him that it is worthwhile in face of the inevitable nonbeing on the other side. No life can answer this challenge unless it is judged to do so by the one whose life it is. But, then, more important than people being gotten to live one way or another, is allowing them to live the way they find to be meaningful and worthwhile. And this implies a moral standard that insists that everyone have the maximum possibility of finding what that life is and then living it—in short, the ideal of individual sovereignty.

I would take this even further. The urgency of the demand to live the life that we find meaningful is not just a brute fact or desire. It is a true imperative—true, because the fact that a being confronts a finite and once-in-eternity chance to live is a good reason for making the best of that life.[16] If it is a true imperative, then we have a translation of the notion that human beings are ends in themselves: their nature is such that it is truly valuable for them to pursue their ends though no further end beyond them is thereby served.[17]

If the truth of this imperative is only really known in the first person, then there is something about human subjects, ourselves and everyone else, that can only be known in the first person, either by being it (in one's own case) or by imagining being it (in everyone else's). Now, it is a requirement of reason that we act with the best available knowledge of the circumstances in which we are to act. And insofar as among those circumstances there are human subjects, it follows that it is a requirement of reason that we act with the special knowledge of them that comes from imaginatively identifying with their first-person reality.

To act with this special knowledge, one cannot allow it to be subtly denatured into a third-person observation, since then its true urgency will be flattened out and distorted and the truth of its imperative will evaporate. Accordingly, acting with this special knowledge means acting subject to the experience of identification with others. But, truly identifying with others will mean experiencing the urgency for them of living a life they find meaningful and recognizing the truth for them of the imperative to do. Recognizing this truth for them means endorsing it as I do my own, and that means recognizing at once the truth of the imperative to live in a way that leaves room for everyone's equal possibility of living the life that he or she judges to be the worthwhile one. This amounts to showing that the ideal of individual sovereignty is a requirement of reason.[18] It also provides a plausible defense of Kant's claim that reason requires us to recognize all human beings as ends in themselves.

Liberalism and Its Critics

There are three critiques of liberalism that I will take up: communitarian, Marxian, and feminist. Each of these perspectives covers various objections to liberalism, from which I shall only select representative samples. There is considerable overlap among the perspectives, so if I don't get to your favorite criticism of liberalism where you normally expect it, I might deal with it under another head.

The Communitarian Critique

Communitarians charge that liberalism, by emphasizing people's freedom from interference by others, by laying down boundaries between individuals where one person's freedom begins and another's ends, assumes and thus conveys that people's interests are antagonistic.[19] This both distorts the true possibilities of communal solidarity and distorts human nature by training people in anticommunal ways. Thus, liberalism is contrary to the value of community.

In my view, the communitarians are making a mistake about the nature of community. To be real, community must be voluntary, it must be a free expression of shared commitment. But to be free, it must arise in just the space that liberalism protects. Those who think that liberalism is community's enemy, and who would instead start by teaching people to share some set of values, would essentially force a conformity on people that is related to true community in the way that forced religious observance is related to true faith. Rather than being contrary to community, liberalism is its precondition. That liberalism protects people's freedom from other people does not imply that people's interests are antagonistic. It implies only that they can be because of the nature of freedom itself. Because freedom *can* be constrained by the acts of others, any guarantee of freedom is a guarantee against invasions by others—even if the guarantee never has to be used.

Unless community is truly and explicitly voluntary, it is a dangerous vehicle of oppression of individuals in the name of the group— that is, the name of other individuals. Some feminists have noticed that two types of supposed community lauded by communitarians for their transcendence of liberal values—namely, family and church—are characteristically oppressive to women.[20]

A related communitarian objection holds that liberalism is excessively individualistic. Separate individuals are not the basic moral unit. Individuals naturally care about and are attached to other individuals and thus they should not be treated as if they had separate interests from at least those others to whom they are attached. Emphasizing their rights to freedom from interference and the rest, then, fails to do justice to the fact that individuals both care about others and only live satisfying lives when they are connected to others. This objection to liberalism fails to take seriously the fact that liberalism applies to the moral requirements. Liberalism does not stop people who care about and want to relate to others or even who wish to submerge themselves in groups from doing so. All it prohibits is requiring that people do this when they are not inclined to. The communitarian critic of liberalism obviously does not believe that people really care enough about others to form communities with them when they are not forced or brainwashed into doing so. If the critic did believe this, then liberal freedom would be enough.

Yet another form of communitarian objection holds that liberalism is based on faulty psychology.[21] Since liberalism insists that people have a reason to live according to principles that guarantee each person the greatest compatible freedom to live according to his or her judgments, it assumes that people can treat their judgments purely formally, that is, with indifference to their particular content. Thus, the objection runs, liberalism mistakenly assumes that people are separable from their deepest beliefs and values. If people's real attachment to their beliefs and values were recognized, they would not (certainly not always) be willing to live according to principles that allowed everyone the right to pursue his or her own ends. For example, if people's judgments (or underlying values) were treated in light of their content, those whose judgments or values were such that they wanted, say, to live under a regime of religious orthodoxy would not have a reason to accept a principle that would allow others (at least others in the neighborhood) to live according to different judgments.

I think this objection throws into relief the true oppressive potential of illiberal communitarianism. Liberalism would allow a community of people who wanted to live according to a religious orthodoxy to do so. People who really were committed to such values would be protected by liberalism in their attempt to form such a community. For such people, liberal values would be enough to protect the value of community. What liberalism would prohibit is forcing religious orthodoxy on those who do not have it as a deeply held value. Thus, the rejection of liberalism along these lines is simply rebellion against not being able to force one's values on others.

For those who recognize that real community is voluntary and who do not insist on communitarian values as a means to forcing conformity on people against their will, liberalism is the foundation of communitarianism.

The Marxian Critique

Marxism holds that if a part of society owns the means of material production available to the whole society, then the part that does not own the means of production will be forced to work for those who do own because they will have no other way of earning a living—which is to say, no other way of living at all. Based on the assumption that time labored is the substance of what is of value in an economy, Marxists can show that, not only are nonowners forced to work for owners, they are forced to work in part for free because they are forced to work more than the equivalent in labor time that they get back in their pay. Thus, all societies in which a part of society owns the means of production and the rest do not are characterized by a kind of slavery, though not always by that particular kind found in the ancient world or in antebellum America.

It was central to Karl Marx's analysis, that this slavery could happen even in a capitalist society in which commodities including labor were traded in a market free of overt coercion. Since the workers own nothing but their labor, and since they have no way of living other than by working for those who own the means of production, even when they enter into free bargains with prospective employers they will have to settle for giving more labor time than they get back, and thus working in part gratis. Consequently, Marxists believe that there is a kind of force that is mediated by private ownership of means of production that can work even when people are not subject to overt coercion. Liberalism, by holding that people are free when they are not coerced, provides ideological cover for the invisible force in capitalism. Liberal freedom allows people, as Marx says, to sell themselves of their own free will, and what they sell themselves into is a kind of slavery.[22] The response to this is that it is not really a critique of liberalism, but a critique *from liberalism* of a certain blindness toward the coercive power of certain forms of property. The critique of the invisible force in capitalism only makes moral sense from a position that is inherently at one with liberalism in its insistence on the right of individuals to control their own lives. I contend, therefore, that Marxism is squarely within the liberal tradition, differing with the main proponents of liberalism not over the ideal of maximum individual freedom, but over what constitutes a coercive threat to that freedom. The conventional liberal fails to see that where ownership of means of production is in the hands of a few and the rest own little more than the muscles in their backs, such ownership is coercive. I contend that such blindness to the coerciveness of property is the substance of ideology in capitalism, and the Marxian critique of what goes on under the cover of this ideology is fundamentally a liberal critique.[23]

Elsewhere I have argued that liberals ought to take seriously the Marxian analysis, and that they can do so by viewing the goods exchanged in an economic system in terms of the amount of labor time that went into producing them.[24] This enables us to see a putatively free market economy as a set of ratios in which people work for one another, and thus allows us to test that economy for the presence of subjugation. I argue further that the appropriate test for this is a version of the difference principle, which, properly understood, turns out to insist that people work as little as possible for others as is necessary to get the largest share of goods back. Obviously, I cannot go fully into this argument here, but the point is that a liberal can take quite seriously the Marxian insight that property is power that threatens the freedom of nonowners.

The Feminist Critique

Some feminists argue that liberalism reflects a male picture of the elements of the moral life. Following upon work such as that of Carol Gilligan, this view holds that young boys typically grow up insisting on their rights, wanting to resolve conflicts fairly, and so on, whereas young girls typically grow up caring about others rather than pressing for their rights against them, wanting to keep conflicts from arising in the first place, and so on.[25] Thus, the emphasis on liberal moral values is a one-sided vision of morality that comes from the fact that moral theorists have been (until very recently) males and reflected typically male experience.

The answer to this is, first, that the business of moral philosophy is not to enshrine in theory everyone's moral experience. Its business is critical. It aims to determine the correct moral rules or proper moral attitudes. Consequently, the fact that any or all moral theories express a conception of morality that parallels the experience of one gender, or for that matter, any segment of humanity and not another's, does not itself imply that that conception is wrong or one-sided. It might be the case, say, that liberalism is correct and that, because of sexism, young girls have been introduced into a false or partial understanding of morality. This was Mary Wollstonecraft's view.[26]

It is worth noting, in any event, that training in liberalism is likely to make one more likely to insist on one's own rights and desires and thus more resistant to oppression, while training in caring and conflict-avoidance is likely to make one less willing to insist on one's own rights and desires and thus more vulnerable to oppression. Indeed, the liberal's insistence that every adult human being has a right to the maximum freedom to live according to his or her own judgments is the core of the feminist's demand for women. Thus, much as I think that Marxism is basically liberalism that recognizes the coerciveness of private property, I think that feminism is liberalism that recognizes the coerciveness of gender roles and the social infrastructure that supports them.

Furthermore, note that the liberalism I have been defending is not presented as a complete moral view. Its domain is the moral requirements, those dimensions of the moral life that can be insisted on by human beings and even forced out of resisters. It lays out the boundaries of freedom, but says little or nothing about how that freedom is to be exercised beyond the fact that it is not to be used to violate the freedom of others. Within the realm of protected freedom, there is nothing incompatible with liberalism in holding that caring and sharing and avoiding conflict (etc.) are more noble and worthy ways to exercise one's freedom than simply fighting about what belongs to whom. In this way, it could be acknowledged that liberalism reflects dimensions of the moral life that are most salient in male experience, and that it is as a result a partial moral view, without having to give up the idea that the liberal ideal is basic to any correct moral view.

This point can be put more positively. Suppose that it is true that young boys grow up insisting on rights and limits, and young girls grow up trying to avoid conflicts and caring more about others than about their own desires and rights. (Actually, the studies, by Gilligan and others, indicate that these are tendencies and that both genders use both approaches, albeit with different frequencies and emphases.)[27] This in turn might simply mean that one gender was more inclined toward the moral requirements and the other toward those aspects of morality that are, so to speak, beyond the call of duty. It certainly would not mean that one gender was superior to the other, or that either could do without learning the part that the other seemed naturally inclined toward. Indeed, such reciprocal learning would be necessary for a full moral life. Since caring and the related attitudes are only worthwhile if they are free, and since the liberal moral requirements protect freedom, liberalism can be thought to establish the preconditions for the full flowering of the aspects of morality, like caring, that go beyond duty. And since the moral life is richer in possibilities than mere meeting of the requirements, the dimension of caring might be thought of as the full flowering of morality, without which morality is just a pale shadow of what it could and should be.

Notes

1. I defend this notion in the context of disputes about the appropriate moral doctrine for Marxism in "An Alternative to 'Distributive' Marxism: Further Thoughts on Roemer, Cohen, and Exploitation," *Canadian Journal of Philosophy*, supplemental volume 15: *Analytic Marxism* (1989): 299–331; and in "Marxism and Moral Philosophy," in T. Carver, ed., *Cambridge Companions to Philosophy: Marx* (New York: Cambridge University Press, forthcoming). I try to provide a complete moral philosophical foundation for this liberal ideal as well as work out its implications for natural and social justice in *Justice and Modern Moral Philosophy* (New Haven, Conn.: Yale University Press, 1990).

2. This argument is developed in detail in *Justice and Modern Moral Philosophy*, 272–308.

3. See the discussion of liberal education in Bruce Ackerman, *Social Justice in the Liberal State* (New Haven, Conn.: Yale University Press, 1980), 139–67.

4. Immanuel Kant, *The Metaphysical Elements of Justice*, J. Ladd, trans. (Indianapolis: Bobbs-Merrill, 1965), 35.

5. "If either a public officer or anyone else saw a person attempting to cross a bridge which had been ascertained to be unsafe, and there were no time to warn him of his danger, they might seize him and turn him back without any real infringement on his liberty; for liberty consists in doing what one desires, and he does not desire to fall into the river" (John Stuart Mill,

On Liberty [New York: Penguin Books, 1974], 166).

6. Mill, 68.

7. See *Justice and Modern Moral Philosophy*, 170–79, 302–3.

8. I criticize Robert Nozick's version of libertarianism along these lines in my "The Fallacy of Libertarian Capitalism," *Ethics* 92, no. 1 (October 1981): 85–95.

9. In *Justice and Modern Moral Philosophy*, I attempt to show that the true principles of justice (which turn out to be liberal principles of the sort defended here) can be found by determining the terms under which rational human beings ought to agree that they are not being subjugated. I also contend that this is the implicit logic of the social contract approach to moral theorizing, and thus it accounts for the perennial appeal of that approach. Rules arrived at by determining the conditions under which people are not subjugated have the unique advantage over other rules of being the only ones that can withstand the charge of being might not right.

10. In *Justice and Modern Moral Philosophy*, I take a different approach and argue that respect is a cognitive attitude that is required for gaining knowledge of human subjects. This cognitive attitude, however, brings with it liberal normative commitments. See especially 112–28.

11. For a more extended critique of the universalizability strategy, in both Alan Gewirth's and R. M. Hare's versions, see *Justice and Modern Moral Philosophy*, 108–12, 314.

12. Thomas Nagel, *The View from Nowhere* (New York: Oxford University Press, 1986), 18 inter alia.

13. Martin Heidegger, *Being and Time* (New York: Harper & Row, 1962), 236–38 pass.

14. I develop this solution to the fact-value problem in *Justice and Modern Moral Philosophy*, 54–63, 199–206. I contend further that this account of human subjectivity provides us with the natural basis of human equality (see esp. 49).

15. Friedrich Nietzsche, *The Gay Science*, trans. Walter Kaufmann (New York: Vintage, 1974), sec. 270.

16. See *Justice and Modern Moral Philosophy*, 59–60.

17. Ibid., 134–40.

18. For a more extended version of the argument (summarized in this and the previous paragraph) that the liberal idea is a requirement of reason, see *Justice and Modern Moral Philosophy*, 112–24.

19. An influential recent version of this objection can be found in Michael Sandel, *Liberalism and the Limits of Justice* (New York: Cambridge University Press, 1982), 30 inter alia. An earlier form of the objection, from a Marxian standpoint, can be found in Robert Tucker, *The Marxian Revolutionary Idea* (New York: Norton, 1970), 42–53. I take up this and other communitarian critiques of liberalism in "Law, Rights, Community, and the Structure of Liberal Legal Justification," in J. R. Pennock and J. W. Chapman, eds., *Justification: Nomos XXVIII* (New York: New York University Press, 1986), 178–203; and in *Justice and Modern Moral Philosophy*, 206–12.

20. See, for example, Marilyn Friedman, "Feminism and Modern Friendship: Dislocating the Community," *Ethics*, 99, no. 2 (January 1989): 275–90.
21. Sandel, *Liberalism and the Limits of Justice*, 19–22, 58–62.
22. Marx writes that the sphere, "within whose boundaries the sale and purchase of labour-power goes on, is in fact a very Eden of the innate rights of man. There alone rule Freedom, Equality, Property. . . . Freedom, because both buyer and seller of a commodity, say of labour-power, are constrained only by their own free will"; but he goes on to describe the wage-worker as a "man who is compelled to sell himself of his own free will," and to characterize capitalism as a system of "forced labour—no matter how much it may seem to result from a free contractual agreement" (Karl Marx, *Capital* [New York: International Publishers, 1967], I, 176, 766; III, 819).
23. This interpretation of Marxism is developed in a series of articles, such as, "The Marxian Critique of Criminal Justice," *Criminal Justice Ethics*, 6, no. 1 (Winter/Spring 1987): 30–50; and "Exploitation, Force, and the Moral Assessment of Capitalism: Thoughts on Roemer and Cohen," *Philosophy & Public Affairs* 16, no. 1 (Winter 1987): 3–41. See also note 1, above; and *Justice and Modern Moral Philosophy*, 243–58.
24. See "The Labor Theory of the Difference Principle," *Philosophy & Public Affairs*, 12, no. 2 (Spring 1983): 133–59; and *Justice and Modern Moral Philosophy*, 272–90.
25. Carol Gilligan, *In a Different Voice* (Cambridge: Harvard University Press, 1982). See also the excellent survey article by Owen Flanagan and Kathryn Jackson, "Justice, Care, and Gender: The Kohlberg-Gilligan Debate Revisited," *Ethics*, 97, no. 3 (April 1987), 622–37.
26. Mary Wollstonecraft wrote, for example, that "the most perfect education, in my opinion, is such an exercise of the understanding as is best calculated to. . .enable the individual to attain such habits of virtue as will render it independent. In fact, it is a farce to call any being virtuous whose virtues do not result from the exercise of its own reason. This was Rousseau's opinion respecting men: I extend it to women, and confidently assert that they have been drawn out of their sphere by false refinement." And further: "Love, in their bosoms, taking place of every nobler passion, their sole ambition is to be fair, to raise emotion instead of inspiring respect; and this ignoble desire, like the servility in absolute monarchies, destroys all strength of character. Liberty is the mother of virtue, and if women be, by their very constitution, slaves, and now allowed to breathe the sharp invigorating air of freedom, they must ever languish like exotics, and be reckoned beautiful flaws in nature" (*Vindication of the Rights of Woman* [New York: Penguin Books, 1982], 103, 121–22).
27. See Flanagan and Jackson, 624–25.

3

Moral Pluralism, Disintegration, and Liberalism

Richard F. Galvin

The term "moral pluralism" has been employed frequently by writers in both the academic and popular press, as well as by political officials and commentators. My present purpose is (1) to argue that there are two distinct senses of moral pluralism, (2) to apply this distinction to a representative argument concerning the alleged connection between moral pluralism and the disintegration of society, and finally (3) to offer some suggestions as to how this distinction can be employed to shed some light on the current rethinking of liberalism, especially in response to attacks on liberalism by communitarians.

I

One sense of moral pluralism owes its genesis to writers in moral theory who attempted to distinguish *pluralistic* moral theories from *monistic* moral theories.[1] Somewhat roughly, a pluralistic moral theory holds that moral judgment or evaluation ultimately involves more than one type of morally relevant factor or consideration. Depending on the theory in question, these factors might include duties, goods, moral rules, or virtues. Pluralistic theories also typically stipulate further that these types of morally relevant factors are irreducible, and hence cannot be accounted for in terms of any other such factor or combination of factors.[2] On the other hand, monistic moral theories maintain that moral evaluation ultimately involves, or at least can be reduced to, a single type of morally relevant factor or consideration.

Examples of monistic and pluralistic views can be found among familiar consequentialist and deontological moral theories.

Since consequentialist theories share the tenet that the moral character of an act is determined by its consequences, whether a consequentialist theory is monistic or pluralistic is a function of its axiology. If, as C. D. Broad assumes, what ought to be maximized are those consequences that are "intrinsically good," then "any theory which holds that there is a non-ethical characteristic which is both common and peculiar to all things that are intrinsically good" is a monistic consequentialist theory.[3] On the other hand, consequentialist "theories which hold that there is no non-ethical characteristic common and peculiar to those things that are intrinsically good" are pluralistic consequentialist theories.[4] Jeremy Bentham's utilitarianism provides an example of a monistic consequentialist theory insofar as there is only one good—pleasure—and anything else is good only insofar as it tends to produce pleasure. G. E. Moore shares Bentham's allegiance to utilitarianism, but rejects his simple hedonism, holding instead that there are multiple intrinsic goods such as knowledge, beauty, and, indeed, pleasure. So while Bentham's utilitarianism is monistic, Moore's is pluralistic by virtue of its recognition of a plurality of irreducible goods.

Similarly, deontological views can be characterized as either monistic or pluralistic. A deontological view is monistic if there is a single duty or rule that determines an act's moral character, or if all first-order moral rules can be generated by a single second-order moral principle. A deontological view is pluralistic if an act's moral character is a function of a plurality of irreducible rules or duties for which no second-order "generating" rule can be provided. Immanuel Kant's view, at least as it has been traditionally interpreted, provides an illustration of a monistic deontological theory. If, as Kant assures us, the various formulations of the categorical imperative are equivalent, then the status of the categorical imperative as the supreme moral criterion provides an example of a monistic deontological theory. W. D. Ross's view, while straightforwardly deontological, is explicitly pluralistic. He holds that (1) there is a plurality of *prima facie* duties that determine an act's moral status, (2) none of these *prima facie* duties is reducible to any combination of other *prima facie* duties, and (3) these *prima facie* duties can conflict since more than one can apply to the same act. An act's moral character is a function of "balancing" those *prima facie* duties that apply to the act. Ross specifies further that there is no overriding hierarchy or principle of adjudication to which we can appeal when attempting to balance competing *prima facie* duties. We may then conclude that Ross's view is pluralistic.

Although the discussion of this sense of moral pluralism has been confined to consequentialist and deontological moral theories, the analysis could be extended to (1) theories that are neither consequentialist nor deontological, such as virtue conceptions of ethics (e.g., Plato's conception of the virtues would appear to be monistic whereas Aristotle's is pluralistic), and (2) moral codes, views, or positions that might not be sufficiently refined or developed to be termed "theories," such as an appeal to the Ten Commandments. But as the above discussion shows, when moral pluralism is used in this sense, it refers to the characteristic, possessed by certain moral theories, codes, views or positions, of admitting that moral evaluation involves a plurality of types of moral considerations or factors.

There is, however, a second sense of moral pluralism that involves no reference to the content or internal structure of specific moral theories or positions. This sense of moral pluralism refers instead to a plurality of moral positions or views within a society, community, or otherwise specified group. Those who use moral pluralism in this sense are concerned with the level of moral agreement within a group. Whether explicit or implicit, the presupposition is that a group is *pluralistic* if there is a sufficient level of moral disagreement or diversity within the group. In contrast, a sufficient level of moral agreement within a group would indicate a moral *consensus* within that group. For there to be a consensus, there must be a sufficiently shared moral view within the group.

While a moral consensus requires a certain level of agreement on substantive moral issues, there is no requirement that the shared moral view have a specific content. Rather, the moral view (whatever it is) must be sufficiently shared. So while in one group there may be a consensus that condemns active euthanasia, in another group there may be a consensus that requires active euthanasia under certain conditions. Nor is there (typically) any requirement that the shared view possess any particular internal structure—the concern is usually with substantive moral issues. We could envision a community consisting of pluralistic utilitarians (in the manner of G. E. Moore) in which there is sufficient agreement on substantive moral issues to constitute a moral consensus. We could also envision a community in which there is a great deal of moral disagreement on substantive issues, but where all members embrace a monistic moral view (they could be equally divided among Kantians, Benthamite act-utilitarians, and followers of the Golden Rule; or, for that matter, they could all be Benthamites who disagree about the consequences of a variety of acts).

It appears, then, that moral pluralism can be used to designate two distinct phenomena. When used in one sense, moral pluralism refers to pluralistic moral views; when used in an entirely different sense, it refers to a plurality of moral views within a group.

II

One common argument in which moral pluralism plays a prominent role is the "disintegration thesis" (DT). In this section, I shall examine, in light of the distinction outlined in Section I, one recent argument that considers the merits of DT.

John Kekes has attributed DT to a number of writers who are fearful of the consequences of our society's moral climate. Citing phenomena such as the "breakdown of moral responsibility" and the "loss of our sense of virtue," these writers find evidence of "disintegration" in that many current moral conflicts concern "the appropriateness of moral considerations" and "whether praise and blame are fitting responses."[5] According to Kekes, DT is the position that "moral change in our society is so deep as to produce widespread moral confusion; the confusion cannot be dispelled, because there is no common ground, no accepted standard or principle to which we can appeal to resolve moral conflicts; hence moral disintegration results."[6] Kekes's response to DT is to grant that while there has been moral change in our society, the type of moral change that our society has undergone is not sufficient to produce moral confusion or disintegration. Rather, our society's morality has changed from a monistic moral view to a pluralistic moral view, and this pluralistic view not only fails to entail horrible consequences such as disintegration, but also actually represents an improvement over our society's old monistic moral view. Kekes characterizes the nature of moral change in our society as our "abandoning the idea that there is a *summum bonum*, . . . and that the task of morality is to teach us how to live it," and adopting the view that "there are many good things," none of which is "reducible to the others."[7] This type of change from a monistic to a pluralistic moral view is not so deep as to produce anything like the moral confusion that worries proponents of DT.

Kekes's argument seems to rely on two empirical claims: (1) there formerly was a shared monistic moral view in our society, and (2) this monistic view has been supplanted by a relatively equally shared pluralistic moral view. Neither claim strikes me as obviously true. The former faces the counterargument that our society has attempted to avoid at least the legal entrenchment of any particular moral view via First Amendment protections and the like, as well as the further argument that our history of cultural diversity would undercut any claims of moral consensus.

The prevalence of moral conflicts cited by proponents of DT would appear to undermine the claim that there is presently any moral consensus at all in our society. But Kekes argues that this is not so: the prevalence of moral conflicts and controversies is compatible with the existence of a moral consensus where the shared view is pluralistic, since pluralistic moral views allow legitimate moral considerations to conflict in specific cases. According to Kekes, current moral conflicts are not at the level of principle, but "about applying principles to individual cases," and conflicts of this sort are inevitable since pluralistic morality "has no preeminent standard for resolving moral conflicts."[8] So where proponents of DT argue that the prevalence of moral conflicts undermines the claim that our society has a shared morality, Kekes responds that the existence of moral conflicts can support the claim that our society's shared morality is pluralistic. Thus, the locus of one disagreement between Kekes and proponents of DT appears to be the proper analysis of the nature of moral conflicts in our society. If Kekes is correct, these moral conflicts involve disagreement over how to balance competing moral claims that all parties to the dispute recognize as legitimate. According to proponents of DT, these moral conflicts indicate disagreement over moral considerations themselves, as well as "what constitutes a moral question."

What is the most plausible analysis of moral conflicts such as abortion, euthanasia, suicide, capital punishment, and promiscuity? Kekes himself admits that disputes in these areas rarely involve the attempt to balance competing claims that each party to the dispute regards as legitimate, and even in those cases, the argument is bound to end in an impasse because there is no moral authority or "preeminent principle" within a pluralistic view to which we could appeal to resolve such conflicts. But the rarity of disputes over balancing competing legitimate claims seems to support the analysis of proponents of DT, since disputes over abortion, euthanasia, suicide, capital punishment, and promiscuity would then be better explained by significant disagreement at the level of fundamental moral principle.[9] This provides some reason to be skeptical of Kekes's claim that there is a shared pluralistic moral view in our society.

How does this bear on Kekes's claim that DT mistakes "moral pluralism" for "moral disintegration"? According to DT, moral disintegration results from there being "no common ground, no accepted principle or standard to which we can appeal to resolve moral conflicts."[10] If DT were based on the claim that a shared pluralistic view results in disintegration, Kekes would have grounds for rejecting DT since although pluralistic views typically lack a preeminent principle for resolving conflicts between legitimate moral considerations, there would be common ground in terms of agreement over the set of legitimate moral considerations, and consequently no disagreement over what constitutes a moral issue. But the DT would fail to establish any link between moral disintegration and a shared pluralistic moral view.

It is important to note that the proponents of DT identified and cited by Kekes are writers in the popular press, and somewhat understandably do not consider the distinction between pluralistic moral views and a pluralism of moral views within a group. And perhaps these authors do hold that a pluralistic moral view, regardless of how widely shared within a group, would indeed lead to moral disintegration. There is, however, a more formidable argument for the connection between moral pluralism and disintegration to the effect that a lack of moral consensus or shared moral view within a group will lead to disintegration. While those proponents of DT mentioned by Kekes might not have argued for this claim, Patrick Devlin and Emile Durkheim have offered elaborate defenses of this position.

Devlin's remarks on this topic have received widespread attention, so I will not belabor the specifics of his argument.[11] That his version of DT concerns the effects of a plurality of moral views within a society is clear from his remark that "an established morality is as necessary as good government to the welfare of society."[12] Shared moral ideas are necessary since "there is disintegration where no common morality is observed and history shows that the loosening of moral bonds is often the first stage of disintegration."[13] Devlin argues further that "without shared ideas on politics, morals and ethics no society can exist. . . . If men and women try to create a society in which there is no fundamental agreement about good and evil they will fail. . . . For society. . . is held together by the invisible bonds of common thought. . . .A common morality is part of that bondage."[14] Durkheim's view resembles Devlin's in the following respect: according to Durkheim, an element of social solidarity is "mechanical solidarity" or the *"conscience collective."*[15] This common conscience is required for social cohesion, since if the common conscience were to lose its energy, the result would be a breakdown of social solidarity. Durkheim's version of DT is that in each society there is a common morality that has a cohesive force without which there would be a breakdown of social solidarity, and the subsequent disintegration of society.

For Devlin and Durkheim, the fear is that the absence of a moral consensus will lead to disintegration. Neither is concerned with the content of the shared moral view (so whether or not it is a pluralistic view is beside the point), but rather with the cohesive power of a shared morality of any sort within society. This version of DT represents a more formidable opponent for Kekes. If Kekes is correct in claiming that within our society there is a sufficiently shared moral view, then even with Devlin's and Durkheim's version of DT there should be no fear of disintegration, which in their view arises from a lack of a shared morality. But then the issue becomes whether there is a sufficiently shared moral view in our society. I have argued above that it is not clear whether the prevalence of moral conflicts in our society is best explained by the existence of a shared pluralistic moral view (as Kekes holds) or by the lack of a shared moral view of any sort in society. While this would appear to be an empirical issue, H. L. A. Hart has argued that for DT to be distinct from the Conservative Thesis, which holds that society has a right to protect its shared morality from essential change, its proponents must provide an account of "disintegration" that is not equivalent to "any essential change in society's shared morality."[16] Hart argues convincingly that neither Devlin nor Durkheim has accomplished this, and that the prospects for doing so are not promising. Similarly, the related notions of a pluralism of moral views and a moral consensus within a community are problematic. I shall mention three related difficulties.

1. Whether a community is pluralistic depends on the level of moral agreement within that community, but the notion of "moral agreement" can be understood in two ways. One might inquire, as do Devlin and Durkheim, as to the level of agreement on substantive issues such as killing, stealing, euthanasia, and the like. However, one might also consider the level of agreement on more structural or theoretical moral issues, such as whether an act's moral status is determined by its consequences, what "the good" is, whether moral rules admit of exceptions, and similar questions. We can conceive of clear cases of moral consensus at all levels within a group, where all members agree not only on substantive moral issues, but also on structural questions—they might all be like-minded Benthamite act-utilitarians. We can also envision clear cases of pluralistic groups whose members are sharply divided on both substantive and structural issues. But in other cases, the distinction is not so easily applied. It is possible that

within a given group, members might be nearly unanimous on substantive moral issues, but be sharply divided on structural issues, or vice-versa. While it is clear that most proponents of DT are primarily concerned with the level of agreement on substantive issues, it is not clear why disintegration should not be equally as likely where a group's members are divided on structural issues as well. And conversely, if disintegration is not likely where there is agreement on substantive issues, why wouldn't agreement on structural issues be sufficient for agreement on "what constitutes a moral question" or a "fundamental agreement on good and evil"? It is odd that no argument for DT even begins to address these questions, which casts serious doubt on the plausibility of DT.

2. Even if questions regarding consensus are confined to substantive moral issues, a further difficulty arises in determining whether a consensus requires agreement of a certain level on *all* moral issues. If a moral consensus were to require this, nearly all imaginable groups would be pluralistic. If agreement on *any* substantive issue were sufficient for a consensus, few imaginable groups would be pluralistic. Hence, there must be some weighted level of disagreement in terms of the range of issues on which members disagree that is sufficient for establishing a lack of consensus. Likewise, a weighted level of agreement would be required for the existence of a consensus.[17]

3. Any argument concerning a moral consensus or moral pluralism within a group must consider what level of agreement on *any* issue is sufficient or necessary for a consensus *on that issue*. Even if there might be clear cases of consensus (unanimity) and pluralism (divided equally), most groups will likely fall somewhere between the paradigms.

It is worth noting that in arguing that there is a shared moral view in our society, Kekes does not address any of these issues. But what is worse is that no proponents of DT address these issues either.[18] What makes this omission so damaging is that DT relies on the empirical claim that a lack of consensus is sufficient for producing disintegration. But before anything resembling a test of this empirical claim could be examined and evaluated, we must be sufficiently clear about what counts as a consensus. Since neither Kekes nor proponents of DT provide an adequate account, it is difficult to determine whether our society's moral conflicts are best explained by the proposition that our society has a shared moral view that is pluralistic, or the proposition that our society exhibits a pluralism of moral views. And as long as this cannot be decided, there can be no clear winner in the dispute between Kekes and proponents of DT.

III

In arguing that neither Devlin nor Durkheim has provided an account of DT that would distinguish it from the nonempirical claim that society has a right to protect its moral code from essential change (the Conservative Thesis), Hart suggests, but does not develop in detail, a counterthesis to DT. Hart refers to the possibility that "divergent moralities" might live together in peace, since "plural moralities . . . might perfectly well be mutually tolerant," and includes among alternatives to DT "moral pluralism" and "permissiveness."[19] In responding to challenges posed by DT, both Kekes and Hart offer responses that are, in essence, statements of one central tenet of liberalism. The reference to, and reliance on, the likes of moral pluralism and permissiveness is fairly commonplace in liberal political theory, and points to both a major concern of proponents of DT (as well as other critics of liberalism) and a major source of difficulty for liberalism. In what follows, I shall offer some brief suggestions about the connection between liberalism and moral pluralism.

Certainly, individual freedom plays a major role in liberal theory. While some liberal theorists also recognize the need for promotion of positive liberty, it is difficult to imagine how a political theory could qualify as "liberal" without a prominent role for negative liberty. One hallmark of a liberal society is the stipulation that there are spheres of conduct that lie beyond the limits of legitimate government interference, entailing in turn that some types of behavior are strictly optional, as opposed to prohibited or required by the coercive power of the state. As a consequence, liberal theory can be viewed as possessing the minimal core features of (1) emphasis on individualism (at least to the minimal degree suggested above),[20] and (2) a requisite degree of neutrality toward and tolerance of divergent points of view on a range of issues. It is this neutrality and tolerance that creates both practical and theoretical difficulties for liberal theory, and provides ammunition for critics of liberalism, including proponents of DT and communitarians.

While neutrality and tolerance might be unobjectionable as far as obviously nonmoral or morally uncontroversial issues are concerned, liberal theory also typically specifies a range of issues on which the state simply "should not take a moral stand"—so-called freedom of conscience, freedom of choice, or life-style issues. It is important to emphasize that liberal theory does not simply identify all such issues as morally uncontroversial or nonmoral; liberal theory's neutrality extends beyond such issues. Here liberal theory encounters two problems: (1) to exactly which issues does this neutrality and tolerance extend?, and (2) on what grounds is this neutrality and tolerance justified? My main (although not exclusive) concern will be with the latter—how liberal theory can justify maintaining neutrality on a range of issues that are neither morally uncontroversial nor uncontroversially nonmoral. The standard liberal party line, endorsed by Kekes and Hart, is that on these issues, the liberal society advocates moral pluralism. It is in this context that I believe a clear connection can be made between liberalism and the two senses of moral pluralism discussed earlier. Not surprisingly, there appear to be two options.

1. In essence, Kekes's response to DT is that a liberal society (which he takes "our society" to be) is pluralistic in the manner of a pluralistic moral view. There is no disintegration since there is a shared morality. This pluralistic morality recognizes a set of irreducible moral considerations that can conflict in specific cases, and at least in some cases there is no reliable uncontroversial decision procedure for resolving the conflict. Here the liberal state "does not take a moral stand," adopts a position of moral neutrality, and must tolerate at least that range of divergent points of view associated with the moral considerations that are in conflict. But this neutrality is not derived from skepticism over the legitimacy of the conflicting moral considerations. If there is any skepticism underlying liberal theory's neutrality, it is confined to the level of resolving or "refereeing" conflicts between legitimate moral considerations in specific cases. When liberal theory is linked to this species of moral pluralism, moral conflicts are akin to what Bernard Williams has called "one-party conflicts."[21] I shall refer to this conception of liberalism as *Liberalism I*.

2. Liberal theory has also been construed as viewing moral conflicts on the model of what Williams has termed "two-party conflicts." If the skepticism or neutrality of liberal theory extends, not only to decision procedures for refereeing conflicts, but also to the legitimacy of moral considerations themselves, then liberalism can be characterized as advocating, tolerating, or being derived from a pluralism of moral views within a society. I shall refer to this as *Liberalism II*.

While either of these characterizations of liberal theory will advocate tolerance of divergent points of view, the grounds for doing so, as well as the range of views tolerated, will differ. Consider an example discussed (although not in this context) by Williams: a conflict between freedom and equality. If liberalism's connection with moral pluralism is in the model of Liberalism I (so that the connection is with a pluralistic moral view), then assuming that freedom and equality are among the set of legitimate moral considerations, the analysis of a conflict between them would run roughly as follows: while freedom and equality are each recognized to be legitimate moral considerations, there is no available decision procedure (at least in this case) for determining which should take precedence; hence, on this issue the liberal society must remain neutral. If, on the other hand, the model is Liberalism II (where the link is to a pluralism of moral views), the analysis would be: since the legitimacy of neither freedom nor equality can be recognized, the liberal society must remain neutral on this issue.

In a sense, this analysis yields two conceptions of liberal theory—one incorporating a pluralistic moral view that grounds and provides the theoretical underpinnings of liberal theory, and another that simply links liberal theory to a society that incorporates or tolerates divergent moral views. Among classical writers, John Locke's view provides a clear example of Liberalism I, insofar as his liberal political theory is derived from natural rights to life, liberty, and property, even if Locke himself was not as forthcoming as he should have been about how these rights can conflict and what society should do when conflicts occur. John Stuart Mill's argument in *On Liberty* for toleration of diversity based on the nature of truth-seeking and the limits of human knowledge fits well with Liberalism II.[22] Examples of each conception of liberalism can also be found in the work of roughly contemporary writers who can be considered liberals in this wide sense. Bernard Williams claims that most disputes about values in our society are one-party conflicts, as opposed to (e.g.) "a body of single-minded egalitarians confronting a body of equally single-minded libertarians."[23] Isaiah Berlin claims that cultures "obsessed by single models are rare . . . and tend to collapse violently when, in the end, their concepts are blown up by reality." Instead, Berlin advocates a society whose picture of moral and social life involves "more than one model."[24] Both Williams and Berlin thus appear to advocate Liberalism I. On the other hand, James Fishkin's reference to the "neutrality required by the liberal state *on ultimate moral convictions*" appears to follow the model of Liberalism II.[25] Similarly, Brian Barry characterizes the "essence of liberalism" as a "vision of society as made up of independent, autonomous units who cooperate only when the terms of cooperation are such as make it further the ends of each of the parties."[26] And P. F. Strawson portrays the liberal society as one "in which there are variable moral environments but in which no ideal endeavors to engross, and determine the character of, the common morality," and in fact encourages the development of many ideal images of life.[27]

So, it is fair to say that each conception of liberal theory is included in the history of liberal thought. It is important, however, to point out a tension between the two conceptions. For example, the analysis of a conflict between freedom and equality shows that while Liberalism I asserts the moral legitimacy of freedom and equality, Liberalism II must refrain from doing so. Tensions of this sort have both created confusion and disarray within liberal thought itself, and provided a target for critics of liberal theory, in particular, proponents of DT and communitarians. In what follows, I shall explore, in light of the two conceptions of liberalism, a few related issues facing liberal theory.

1. In advocating a pluralism of moral views, Liberalism II serves well the liberal goal of maintaining neutrality on life-style issues and protecting the freedom of the individual. But the danger appears to be the type of "moral anarchy" that worries proponents of DT and the "eroding of moral fabric" or "moral malaise" that worries communitarians. In order to avoid the charge of moral anarchy, liberal theory must maintain that not just any life-style or moral position is to be tolerated—some types of behavior simply must be restricted. But it is difficult to determine what types of behavior should be restricted, and the grounds on which those restrictions are justified, in the absence of an appeal to some type of background moral theory (however minimal), which entails that some types of behavior should not be tolerated. For instance, how can liberalism maintain that intolerance (perhaps above all) should not be tolerated? It appears that Liberalism II is vulnerable to the moral anarchy charge, and rebuttal almost invariably invokes some type of background moral theory, in the manner of Liberalism I.

2. While Liberalism I fares better against the moral anarchy charge, it is not without its own set of problems. Since Liberalism I incorporates a pluralistic moral view, this view itself stands in need of justification. In order to minimize controversy at the level of background theory, one standard liberal tack is to endorse a fairly limited or "thin" background moral theory, perhaps in terms of the good (John Rawls) or individual rights (Robert Nozick). Although Rawls's lexical ordering departs from this model to a considerable extent (but by no means completely), Liberalism I generally allows that when conflicts between moral considerations identified as legitimate by the background theory conflict, the liberal society should remain neutral. But two potential pitfalls await Liberalism I: (1) while a relatively thin background theory will probably prove less controversial than a relatively thick background theory, the thinner the background theory, the more bite there is to the moral anarchy charge. (2) While a relatively thick background theory would lessen the impact of the moral anarchy charge,

it is likely to lessen as well the range of life-styles and points of view tolerated within the liberal society. And there must be some requisite degree of neutrality, in terms of both the range of issues on which the state is neutral and the range of points of view tolerated on those issues, for a theory to qualify as sufficiently liberal.

3. In the model of Liberalism II, liberal theory appears largely procedural, that is, as a *process* of accommodating a variety of divergent points of view within a society. On the other hand, Liberalism I's reliance on a background moral theory looks to be more of a substantive view. The difficulties here are essentially similar to those raised above: if liberalism is largely procedural, the moral anarchy charge looms large, whereas if liberalism is substantive, the difficulties include justifying its background theory and determining to what extent certain points of view are excluded on those issues where liberalism does take a stand, even if the stand is limited to recognizing only a few points of view as legitimate. According to Liberalism II, any number of substantive results might be justifiable provided that they are arrived at by employing certain procedures—those conducive to maintaining a pluralism of moral views. According to Liberalism I, the justificatory "arrow" points in precisely the opposite direction: procedures can be justified only by reference to a background (substantive) moral theory, so that if a certain procedure yields (substantively) indefensible results, the procedure must be rejected. This would explain how some liberal theorists characterize the view as a "pluralistic theory of democracy" and "a process of political accommodation," while others insist that liberalism includes "some kind of moral foundation" and involves "balancing liberty with other goals, like equality and social justice."[28]

4. On at least some points Kekes is correct—there is a sense of moral pluralism that refers to pluralistic moral views, and proponents of DT frequently, if not invariably, fail to consider this sense of the term in arguing that moral pluralism leads to disintegration. Likewise, Kekes is correct in pointing out that if some proponents of DT are concerned that disintegration will result from a pluralistic moral view, they have provided no solid ground for their concern. Kekes also believes that our society has a shared morality that is pluralistic, but I have argued that we should be skeptical of this claim. And what actually worries proponents of DT, such as Devlin and Durkheim, are the effects of a pluralism of moral views. So it would be fair to say that proponents of DT are fearful of the effects of Liberalism II, and Kekes's response is that their concerns should not extend to Liberalism I.

How then should we understand the concerns of communitarians, whose dissatisfaction with liberalism resembles that of proponents of DT in any number of respects? At least some communitarians appear to be concerned about the effects of pluralistic moral views. In *After Virtue*, Alasdair MacIntyre mentions both "moral pluralism" and "moral disorder" as sources of difficulty in contemporary (i.e., liberal) society, and at times uses the terms as if they were virtually synonymous. And while MacIntyre could be understood as referring instead to a pluralism of moral views, he characterizes the source of his concern as follows: "There seems to be no rational way of securing moral agreement in our culture."[29] The context of this remark indicates that while moral disorder resulting from a pluralism of moral views would be sufficient for our inability to secure moral agreement, any type of pluralistic moral view that fails to provide a decision procedure for adjudicating conflicts between conflicting moral considerations would as well fail to allay MacIntyre's concerns, as indeed might any moral view that allows legitimate moral considerations to conflict in any way whatsoever.[30]

Here the response of liberal theory must be twofold: (1) MacIntyre's misgivings appear to be directed not so much at liberal political theory as modern moral philosophy. While there is no doubt a connection between the two, the issues are distinguishable at least in principle, and it is a mistake simply to equate the moral theoretic dispute with issues in political theory. (2) When communitarians argue their case against what MacIntyre calls "moral disorder," the argument proceeds from the assumption that the proper conception of liberal theory is Liberalism II. From this the implication is drawn that liberalism involves not much more than abstract individualism and skepticism about the good.[31] While I have not addressed the question of individualism here, there appears to be no necessary connection between liberalism and abstract individualism, and indeed many contemporary liberal theorists explicitly reject abstract individualism.[32] And as we have seen, Liberalism I involves no skepticism about the good. As with proponents of DT, there is precious little argument by communitarians to the effect that pluralistic moral views will lead to anything like the describable conditions associated with moral disorder. Therefore, Liberalism I appears undamaged by this species of communitarian criticism.

5. The criticisms of proponents of DT and communitarians do provide a valuable lesson for liberal theorists. In responding to these criticisms, liberals must remain mindful of the two conceptions of liberalism, and hence of the two senses of moral pluralism as well. In

short, liberals should not permit the debate over *justifying* liberal theory to be cast in such a way that Liberalism II is taken as *the* foundational or justificatory premise for liberalism. On the question of justification, Liberalism I can provide a theoretical underpinning for Liberalism II in the following way. It is because of liberalism's commitment to a pluralistic moral view that as a matter of policy, a liberal society will accommodate a pluralism of moral views among its members. A political morality grounded in a pluralistic moral view will then provide that what a society should do is permit a pluralism of moral views on those issues that cannot be decisively resolved by the pluralistic moral view. Thus, in a liberal society there is room for tolerance of diversity and perhaps even encouragement of it. But this diversity is not to be equated with moral license or moral anarchy since those points of view that a liberal society tolerates must lie within the confines of the pluralistic view that grounds liberal theory. Hence, it is a bit misleading to refer to Liberalism I and II as "characterizations" or "conceptions" of liberal theory—they are more properly two "domains" or "spheres" of liberal theory. Liberalism I can provide the background theoretical justification for employing the policies of Liberalism II that include tolerance of divergent points of view on "freedom of choice" issues. Liberalism I and II are interrelated in being subsets of liberal theory proper, but distinct in their structure and role within liberal theory.

6. Of course, what I have said above is ultimately speculative and devoid of any troublesome specifics. But it does fit well with much of the recent "rethinking" of liberal theory. For example, Ronald Dworkin concludes that "liberalism cannot be based on scepticism. Its constitutive morality provides that human beings must be treated as equals by their government, not because there is no right and wrong in political morality, but because that is what is right."[33] If part of what it means to "treat human beings as equals" includes tolerance of a range of points of view on certain issues, this view is consistent with the picture I have presented. And along similar lines, J. Roland Pennock argues that liberalism is committed to a set of principles, but includes the stipulation that "no single principle . . . should serve as *the* foundational principle of liberalism."[34]

Elsewhere I have argued for a version of "legal moralism" that is roughly extensionally equivalent to Mill's Harm Principle.[35] According to "Limited Legal Moralism," the law is justified in restricting a type of behavior only when there is a consensus of rationally defensible moral views that condemns that type of behavior. While I do not address the issue of what specific behavior will be tolerated, the view could be extended to stipulate that in those areas where society is neutral, any behavior that can be made consistent with some rationally defensible moral theory should be permitted. Here there would be a type of "second-order moral consensus" that justifies a set of prohibitions roughly equivalent to those of the Harm Principle, thus avoiding the moral anarchy charge, while simultaneously identifying a set of life-style areas of tolerance of a range of acceptable points of view, and also providing a moral theoretic foundation for doing so. This moral theoretic foundation would almost undoubtedly be pluralistic, since there will be conflicts between those moral considerations identified as legitimate by the set of rationally defensible moral theories, and the policies sanctioned by Limited Legal Moralism will coincide with those of Liberalism II.

Thus, I conclude that the distinctions outlined at the beginning of this paper are important in providing a defense of liberalism against the criticisms of proponents of DT and communitarians, and in providing a direction in which those who are currently "rethinking" liberal theory should proceed.

Notes

1. This discussion owes much to C. D. Broad's *Five Types of Ethical Theory* (Oxford University Press, 1930), esp. Chapter 7.
2. This should not be taken to entail that for a theory to be pluralistic it must countenance (e.g.) both duties *and* goods. So-called mixed views would clearly be pluralistic. But as we shall see below, there are examples of pluralistic theories that recognize only goods or only duties, but hold that there is a plurality of goods or duties.
3. Broad, op. cit., 280. Broad's point applies nonetheless to consequentialist theories that eschew talk of reductionism and intrinsic goods.
4. Ibid.
5. John Kekes, "Is Our Morality Disintegrating?," *Public Affairs Quarterly*, 1, no. 1 (1987): 79–94.
6. Ibid., 89.
7. Ibid., 80.
8. Ibid., 90.
9. See, for example, Louis B. Schwartz, "Morals, Offenses and the Model Penal Code," in Richard Wasserstrom, *Morality and the Law* (Wadsworth, 1971), 86–106.
10. Kekes, op. cit, 89.
11. See, for example, Carl Cranor, "The Hart-Devlin Debate," *Criminal Justice Ethics* 2, no. 1 (1983): 59–65.

12. Patrick Devlin, "Morals and the Criminal Law," reprinted in Wasserstrom, op. cit., 36.
13. Ibid.
14. Devlin, op. cit., 33.
15. Emile Durkheim, *The Division of Labor in Society*.
16. H. L. A. Hart, "Social Solidarity and the Enforcement of Morality," in Tom L. Beauchamp and Terry P. Pinkard, eds., *Ethics and Public Policy*, 2d ed. (Prentice-Hall, 1983), 62–75.
17. While this might appear to be a semantic issue, it is not *purely* semantic since proponents of DT proceed to argue for the empirical claim that disintegration will occur in the absence of a consensus.
18. Devlin does say that a consensus exists when it would be reasonable to expect that twelve people chosen at random would be unanimous on an issue. While this might be sufficient for a consensus, if we take "reasonable" to mean something like "has a probability of greater than .5," his criterion would require agreement at least in excess of 92.5 percent. It is not clear how seriously even Devlin takes this proposal.
19. Hart, op. cit.
20. See Steven Lukes, *Individualism* (Harper and Row, 1973).
21. Bernard Williams, *Moral Luck* (Cambridge University Press, 1981), 72.
22. See Isaiah Berlin, "John Stuart Mill and the Ends of Life," in *Four Essays on Liberty* (Oxford University Press, 1969). This "epistemological" argument is based on the "empiricist" tenets that "we can never tell (until we have tried) where greater truth or happiness (or any other form of experience) may lie" (182), that "there is no absolute truth, only different roads towards it" (188), and, hence, "without full freedom of discussion the truth cannot emerge," since "new observations could in principle always upset a conclusion founded on earlier ones" (187). Still, Berlin argues that Mill's argument is ultimately best understood as based on the tenet that there is a multiplicity of things that are good, hence a pluralistic conception of the good, rather than on skepticism about the good.
23. Williams, op. cit., 73.
24. Isaiah Berlin, *Concepts and Categories*, (Viking Press, 1978), 159–60.
25. James Fishkin, *Beyond Subjective Morality: Ethical Reasoning and Political Philosophy* (Yale University Press, 1984), 154 (my emphasis).
26. Brian Barry, *The Liberal Theory of Justice* (Oxford University Press, 1973), 166.
27. P. F. Strawson, *Freedom and Resentment* (Methuen and Co., 1974), 44.
28. Karen J. Winkler, "Scholars Rethink Liberal Theory," *The Chronicle of Higher Education*, 22 April 1987, 6–8.
29. Alasdair MacIntyre, *After Virtue: A Study of Moral Philosophy* (University of Notre Dame Press, 1984), 6.
30. MacIntyre's argument in *After Virtue* bears more than a passing resemblance to Elizabeth Anscombe's argument in "Modern Moral Philosophy,"

reprinted in Judith J. Thomson and Gerald Dworkin, eds., *Ethics* (Harper and Row, 1968), 186–210. And the argument in the later *Whose Justice? Which Rationality?* (University of Notre Dame Press, 1988) is even more explicit in this regard. Here MacIntyre characterizes liberalism as the view that "every individual is to be equally free to propose and live by whatever conception of the good he or she pleases, derived from whatever theory or tradition he or she may adhere to, unless that conception of the good involves reshaping the life of the rest of the community in accordance with it" (336). But his major misgivings are that in liberalism "no overall ordering of goods is possible" (336), which he identifies with "this kind of increasingly emotivist culture" (343).

31. See Lukes (op. cit.), Chapter 11, for an account of "abstract individualism," as well as more than a dozen distinct varieties of "individualism."

32. See J. Roland Pennock, "Liberalism Under Attack," *The Political Science Teacher*, 3, no. 1 (1990): 1, 6–10.

33. Ronald Dworkin, "Liberalism," in Stuart Hampshire, ed., *Public and Private Morality* (Cambridge University Press, 1978), 142.

34. Pennock, op. cit., 8 (emphasis in original).

35. In "Limited Legal Moralism," *Criminal Justice Ethics*, 7, no. 2 (1988): 22–36.

4

Romantic Communitarianism: Blithedale Romance Versus the Custom House

Nancy L. Rosenblum

> It is my firm belief and hope that these terms of roof and hearthstone, which have so long been held to embody something sacred, are soon to pass out of men's daily use, and be forgotten.
> —Nathaniel Hawthorne, *The House of the Seven Gables*

Introduction: Hawthorne and Communitarianism

Waves of communitarianism, like the intense period of community-building in the first half of the nineteenth century and again in the 1960s and 1970s, are unique to American political culture.[1] We know from historical and sociological studies of utopianism that these communities differed wildly: some were erected by other-worldly millenarian groups transplanted from Europe, attracted here by religious toleration and cheap land; others were secular experiments in utopian socialism whose ideas were imported but whose members were erratically drawn from the various social strata of America; and, in addition, there were a host of "romantic communities"—self-governing friendship groups and expressive life-style enclaves uncommitted to any ideology. John Humphrey Noyes, the founder of Oneida and author of *History of American Socialisms* admitted that he was writing a history of failures; he called his work an inquest: "all died young, and most of them before they were two years old." It is true that relatively long-lived communities like Oneida are rare, and that these wide-ranging experiments in everything from property arrangements to "amative sexuality" have not introduced permanent social reform.² Nonetheless, from the broader perspective of American political thought elective communities are not at all trivial. Communitarianism is one manifestation of the dominant perfectionist American style, and the communal wish is always present in periods of democratic revitalization.³ And the motivations that inspire communal experiments along with the political conditions that make them possible are key to American political identity.

Elective community has not found its political theorist, though, and it is clear that contemporary political theorists of community (whom we call "communitarians") disregard elective community altogether. Nothing in the recent literature indicates interest in the historical presence of this form of communitarianism, or even acknowledges that community has often referred to groups voluntarily formed by individuals oriented by subjective values, personality, and affective desires.⁴ Indeed, contemporary communitarian theory may be conceptually unequipped to take elective community into account even if it would, for the notion of elective community unsettles familiar categories and distinctions: the individualism/holism divide, for example, or the contrast between constitutive community and consensual liberal democracy. One implication of this essay is that the conceptual framework of communitarian theory needs complicating. Another is that elective community raises questions about the adequacy of notions of the self that lie at the heart of contemporary communitarianism's theoretical enterprise.

Consider how elective community, and particularly its romantic variants, points up the inadequacy of standard accounts of individualism. The romantic sensibility seldom appears in discussions of individualism as atomistic or autonomous, yet it is the epitome of the sole self resisting found social contexts and disavowing inherited attachments, the model self-made individualist. When we think of romanticism, it is usually in terms of heroic individualism—as defiant exhibitionism or extravagant privatization and retreat. Things are complicated further by the fact that romantic individualism has a communitarian face. The lure of holism is definitely there, and romantics are attracted to elective community by the promise that the inner self can find expression in public life. Social studies of elective communities confirm this; R. M. Kanter described elective community in these terms: "both what is given to the group and what is received from it are seen by the person as expressing his true nature and as supporting his concept of self."[5] And, "what was going on was the collective making of a more authentic type of self . . . the prospect of a wholeness of identity not possible elsewhere."[6] In romantic community, we see what it means to want not just self-expression, which can take any number of lonely and apolitical forms—but genuine correspondence between inner self and outer world.

This sort of expressive holism is, of course, what contemporary communitarian theorists extol but associate exclusively with traditional or "constitutive" communities. A familiar contention of contemporary communitarian theory is that identity is found and not freshly created in accord with some imaginative vision or the imperatives of the law of the heart. As it is used today, the term "community" indicates more than just shared norms and practices. It evokes deep psychological attachments and developmental processes by which individuals are embedded in a communal context, penetrated by it, socialized into it, or identified with it. This association of community with unchosen, formative identity groups is apparent when political theorists speak of communities bound together by tradition and culture, or designate ethnic groups communities, or refer to ascriptive "communities" of blacks or women. And in recent discussions of democratic community too, we find this preoccupation with the formative effects of community on its members. Democratic theorists offer different catalogues of civic virtues, but they are united in the claim that democracy depends on the conscious reproduction of citizens. On this view, the constitutive function of democratic community is one of its defining features and what distinguishes it from liberal society.

Charles Taylor wrote in this connection that the least alienated human life is lived in communities "where the norms and ends expressed in the public life of a society are the most important ones by which its members define their identity as human beings."[7] Either this formula delineates a broader spectrum of unalienated life than Taylor seems to have intended, or it is an inadequate account of both community and identity. I will show that one public norm of American democracy is precisely self-made identity unencumbered by hereditary conditions, and another is voluntary association. Together they suggest that elective community is a rare but exemplary expression of the public life of American society, a distillation of the distinctive relation between democratic society and personal identity.

My main object in this essay is not conceptual analysis, though. I explore the relation between communitarianism and American democracy, and the pivotal part romanticism plays in this dynamic. There is no better entree to American communitarianism than the writings of Nathaniel Hawthorne. He saw variations of community all about him: in the still vivid heritage of his Puritan ancestors' city on the hill; in the revolutionary ideology that cast America as an experiment in democratic community (revived in his time by Jacksonian Democrats); in the spate of romantic retreats from society to communal life, Brook Farm among them. He provides the materials with which to compose a portrait of American political identity as a dynamic interaction of romantic, democratic, and communitarian elements, and the phases of this dynamic are brought to life in his work.

We read in *House of the Seven Gables* how even in its expansive Jacksonian era, democracy in America appeared to have failed to deliver on its promise of self-made identity unencumbered by inheritances and elective rather than found community. For those who took these revolutionary ideals to heart, America had devolved into a "Custom House." Hawthorne was its Surveyor.[8] The most familiar romantic response to the sense of aridity and dread closure were Promethean defiance or isolationist retreat, like Henry David Thoreau's. But another response was the romantic attempt to redeem the promises of democracy in elective community, and *Blithedale Romance* is the life-history of one.

The creation of communities such as Brook Farm is only part of the story. Hawthorne is a master narrator of the unintended, often cruel, and always self-defeating consequences of pursuing a romanticized wish for community relentlessly. He cast a cold eye on the excesses of perfectionism and the law of the heart when they are given free reign. Blithedale is an understandable romantic reaction against society experienced as a Custom House, but the Custom House offers relief from romantic community in turn: "Even the old Inspector was desirable, as a change of diet, to a man who had known Alcott," Hawthorne confessed.

Utopians such as Noyes took *Blithedale Romance* as evidence of Hawthorne's unmitigated hostility toward elective community, but the book is not unsympathetic to communitarianism, much less a satire. It is a psychologically and politically astute analysis of communal longing and disillusion. Certainly, Hawthorne never diminished romantic communitarianism by idealizing its adversaries; he was no Whig or skeptic. And he granted Jacksonian democracy its "proper respect and natural regard" because he thought there was room in ordinary democratic society for self-made identity and expressivism—the things that had made elective community compelling in the first place.[9] Through Hawthorne's fiction, we are able to follow the course from romantic repudiation to reconciliation to the real world of democracy.

In my earlier study of the romantic face of liberalism, I did not elaborate a methodological justification for using literature to discuss political theory; after all, literary expressions are our acknowledged "way in" to the romantic sensibility.[10] Here, my subject is the dynamics of American communitarianism, which can be described as a continual process of romanticization and chastening, and once again literature is crucial. Novels, which show us the changing lives and thoughts of characters in relation to one another, may be the only way to get a dynamic picture at all. We must meet Westerveldt to see why Blithedale might be attractive and Hollingsworth and Coverdale, Zenobia and Priscilla for Blithedale's own cruelties to be forcefully understood.

Hawthorne's grim account of the unintended effects of exquisite sympathy and sincerity on communal relations is of particular interest because it offers a sober corrective to current enthusiasms for an ethic of empathy and care and for communitarianism modeled on friendship. The confrontation between psychological reality as portrayed in a romance and the fantasy of close community we find in philosophy would be impossible outside of a novel. For the limitations of transparency and sincerity only emerge full force in a setting deliberately designed to achieve correspondence between the inner self and community, a setting that exists for most of us only in fiction.

There is a further reason for using literature to think about political theory here. It seems to me there is a close connection between Hawthorne's literary forms and a certain view of American democracy. In his allegorical tales and novels with allegorical overtones, seemingly arbitrary objects are made to stand for other things and to take on surprising meaning.[11] This prepares us for the idea that the self is expressed in an unexpected array of perfectly ordinary actions and institutions, and reinforces the thought that romantic expressivism is compatible with the plain face of democratic society. In "The Custom House" introduction to *The Scarlet Letter*, Hawthorne links his literary theory of romance explicitly to his notion of the democratic life, and says that the peculiar excellence of both romance and democracy is the creation of a balance between imaginative longing and the mundane.

Hawthorne's fictional counterpart, Coverdale, tries to strike this balance literally by moving back and forth between the Roxbury farm its members call Blithedale, and Boston. His strategy is unsuccessful, of course, but his explanation for alternately engaging and self-distancing captures Hawthorne's point: "No sagacious man will long retain his sagacity, if he live exclusively among reformers and progressive people, without periodically returning into the settled system of things, to correct himself by a new observation from that old standpoint" (156).[12]

This is not to suggest that Hawthorne is a political theorist, only that his novels are resources for thinking about the way in which romanticism, democracy, and community come together in American political identity.

The Two Faces of Romanticism

Before turning to the connection between communitarianism and democracy, it is worth emphasizing that romanticism has two aspects. The sensitive soul seeking the infinite and finding only the finite at every turn is a familiar theme in modern European and American literary and intellectual history. The romantic sensibility is marked by a sense of its own boundless potential, by revulsion at constriction and closure and at the very thought of being definitively constituted. In American thought, romanticism is most often captured in visions of the imperial self or the infinitude of the private person. We get our heroic individualism from Emerson, Thoreau, and of course Whitman, the most expansive and exhibitionistic of them all.

Yet romanticism is also characterized by the desire to have inner multiplicity reflected outside rather than thwarted, to find an external correspondence for the inner self. In English and Continental romanticism, accommodation to the rest of humanity and history exploits the heroic individualist's grandiose isolation instead of overcoming it: the poet is legislator, or prophet, or Promethean recreator of a disenchanted world. When European romantics do identify with some community it is with imaginative recreations of a frankly aristocratic past: beautified medievalism, or Athens "rising above the foamy tide," or Schiller's republic of letters—that exclusive company of great souls.

American romantics were embarrassed by these overtly antidemocratic visions, by claims of genius, and by their own inclinations to aesthetic isolation and retreat. Stifled by his tenure in the Salem Custom House, Hawthorne comforts himself with the thought "I am a citizen of somewhere else," meaning that he is really at home in his imagination, but he instantly takes back this traitorous idea and chastises himself for being unable to find literary inspiration in the dull Custom House routine. The result is a characteristically American set of romantic scenes of belonging that avoid identification with democratic society as it is without being defiant or confrontational.[13] Emerson went back and forth between the "infinitude of the private man" and "representative man"—heroic individualism once removed from ordinary people but not rejecting. Thoreau frankly preferred immersion in nature to any regular association or cooperation, but managed, for the most part, to avoid the accusation of misanthropy. Whitman had the boldest solution: merging with every element of teeming democracy. Whitman's is a limitless "I." He "contains multitudes." D. H. Lawrence saw this as a pathetic loss of self—Walt was leaking out all over; others have seen it as narcissistic engulfing, gigantic self-enlargement.[14]

Hawthorne recognized the seductiveness of this vision of fusion with a romanticized democratic mass. In *House of the Seven Gables*, Clifford, the exquisitely sensitive aesthete, watches a political procession from the balcony and finds the democratic spectacle so enchanting he is ready to plunge down into the "surging stream of human sympathies" to his death. Hawthorne explains: "by its remoteness, it melts all the petty personalities, of which it is made up, into one broad mass of existence—one great life—one collected body of mankind, with a vast, homogeneous spirit animating it" (147). It is as if he were commenting, acidly, on the romantic propensity for portraying the plain face of democracy as sublime in order to make it palatable at all.

Hawthorne knew all about the embarrassed antiworldliness and the whispy connectedness of romantics, transcendentalists among them. Revolted by prosaic democratic society but uncomfortable with heroic individualism, attracted to holism but not to an idealized European past, American romantics seem caught between privatization and airy, aestheticized democracy. Henry James explained the tendency to introspection as the only resource for sensitive souls in a society that provided little external entertainment; finding the self interesting could help to make life interesting, he wrote.[15] Emerson and Thoreau were not pure introverts, and their writings inspired reformers in practice. But they plainly dissociated themselves from democratic politics; Thoreau declared his intention to stand aloof from cooperation even when it aims at correcting the most enormous wrong. Coverdale, the minor poet in *Blithedale Romance*, puts it exactly when he described Emerson's essays, *The Dial*, Thomas Carlyle's works, and George Sand's romances as "the cry of some solitary sentinel, whose station was on the outposts of the advance-guard of human progression"(75–76) and Hawthorne casts a cold eye on this outpost in "The Celestial Railroad."

The concrete array of elective communities that sprang up in the first half of the nineteenth century indicated that alternatives to Promethean defiance or privatization and retreat were conceivable.

Religious revivalism and collective awakenings were another fact of society, and Perry Miller identified the Second Awakening with romanticism. His reasoning is instructive. Revivalism grew, in part, out of the romantic appetite for self-examination and expressivism, but he insisted that it was not escapist. Radical personal conversion was public not private, occurring in community, not alone, and meant to usher in a new America.[16] Miller called its religious aspect "romantic evangelicalism" and its broader outlook "romantic nationalism." It aimed at establishing the importance of the inner man and woman of feeling for America. In the same way, romantic community was directed against democracy devolved into a Custom House; Hawthorne disparagingly called those who felt most at home there "legitimate sons of the revenue service"; they had the rigidity of dead corpses, and were without imagination, fancy, or sensibility. The idea was to reassert heart over head, spontaneity, excitement, vigor, warmth, life-giving energy, and imaginative vision; to glorify sincerity and the law of the heart as both personal qualities and an alternative social glue.

"Elective" community brings to mind classic liberal notions of the origin of authority and obligation in consent, and it is true that Jacksonian Democrats reminded one another all the time that further progress in the spirit of 1776 would only follow from aggressively pursuing the voluntary principle and "untried experiments."[17] For romantics who took the democratic wish to its extreme, however, the problem with found order and constitutive contexts is not fully captured by roles and obligations as arbitrarily imposed or mutely inherited, which is why even Thomas Paine's radical prescription for a revolution in every generation fails to capture romantic expectations. Involuntariness is important, but expressivity is key. Elizabeth Peabody, writing about Brook Farm, described "a few individuals . . . unknown to each other, under different disciplines of life, reacting from different social evils, but aiming at the same object,—of being wholly true to their natures as men and women."[18]

Being true to one's nature is the romantic answer to one of the central problems of American politics—how to form a political community from a company of strangers who did not share and did not wish to share religious beliefs, kinship, or loyalty to traditional authorities. What is the glue if the available alternatives—rights and contracts, impersonal market relations, or distant democratic elections—are also repulsive? Free of the custom house, the thought goes, the inner man and woman of imagination and feeling will unite spontaneously with others. That is why, despite the term "elective," romantic community is perfectly consistent with involuntary obedience to the law of the heart, or irresistible attraction to some perfectionist vision. Romantic community aims above all at complementarity between the singular self and the world, and as George Santayana remarked, in America "this metaphysical illusion has a partial warrant in historical fact." Its warrant comes from the public promises of democracy. With characteristic extravagance, romantic communitarians intend to make good the promise of uninherited identity and elective community for themselves.

Hereditary Conditions: Property, Genealogy, and Gender

The essence of Americanism was disavowal of hereditary conditions, and repudiation of inherited identity was an aspect of revolutionary ideology forcefully proclaimed during the Jacksonian era. The issue was not whether strong constitutive forces, material and cultural, were at work in society; clearly there were. Simply, none was supposed to be finally constituted by these found conditions or fully identified with a given social role.[19] Individual identity was infinitely variegated, mysterious, and always surprising. And these qualities of American character were thought to correspond to fluid external conditions. In romantic formulations of the idea, there is an unbounded private self of feeling and imagination, which has a powerful claim to expression in the public life of democracy.

Tension between the democratic wish and the persistence of inheritances preoccupied Hawthorne. He saw the strong grip of kinship, estate, and hereditary traits all about him in a political society that pretends they have been erased. Not everyone was attuned to these forces. Henry James thought that the past had time to produce so little that it attracted scant attention: America did not have ancient classes, castes, manners, or institutions, and his famous litany of what is lacking continues on. America was a "thinly composed society," and James had compassion for Hawthorne (and for himself) struggling to draw romance from such meager elements. To Santayana, it seemed as if Hawthorne wrote in an utter social vacuum; his genius was employed in "digestion of vacancy." In the same spirit, Irving Howe argued that like all American novelists, Hawthorne was reduced to treating politics as a form of personal experience because there was not enough real political material in the environment. And Lionel Trilling described the lack of solidity of American society, the absence of palpable weight and force.[20]

By contrast, Hawthorne was excruciatingly conscious of the pressure of American history and genealogy on imagination. He knew the weight of antiquity and longing for pagan beauty had not been lifted off everyone; *The Marble Faun* tells that story. Certainly America had enough in the way of inheritance and unearned privilege to foster the pretense of nobility, to undermine the social ethos of voluntary association, and to make the ideal of self-made identity seem like a chimera. *House of the Seven Gables* is an extended narrative on the theme, "how much of old material goes to make up the freshest novelty of human life" (12). In part, this echoes the standard political rhetoric of Jacksonian democracy: the American revolution is unfinished; a "regal fungus" survives and so do features of feudal Europe— "entails, nobility, hierarchy, and monopolies."[21] The difference is that Hawthorne was less interested in transferring social status and political influence from a "paper aristocracy" to laboring classes than in understanding the social psychology of democratic expectation and disillusion in the face of inherited conditions. He showed just how the public ideology of self-made identity fostered two rival romantic illusions: the subversive dream of aristocracy and the wish for perfectly unencumbered, expressive individuality.

Inheritance begins for Hawthorne with the externals: material legacies and legal privileges. Wherever there is property to be passed on, expectation of ownership will define the character of owner and heir. In practice, inherited property ceases to be alienable and becomes constitutive. Imagination can cling to a prerevolutionary grant of crown lands even when the deed is lost, and a seedy house in Salem can serve as well as a feudal castle as carrier of class and character. *House of the Seven Gables* shows just how social attributes attached to inherited property including snobbery, idleness, gentility, exquisite aestheticism, and political bullying work themselves out in three morally crippled Pyncheon cousins. Inheritance is corrupting and a plain affront to democratic equality; Judge Pyncheon's paternalistic benevolence masks a ruthlessness that Hawthorne associates with unearned wealth.

For Hawthorne, the disastrous effects of inheritance on the heirs themselves is the most telling and least appreciated consequence of hereditary property in democracy. The inability to dissociate oneself from inherited social status results in an incapacity for self-preservative change in the face of changed external circumstances, which are inevitable. Hepzibah's aristocratic elevation of uselessness into an ideal of good character, her notion that gentility is soiled by trade (or, what is still more inconceivable, working for others) made her poverty abject and ridiculous.[22] Imagined nobility was paralyzing. So was dependence on public office. The officials working under the gaze of the Custom House eagle are Hawthorne's embodiment of republican hopes gone to seed; the Custom House officials forfeited their powers and capacity for self-support, Hawthorne wrote; they lived in terror of party changes and loss of favors (107). The most resilient character in his novels is the plebeian Phoebe, who is self-reliant, utterly capable in practical affairs, and stands apart from her Pyncheon cousins because she has no expectations of property, indeed, no fixed expectations at all. Hawthorne casts the very survival of any self insufficiently identified with democratic independence in doubt.

If one aspect of inheritance is conservatism, its opposite is social extinction, and Hawthorne understood why the loss of fortune was such a central drama in American society. Inheritance is materialism devoid of the "spiritual existence" and presumptive virtue associated with European nobility. The would-be American aristocrat could no more lay claim to honor than he or she could to proud self-reliance, so without wealth, he or she has no social standing at all. That is why loss of fortune is experienced as a final loss, a sort of social death, and in a republic, someone is always on the point of drowning (39).

Hawthorne did not subscribe to every element of Jacksonian ideology. Neither the portrayal of democratic society as a conflict between rich and poor nor the rhetorical image of a single democratic people free of classifications and enjoying a consensus had much appeal for him. He did share the Jacksonian notion of true and false social hierarchy but without the Democrats' absolute confidence in meritocratic striving. He worried that after the Civil War, military merit ("or rather, since that is not so readily estimated, military notoriety") would become the sole measure of civil distinction.[23] He admitted to finding nothing more foolish "than the eagerness with which gaunt and goslin-like youths strive to break through the barriers."[24] One source of his skepticism is the thought that identity is not fully comprised by what we do. There is more to the unencumbered self than the independence of earning one's living, which is why his notion of democratic character does not begin and end with productive work. Like romantics, Hawthorne was interested in the innermost self, or heart, and whether it could find genuine public expression.

There are metaphysical and cognitive reasons why the true self is impossible to discover, but Hawthorne has still more to say about the social obstacles at work in democracy. Hereditary property is the most obvious compromise of the public ideal of unencumbered identity but it is not the only one. Family per se is inheritance, and habits and traits acquired in the fabric of families can have all the force of genetic makeup. Physical likeness and physical mutilation are Hawthorne's way of describing the ineradicable power of these attachments. Descendants of leading families whose reputations were based on revolutionary leadership enjoyed inherited status and political influence. The Hawthorne family is a reminder that impressive political genealogies did not begin with the revolution, and that there is another, older source of status based on piety. And Hawthorne looked forward to the upset of Southern dynasties if the North were victorious in the Civil War.[25] Moreover, personal past may operate powerfully whether or not one's ancestors are ancient or illustrious. Holgrave, Hawthorne's model democratic individualist, is motivated by the desire to avenge a wrong inflicted on his family by the Pyncheons generations ago, and it does not matter that the Mauls have no claim to public notice.

Names are our universal inheritance. His family's 225-year history had an unmistakable hold on Hawthorne. In keeping with the democratic wish for self-made identity, Hawthorne, born on the Fourth of July, changed his. In keeping with his chastened hopes for pure self-made identity, Hawthorne wrote about his past. Still, if pure self-creation is an illusion, so is found identity; it would be equally immature to experience his Puritan ancestors as an incubus or to disavow them carelessly. (Though of the two, Hawthorne had less tolerance for the dumb, delusive, "oyster-like tenacity" with which some people cling to family and settled expectations.) The truth is that imagination is as much at work on personal history as it is on creating visions of the future, and Hawthorne described his own imaginative appropriation of the past, his dream of his "official ancestor" giving him the document, the "scarlet symbol," which resulted in *The Scarlet Letter*. Hawthorne thought that telling the story was a filial duty, but it emerged as something all his own—a sober estimate of the cruelty and the dignity of Puritanism. In contrast to Hawthorne's account of identity, both found and self-invented, the contemporary notion of the "constituted self" seems simplistic; no psychologically true conception of identity-formation can exclude imagination, or the power of the democratic wish that gives imagination license.

To inherited property and family, Hawthorne adds sexual identity. Gender and institutionalized expressions of patriarchy are blatantly antidemocratic; they are also among the most inescapable of hereditary conditions. Zenobia points out to an oblivious Coverdale the facts of the division of labor at Blithedale: "to bake, to boil, to roast, to fry, to stew,—to wash, and iron, and scrub, and sweep,—and, at our idler intervals to repose ourselves on knitting and sewing" will be feminine occupations until the coming of paradise (43–44). She means until the end of the world. Not even utopia overturned *this* inherited state.[26] Patriarchy entails more than a laundry list of customary tasks and roles, of course; it involves predictable patterns of submission and the vulnerability of women to arbitrary abuse. None knew better than Hawthorne the roots of vicious sexism in religious ideology, in particular, Puritanism's horror of female sexuality. But Hollingsworth and Coverdale are both modern, secular types, proof that Hawthorne never imagined that throwing off the Puritan yoke, or brave declarations of sexual liberation by women like Zenobia, would bring sexism to an end. Sometimes he seems to have thought that patriarchy was the most formidable obstacle to self-made identity, and to community.

Social characteristics so deep that they may effectively define the self, transmitted through family, property, and gender—not a new idea, but a stern commentary on a political culture that publicly repudiates hereditary conditions. (Remarkably, Hawthorne had nothing to say in this connection about slavery.) For romantics who experienced society as a Custom House most keenly, the impetus to disavow inheritances and to reveal the significance of the private man and woman of feeling for a rehabilitated public life was the inspiration to elective community.

In *Blithedale Romance*, every disavowed inheritance reemerges with a vengeance. Hawthorne does not let us forget that elective communities were frequently supported by inherited wealth, Blithedale by Zenobia's. Concealed family ties (and names) give the narrative its melodramatic movement: a lost fortune and a secret marriage are the dark and dirty past Coverdale tries so hard to uncover. Their hiddenness is what makes them so seductive to him, since even in elective community knowing someone means discerning who he or she has been.[27] Not even the defiant Zenobia experiences herself as unencumbered; she finds her past shameful. Hawthorne's thought is that *any* past is a guilty burden. The public ideal of self-made identity, romanticized and made the reason for elective community, insures that will be the case. Zenobia was determined to disavow unchosen attachments but could not, and their continued power in her life violates the norm of transparency and elective affinity. At the same time, to the extent that she can be "born again," she is guilty too, since self-made identity means betraying her family and abandoning those who have done her no deliberate wrong.

Patriarchy reasserts itself in Blithedale as well. Hollingsworth is usually cast as a fanatical social reformer, but his vanity and what is at bottom, his profound conventionality, emerge plainly in his unrepentant sexism: "All the separate action of woman is and ever has been, and always shall be, false, foolish, vain, destructive of her own best and holiest qualities, void of every good effect, and productive of intolerable mischiefs! Man is a wretch without woman; but woman is a monster—without man as her acknowledged principal" (139–40). Conventionality is too weak a description for his vicious misogyny. Many of Hawthorne's tales turn on the forcible, often sadistic repression of female sexuality by men. The most horrible is "The Minister's Black Veil," with its rejecting patriarch, transvestism, and suggestion of necrophilia. In *Blithedale Romance*, Hawthorne has something to say against virtually every millennial hope for deliberate personal and social reform. Yet he is sympathetic toward Zenobia's feminism. Her question pointed to the best reason for leaving the Custom House society for the experiment of elective community: "Did you ever see a happy woman in your life?" (82). Hawthorne created a happy girl in Phoebe, but she is a simple soul who does not defy the limits of gender as Zenobia did; and *House of the Seven Gables* ends before we see what marriage and inheritance will mean for Phoebe.

It is even less surprising that the Custom House reasserts itself in elective community once we recognize that the motivations to join were not always romantic. In addition to freeloaders and desperate social misfits, there are men and women comfortable with the ordinary material promises of democracy who elect community for a second chance, not a second self. In "The Canterbury Pilgrims," it turns out that the handful of hopeful travelers to a Shaker village are not religious believers and that they neither want to escape the world nor to reform it. Instead, the ruined merchant hopes to manage Shaker trade, the poor farmer and his wife hope to find material security, the obscure poet hopes for recognition (1198–99). They are not wrong to seek the mundane in utopia. Hawthorne knew that communities either depend on patronage or support themselves by competition in the marketplace, so that as Coverdale observed, "we stood in the position of a new hostility to society at large." Another unintended consequence of life in elective community is immersion in ordinary affairs and the subordination of expressivity to productivity. "The peril of our way of life was not that we should fail in becoming practical agriculturalists, but that we should probably cease to be anything else" (87). It has been observed that the discipline of work in communal settings looks more like a tactic for integrating marginal types into society than like counterculture.[28]

Coverdale knows that romantic expectations cannot be satisfied by voluntariness alone, that election is not enough. Choosing labor for personal reasons rather than economic necessity makes physical work palatable to Coverdale as it was not to the Roxbury farmers, but it is the expressive nature of the choice that matters. Labor could never reflect some beautiful aesthetic vision or the law of the heart, no matter how cooperative or justly distributed: "the clods of earth, which we so constantly belabored and turned over and over, were never etherealized into thought. Our thoughts, on the contrary, were fast becoming cloddish" (88). The idea that *anything* "belabored and turned over and over," like the idea that "we should practically cease to be anything else," is abhorrent. Democratic identity is fluidity, romantic in its resistance to definition.

The historical presence of elective community, and his own experience at Brook Farm, enabled Hawthorne to survey the damage of the romanticized democratic wish for self-made identity, personal and communal. An untempered law of the heart results in vulnerability and paralysis, and the inexorable demands of imagined perfection are tyrannical. The tyranny of aesthetic vision is abroad in private life, of course; we see insane imagination at work in Aylmer, the villain of Hawthorne's ghastly story "The Birthmark," who was so in love with beauty that he murdered his wife trying to remove her one imperfection, the "bloody hand" imprinted by nature on her cheek. But the consequences of imagination and feeling for public life are distilled in romantic community, where they are given free reign.

Perfectionism and the Persecuting Spirit: "Keep the imagination sane!"

Hawthorne is unsurpassed as a psychologist of the hypocrisy and moral cruelty of perfectionism, which has so often inspired elective community. Early American religious settlements fit this description, of course, and *The Scarlet Letter* dissects the hardness of Hawthorne's own "first ancestor" in the first "city on the hill," whose persecuting spirit was passed on to the son "who made himself conspicuous in the martyrdom of witches" (89). Beyond this, Hawthorne alerts us to just how pervasive the "iron heart and strong will" continue to be in a political culture that invites experiments, and in which personal and collective identity is often tied up with imagined perfection. The Quaker mother persecuted by the Puritans in "The Gentle Boy," turned out to be as ferocious as her conscientious tormentors—she had no desire to avoid martyrdom, and her abandoned son was the only innocent victim of all that godliness. Hawthorne saw the same hard-heartedness around him in contemporary religious communitarianism ("The Shaker Bridal"), and in revivalism and millenarianism ("Earth's Holocaust" and "The Celestial Railroad"). It also was at work in the founding of secular communities; Hollingsworth's philanthropic dreams brought him to Blithedale and made everyone there miserable.

The hypocrisy of perfectionism was one of Hawthorne's preoccupations: the appalling self-delusion of people who never doubt that their imaginative visions are creative and inspired by divine grace, inner light, or the law of the heart. Perfectionism is a sort of grandiose egotism; the visionary's imagination IS a mirror, but of his or her own "haunted mind," not nature or God. Zenobia recognizes Hollingsworth's idealism as "nothing but self! Nothing else; nothing but self, self, self!" Hollingsworth was as fanatical as a Puritan magistrate, but Hawthorne was kinder toward his ancestors. They were redeemed somewhat by piety and humility in the face of an inscrutable God, if not other men.[29] Moreover, the Puritans stood firm in the grim knowledge that perfection was incompatible with worldly happiness; their cruelty was mitigated by fortitude. Hollingsworth is so absorbed by his reformist vision and so unattuned to actuality that he is unaware of his cruelty; fantasy overruns the private person of feeling, and Hollingsworth is barely human.[30] Coverdale observes that in all reformers an overruling purpose "does not so much impel them from without, nor even operate as a motive from within, but grows incorporate with what they think and feel and finally converts them into little else save that one principle. . . . They have no heart, no sympathy, no reason, no conscience. They will keep no friend . . ."(92).

Not all romantic visions for self and community echo religious perfectionism in this way. On the other side, communitarians who determined to elicit the real private feelings of others and to draw them into a company of friends are driven by fantasies of their own, as I will show, and Coverdale is another kind of persecuting spirit. He was as attracted to the dream of transparency and intimacy as Hollingsworth was to the dream of prison reform. He was no less manipulative than Hollingsworth, and more intrusive.

Both of these types work on the weak, on selfless selves like Priscilla, the perfect mesmeric subject, the epitome of blankness. Hollingsworth, greedy for disciples in the cause of reform, is no better than Westerveldt, the charlatan obsessed with money, self-promoting, and exploitative—the worst of the "western world." For poor souls like Priscilla who are insensibly drawn to the heroic individualism of the strong, submission to Hollingsworth is no more elective than enslavement to Westerveldt. And for everyone else, the pressure of these persecuting spirits—endless indoctrination by Hollingsworth and perpetual scrutiny by Coverdale—is inhibiting. Blithedale began as an experiment in expressivity and rapidly became claustrophobic.

The Chillingworths, Hollingsworths, and Coverdales of elective community make ordinary social climbers, snobs, rigid civil servants, and bullying politicians seem like not such bad types after all. Hawthorne offered up biting portraits of his fellow Salem officials for whom democratic society is literally a Custom House, found not elected. Their business encouraged them to be corrupt, and they were vulgar to a man: the stupid military veteran, the inspector who was the perfect animal nature, "so shallow, so delusive, so impalpable, such an absolute nonentity," the man of business bred up from boyhood in the custom house, which was his proper field of activity (94, 98). Still, it turns out that to be "thoroughly adapted to the situation which he held" is only one way to be unfaithful to the democratic promise of self-made identity and elective community. At least it claims fewer victims than imagination gone insane.

Romantic Expressivism and the Law of the Heart

We know from the ardent Zenobia that there is more to romantic communitarianism than perfectionist visions and persecuting spirits. Zenobia is independence, imagination, sexuality, natural beauty, physical exercise. She must contend not only with Hollingsworth, whose obsession with reform blinds him to her attractions, but also with Coverdale and Priscilla. They are drawn to her erotic energy, but without knowing why, and are blind to the dangers eroticism holds for community as they imagine it. Coverdale is a different sort of follower of the law of the heart, who imagines a tender community of friends, where strangers are bound together by sympathy and are committed "first of all" not to some program but to replace pride with familiar love (46, 85). Heart and hearth are the sources of what is expected to be a benign, extended domesticity.

Zenobia could not abide the familial ideal of community in which she was cast in a maternal role; she turned away from a nurturing ethos as fiercely as she did from a paternalistic one. Certainly, the model of caring as mothering, which describes relations in terms of responsibility for a child's growth into individuality, has no appeal for her; elective community is supposed to be a scene of free self-expression, not development. For Zenobia, community meant strong friends, creative work, and passionate love. She is the good face of romantic Prometheanism in Blithedale and of the untamed law of the heart. But the dominant impulse behind Blithedale was to associate free expression of feelings with a milder, warmer set of feelings, with sentimental friendship and domesticity.

This is a familiar thought, since moral theorists today propose that we should draw on the personal realm for standards of community in just this way: caretaking, nurturance, empathy, and connectedness are said to provide new models of egalitarian relations. The core idea is that sympathetic attention to others is the sole source of genuine insight into their interests and desires, and that appreciation of subtle, individual differences is the necessary prelude to assessing obligations. The line of thought clearly goes beyond Bernard Williams's more modest proposition that equal respect requires genuine efforts at understanding, putting oneself in another's shoes.[31] Instead, empathy is supposed to produce active caring; the disposition to care is supposed to follow as an immediate and powerful response to empathy's knowledge. We see in contemporary moral theory how attentiveness to individuality and close connection come seamlessly together. Hawthorne shows these ideas at work in *Blithedale Romance*, to unhappy effect and we see there why the formula of sympathetic attention is radically incomplete.

For one thing, appreciation of individuality depends not only on attention but also on the inclination and capacity of others to express, if not purposefully communicate, their true selves, and Hawthorne describes limitations on expressivity as *the* moral problem of community. Ordinary selfishness can be transcended in community much more easily than self-deception, secretiveness, deceit, and sheer emotional and sexual inhibition. Attuned to the severe demands of Puritan conscience and the hypocrisy it engendered, Hawthorne knew all about how guilt and repression act as barriers to both self-understanding and self-revelation.

In Blithedale, Coverdale comes closest to prefiguring the exquisite sensitivity of a Henry Jamesian character and the view that empathy, moral knowledge, and close community come together. For him, "generous sympathy" is a duty and fine attention a prelude to any action: "Zenobia should have been able to appreciate that quality of intellect and the heart which impelled me (often against my own will, to the detriment of my own comfort) to live in other lives, and to endeavor—by generous sympathies, by delicate intuitions, and by taking note of things too slight for record, and by bringing my human spirit into manifold accordance with the companions whom God assigned me— to learn the secret that was hidden even from themselves." But Zenobia is insufficiently open, even to his delicate intuitions, and Coverdale is reduced to trying to read her by the flowers she wears.

The implications for empathic attention and effective caring are plain. Moral discernment is supposed to take us beyond appreciation of general needs to insight into individual desires. But attention's insights and beneficent effects will be limited, even badly mistaken, if others are deceptive or shy, or put up a self-protective front. Emotional and moral perceptiveness is not clairvoyance, after all. Certainly, where transparency is the chief value, the burden is on the expressive subject. That is why utopian theorists have gone in the other direction and institutionalized confession rather than keen attention. For Charles Fourier, whose writings were most influential in American communitarianism, the distribution of pleasure in the phalanx depended upon declaring one's erotic desires, and his bizarre writings are all the evidence we need of the elaborate machinery required to create conditions in which no longing would be shameful and no confession a source of vulnerability. Attentiveness is not enough.

Elective community also brings out the fact that attention, sincerity, and caring may conflict with the communal warmth and extended domesticity suggested by heart and hearth. Sincere responsiveness is predictably harsh when it aims at correction, even if it is inspired by "generous sympathy." We know from Noyes's account of mutual criticism at Oneida that sincerity meant holding up to others a mirror of their faults, and that the most difficult ordeal was to *receive* criticism attentively and in silence. Noyes was frank about the painfulness of sincerity. He defended it on the grounds that mutual criticism is less awful than ordinary social backbiting and, more convincingly, that it is less painful than the false imaginings of sensitive souls with a propensity to self-accusation.[32] But this means that the other side of attention and caring is mortification. Mutual criticism does involve a sort of intimacy and mutual concern, and it is directed at men and women personally and individually, but it is not domestic warmth. Zenobia gives and takes personal criticism fiercely and truthfully, but it does not earn her love or even friendship. In contrast, the vacant Priscilla is the epitome of unalloyed empathy. She "loves everybody"; she is openheartedness devoid of moral or intellectual approbation, which, Hawthorne observes, always carries latent criticism. Priscilla's perfect sympathetic attention first to Zenobia and then to Hollingsworth has the appearance of stupidity and the worst self-effacement; Westerveldt is able to enslave her with his unblinking attention—his mesmeric eye. D. H. Lawrence calls her a "prostitute soul."³³

Finally, *Blithedale Romance* helps us see how theories of connection based on empathy and expressivism claim too much, first by assuming the presence of uniquely individual needs and feelings that must "out," and then in a further step assuming that sympathetic insight automatically translates into the imperative to take benevolent action, to care. This overlooks the plain psychological possibilities of inner vacuity and ambivalence, to which there is no right response, moral or emotional. Once again Coverdale is key. Ostensibly he is *the* sensitive soul–poet, transcendentalist, the member most absorbed in studying the real private selves of others and relating to them directly in friendship. Yet Coverdale can't distinguish cold analysis from sympathetic attention, caring from curiosity, even in himself. The cognitive problems with empathy's knowledge go well beyond the philosophers' separateness of persons: "A man cannot always decide for himself whether his own heart is cold or warm" (168). Coverdale cannot tell whether he loves Hollingsworth, Zenobia, or Priscilla, or none of them, and the result of his uncertainty is paralysis: "The greatest obstacle to being heroic is the doubt whether one may not be going to prove one's self a fool."³⁴ For all his efforts to "bring his spirit into manifold accordance" with others, Coverdale remains to the end uncaring and uncared for. In retrospect, he concludes: "It now impresses me that, if I erred at all in regard to Hollingsworth, Zenobia, and Priscilla it was through too much sympathy, rather than too little."

Commentators have attributed Coverdale's human failure to aesthetic distancing, cold intellectual analysis, repressed sexuality, and in one instance to Hawthorne's own irrational fantasy life.³⁵ They may all be right. But more interesting is how his ambivalence and paralysis cast doubt on the moral efficacy of sympathetic attention to the real selves of others. We are not meant to think that Zenobia would be transparent to Coverdale if only he were less of an artist or intellectual or had been well analyzed. Hawthorne wrote repeatedly about the limitations of fine attention on the one side and self-revelation on the other. We know from Hawthorne's favorite metaphor of the secret heart that he doubted whether individuality was communicable—for reasons that go beyond the incommensurability of language to capture moral and emotional truths about the self.³⁶ "How little I have told!—and, of that little, how almost nothing is tinctured with any quality that is exclusively my own! . . . So far as I am a man of really individual attributes, I veil my face." He observes that what he tells about himself, and what is most likely to be understood by his readers, are those things diffusely shared by them.

But Hawthorne is not morally dismayed by the limits on self-expression, hence, on insight into particularity. In "The Custom House" he assesses the autobiographical impulse that "took possession of him" as he composed the introduction. There are good reasons to want the thawing of native Boston reserve—convincing readers of the authenticity of his narrative was one. But it is unpardonable to lift the veil from "the inmost ME" (85). Why is it unpardonable? There is always more than goodness underneath, for one thing; none knows what fear, evil, or unbearable sorrow will be horribly revealed. More importantly, no good can come from transparency. There is no earthly reason to confess. And, as I hope to show, what *can* be expressed in democratic society suffices. Hawthorne said as much. Authors who indulge themselves in "confidential depths of revelation" are hoping to find a reader who is "the one mind and heart of perfect sympathy." They are like romantics in search of a community of perfect transparency and intimacy. Hawthorne explains that he tempered his expectations and imagines a reader who is a friend, "a kind and apprehensive though not the closest friend" (88).

This is not to say that the full force of the romantic law of the heart is never felt or obeyed. It does operate powerfully and precisely among strangers. That is the mystery of love. It is uncaused and its objects unelected. Not even obedience to the law of the heart insures closeness, though. Nothing is more pathetic than Hepzibah lavishing her love on Clifford, who is so repulsed by her ugliness that the very sight of her is a grief to him. Zenobia points out that "a little more love than one can conveniently dispose of" is the most troublesome offense you can offer to a woman (59). Undisposable love of one's own is truly unbearable, and Zenobia drowns herself. The law of the heart may be as tyrannical as perfectionist imagination, overwhelming every other, equally genuine, aspect of the self: Zenobia's formidable intelligence and wonderful pride were extinguished by her longing for Hollingsworth. She is undone by natural law, the dark erotic underside of the sentimental law of the heart, and she returns to nature—to the "weedy and slimy" Black River of Death.

The alternative, recommended by Fourier and adopted in many elective communities, is communal regulation of sexual relations and intimacy. But it is severely impersonal, prohibits exclusive affections, and is always authoritarian. Nothing could be more abhorrent or further from romantic expressivism, which is all about unique and irreplaceable individuality, than Noyes's group marriage. Hawthorne tells the same story over and over. In "Shaker Bridal," the community repeatedly forbids a woman from acting on her love and sexual desire in the higher name of general friendship. "Canterbury Pilgrims" is the last word on the subject. Pilgrims to the Shaker village hope to find the worldly success and comfort that eluded them outside. On the road, they pass a young couple escaping the Shaker village in which they were raised because the community outlaws "selfish love." The irony is that the couple *will* find privacy and freedom for romantic love outside, in the Custom House society. In marriage, singularity and elective affinity enjoy the protection of law.

In fact, Hawthorne shows that the spontaneous caring and close personal attachments romantics look for in elective community are commonplace in democratic society: Phoebe's kindness and affection for the elderly Pyncheons, or the simple decency of the couple in "The Gentle Boy." There *is* a spontaneous, beneficent law of the heart. It is wonderful and perfectly conventional at the same time. Hawthorne was a true believer in the law of the heart. His good souls are not highly refined moral sensibilities, puzzling out one another's intentions and needs, as Henry James describes moral interaction. Coverdale is the sobering example of self-conscious and highly refined sympathy; in contrast, goodness is simple and unself-conscious. Phoebe is sufficiently perceptive and sympathetic but she is not altruistic, in fact she does not have to *do* very much. She just *is* good; her presence is a solace and a real kindness to Hepzibah and Clifford. Neither duty or rule on the one side nor an attitude of keen empathic attention on the other captures her moral identity. Instead, Hawthorne portrays the spontaneous attraction of good hearts to one another, and their instinctive recoil from those who would do them harm. Hawthorne's victims are not stupid, only powerless.

The Transitory Life: Blithedale Romance and the Custom House

Elective community neither satisfies romantic longings nor proves that the wish for unencumbered selves and elective society is errant. It only shows that the wish cannot be deliberately pursued, though some people will always try. Part of the significance of elective community for American political identity is cautionary, then. But Hawthorne saw the psychological truth in romantic communitarianism and its effective origin in the democratic wish. So on the positive side, the *possibility* of elective community reinforces healthy impulses to resist hereditary conditions and to seek expressivity in public, not just private life. A distillation of the democratic idea of fresh starts and exemplary differences, the actual presence of elective communities is also a measure of how well America preserves its fundamental tolerance and liberality. But romantic communitarianism is a transitory life, and the best possible result is that members returning to democratic society see it from an altered, chastened perspective, so that it no longer appears as just a Custom House to which they must be bleakly resigned. Movement in and out of elective community is a prism for the larger theme of a "transitory life." Transitoriness is a practical response to the vicissitudes of life in democratic society, but beyond that, it says something true about identity—about the unbounded self free of encumbrances and its possibilities for expression.

Hawthorne describes his own shifting involvements and perspectives in just these terms. Isolated and alienated in Salem society, he imagined romantic affinity. But involvement with the transcendentalists and especially life in elective community tempered these longings. In the Custom House introduction, Hawthorne confessed that he was satiated with "toil and impracticable schemes with the dreamy brethren of Brook Farm . . . the subtile influence of an intellect like Emerson's . . . wild free days indulging fantastic speculations with Channing . . . talking with Thoreau about pine-trees and Indian relics . . . growing fastidious by sympathy with the classic refinement of Hillard's culture . . . becoming imbued with poetic sentiment at Longfellow's hearth-stone" (98–99). It was time to nourish himself with foods for which he had previously had little appetite. In "The Custom House" Introduction, Hawthorne acknowledges that the drudgery of civil service caused him to see things from a new perspective: he came to "think and feel and learn things that are worth knowing, and which I should not know unless I had learned them there; so that the present position of my life shall not be quite left out of the sum of my existence."

"Not quite left out of the sum of my existence"—the stress is not on summation but on inclusion, leaving nothing out. Neither adaptation to the Custom House society nor electing Brook Farm are transfiguring or fully self-expressive by themselves. As alternating experiences, however, they illuminate partial truths about the self and democracy. Hawthorne goes on about the Custom House: "It might be true, indeed, that this was a life which could not with impunity be lived too long; else, it might have made me permanently other than I had been without transforming me into any shape which it would be worth my while to take." That is why "I never considered it as other than a transitory life."

Hawthorne's fictional embodiment of American identity is Holgrave in *House of the Seven Gables*. The familiar romantic characteristics that he parcels out among his other characters—nostalgia for antiquity (especially pagan beauty) in Hilda in *The Marble Faun*, imagined aristocracy in the Pyncheons, Promethean vision in Hollingsworth, passionate intensity in Zenobia—are absent in Holgrave. In their place is an array of ordinary democratic traits, made romantic by their gigantic variety. Holgrave is the democratic person because he is the boundless, unencumbered self. Holgrave, we learn, is self-made: self-educated, self-dependent and willful, traveled, forward-looking, an artist—a practioner of the new art of daguerreotype—but formerly (already, at the age of twenty-two) a schoolmaster, a salesman, a newspaper editor, a peddler, a practitioner of dentistry, a traveler, a short-term member of a community of Fourierists, and a public lecturer on mesmerism. Hepzibah and Phoebe struggle to understand him: he is not lawless exactly, but lives by a law of his own. Yet he does not employ his strong will to mesmerize others, even when he could. His may turn out to be the false brilliancy of youth, Hawthorne warns, but reknown is not important. The only time insignificance is contemptible is when men and women fail in their first attempts at something and never exert themselves again.[37] Holgrave's crucial characteristic is that "amid all these personal vicissitudes, he had never lost his identity . . . he had never violated the innermost man" (157).

Here is a vision of correspondence between self and world: responsiveness to the vicissitudes of democratic society is at the same time the condition for consciousness of one's true identity. It stands in sharp contrast to the conventional romantic view that the ordinary business of democratic society is compromising, and that shifting involvements is a sign of hypocrisy. For Hawthorne, change in response to "fresh atmosphere" is precisely our way of knowing and revealing ourselves. Without shifting involvements, we have no experience of the self, only found "constitutive" conditions on the one hand or solipsistic inner worlds on the other. And in contrast to Whitman's engulfing "I," Hawthorne insists that the democratic self is more than a "reservoir of potentiality," dissonant and contingent, "containing multitudes." Coverdale has a secret heart, an individual identity and innermost self.

Hawthorne was not troubled by the thought that lack of permanent attachments and defining commitments implies radical contingency or a thin self. The greater danger is fixity, or "profound fiddling on one string." A transitory life is what democratic identity is all about, so much so that *resisting* change is a deliberate election. Singleness and constancy are always associated with insanity in his work. To be identified too deeply with some social attribute or role, to be fully constituted by a vision (Hollingsworth), exquisite aesthetic sensibility (Clifford), property (Judge Pyncheon), identification with one place and one affection (Hepzibah) is to suffer the "disease of inner solitude." In every case, it is madness or imbecility. It is the result of imagination wildly distorting the social reality of American democracy.

The private man and woman contain powers of imagination and feeling that emerge in surprising ways when aroused by "fresh outward atmosphere," and if American society is not a fully open, continuously elective political community still, the Custom House is dilapidated; Salem had changed dramatically in just fifty years. Even old Hepzibah, the mustiest lunatic of them all, left the house of the seven gables for a new life. The view that old age is as malleable as youth—Hawthorne's stunning disconnection of romantic self-expression from its usual association with adolescence—is quintessentially American. Elective community is simply the most dramatic expression of it: Blithedale's Coverdale was a not so young poet; Holgrave and Phoebe are joined in their move to the country by Hepzibah, Clifford, and Uncle Venner. In practice, this ultimate American resistance to closure culminates in the communities of the elderly that began to spring up in the United States in the 1960s.

What are the public, institutional complements of the chastened but still determinedly unencumbered self? The social institution that comes closest is marriage; Phoebe and Holgrave fall in love and end a generations-long feud between their families. The family is the ever-present frontier. Hawthorne calls it a "neutral territory." *There* is the law of the heart binding strangers. There too is the start of another round of inheritance; Holgrave would become a conservative when he married Phoebe, though his household will not last forever, either.

The pure political expression of the transitory life, of course, is democratic elections and the recurrent movement of political ins and outs. What struck Hawthorne most about the patronage officers of the Custom House was their passive vulnerability to the "periodical terror of a presidential election." Hawthorne was repulsed by the bloodthirstiness of the victors who wield the "political guillotine"; it is an example of the worst human trait— the tendency of people to grow cruel simply because they have power to inflict harm (90–93). Even so, electoral rotation and the impermanence of patronage jobs was a perfectly good subverter of hereditary influence and a boon to broader democratic participation.[38] Burdensome as it was, officialdom had gotten Hawthorne out of his interminable artistic isolation, and being ousted from the Custom House had gotten him out of what had become unbearable drudgery.

Hawthorne did not reclaim for democratic politics any romantic hopes for perfectionism, personal or communal, though. He knew better than to portray democracy as a faithful reflection of revolutionary wishes—as actual self-government, say, or to pretend that political office attracts goodness. Raw ambition, ignorance, absence of public spirit permeate democratic politics. And they are not the worst of it, either; Judge Pyncheon is his portrait of a thoroughly despicable political campaigner. Hawthorne worried that after the Civil War, "one bullet-headed general will succeed another in the Presidential chair; and veterans will . . . fill all the avenues of public life."[39] He had little faith in the electorate, which on the whole chooses blindly and amiss; in this, too, Hawthorne distanced himself from Jacksonian ideology.

But if democracy would never be a utopia, it was the best possible political life. It was without the worst distinctions, aristocratic pretensions, and tyrannies. Unlike the transcendentalists who were repulsed by democracy in practice, Hawthorne saw some personal and political good even in parties and spoils. He was quite clear about the good political participation may do us. The aesthete Clifford might die by plunging into the democratic melee but he is the romantic sensibility at its most exotic; he is demented.

The effect democratic politics had on Hawthorne is representative. It forced him to mix it up, and he boasted: "I look upon it as evidence, in some measure, of a system naturally well balanced, and lacking no essential part of a thorough organization, that with such associates to remember, I could mingle at once with men of altogether different qualities and never murmur at the change." In fact, he was an unabashed partisan and called himself a "locofoco" surveyor.[40]

A "transitory life" characterizes democratic political identity. We can see how romantic sensibilities are affirmed by it: boundlessness and expressivism are built in. But what recommends it, once perfectionism and the pure law of the heart are rejected as impossible, and if self-made identity and elective community have no apparent direction or purpose besides resistance to closure and opportunities for self-expression? For what vision of the world does democracy's concession to romanticism make moral sense?

We know from everything he wrote about communitarianism that

Hawthorne was appalled by moral certainties and even more by their projection into public life; it was in Puritan communities and again in the revivalism and communitarianism of his age that grand historical claims of progress and infinite perfectibility on the one side or apocalypse on the other were acted out. Hawthorne had had enough of the thought that America was a chosen nation or the scene of the millennium; unlike Whitman, he did not imagine that his nation "culminates history."[41] Hawthorne's vision of time and change has seemed black enough to many readers, since no change could interfere with the recurrence of evil. In "Earth's Holocaust," the human heart survives the apocalypse, and reengenders "all the shapes of wrong and misery." (On the other hand, D. H. Lawrence complained that Hawthorne's vision was not dark enough; true realism requires confronting the fact that America's destiny is to destroy, not to produce.[42])

The ineradicability of evil, like the ineradicability of inheritance, is perfectly clear. But so is the fact that the constancy of evil did not strike Hawthorne as a reason for grim resignation or antiworldliness. Neither God nor nature is ranged against us. There is a constantly shifting moral balance between benevolence and cruelty. In the transitory life of democratic society, with all its vicissitudes, goodness and evil both are likely to be tempered.

In fact, Hawthorne was cautiously optimistic: "There was always a prophetic instinct, a low whisper in my ear, that within no long period, and whenever a new change of custom should be essential to my good, a change would come" (99). He wrote this about himself and about America. Hawthorne was no abolitionist, and for once he was too sanguine. He thought that the end of slavery should not be deliberately pursued and that if slavery were left alone, "it would by some means impossible to be anticipated . . . vanish like a dream." It would have to vanish like a dream, since Hawthorne was convinced that "no human effort, on a grand scale, has ever yet resulted according to the purpose of its projectors." Yet he was unwilling to write off the possibility of goodness and its effects. Against Northern doubters, he was sure that union would be restored after the war: a rough courtship would bring "love and a quiet household." He imagined that educating the hearts of Southern whites would be the unplanned outcome of the war: "Whether we intended it to or no, they have a far greater stake on our success than we can possibly have," he wrote, for the South would rise to "the degree of mercy and benevolence that exists in us."[43]

"Wherever a new change of custom should be essential to my good, a change would come" has nothing to do with divine grace or utopian reform. It has to do with the nature of the self and democratic society. When the boundless inner self needs "fresh atmosphere," it will find it in the plenitude that is democratic society. And, when democracy needs some goodness, it will sometimes be forthcoming. Lincoln was an accident:

> It is the strangest and yet the fittest thing in the jumble of human vicissitudes, that he, out of so many millions, unlooked for, unselected by any intelligible process that could be based upon his genuine qualities, unknown to those who chose him, and unsuspected of what endowments may adapt him for his tremendous responsibility, should have found the way open for him to fling his lank personality into the chair of state.[44]

Here once more, this time in the context of national politics, we find the romantic notion of correspondence between democracy and the inner self, confidence in the complementarity of personal expressivism and public life. It is strange in light of the number of Hawthorne's stories in which unveiling the heart is an unhappy prospect. When he wrote that it is "instructive to take the woman's, the private and domestic view, of a public man," he was issuing a sober warning: beneath the "admirably arranged life" lies a "secret abomination," some rigidity or one-sidedness and moral skewing. Judge Pyncheon's public paternal benevolence concealed a sadistic personal life (111). Hawthorne created many other haunted characters whose private obsessions would be horrible crimes if they were acted out on a public scale. His hope for romantic correspondence only makes sense if we accept Melville's perception of the "depth of tenderness" in Hawthorne's description of men and women and Henry James's characterization of a "curious evenness" in his view of human nature.[45] It is true that public goodness can be shown to conceal private viciousness, and Hawthorne could outdo any romantic on the subject of hypocrisy and its social props. But the other side of unveiling is the perfectly ordinary public exposure of the good heart. Making that imaginable to us, and democracy lovable, was part of his moral business as a writer. Holgrave and Phoebe go off to recreate domestic life in communal living with friends on their country estate. But we cannot help thinking that Holgrave might return and run for office; he has done everything else, after all.

Hawthorne recommends "proper respect and natural regard" for democracy because it was as hospitable an atmosphere for the unbounded self as political society could be. Political community really is not constitutive even if it is not perfectly elective, and it is nothing more than the characters of its individual members that are self-made. That is the best that can be said of representative democracy, and he thought it ought to be enough to satisfy chastened romantics.

Conclusion

I have argued that romanticism is key to the dynamic relation between American democracy and communitarianism. For Hawthorne, the romantic sense of an unbounded self is the deep justification for democratic society—together with the moral judgment that goodness and evil are inescapable but are tempered by a transitory life and "fresh atmosphere." On this view, democracy corresponds to the truth about the self and our relations better than any traditional political form, and better than the romanticized democratic wish with its impossible projects for perfectionism and confidence in the law of the heart. There will always be communitarian longings, for the reasons I have shown, and these will be expressed most harmlessly in communal experiments, which will always be transitory. Mostly, however, the romantic self can find expression in the ordinary life of democratic society, so long as it remains reasonably faithful to the ideal of self-made identity and elective community.

All this is alien to contemporary communitarian political theory. It, too, is about identity politics and the expressive relation between self and public life. But the romantic heart of identity—its resistance to closure and its susceptibility to the workings of imagination—is rejected; instead, personal and political identity are said to be socially constituted. If it is acknowledged at all, the thought that individuals are not fully formed by found attachments is interpreted narrowly to mean that individuals are able to reflect critically on their shared meanings. Even when crucial aspects of personal identity and cultural community are thought to result from historical oppression, communitarian theorists prize the collective identity politics of group membership and communal belonging.

Certainly, the thought that liberal democratic society provides resources for a "transitory life" is viewed as its weakness, not its strength, and the wish for self-made identity is seen as virtually pathological. As one half of the dichotomy that puts Hobbes's metaphor of men springing up like mushrooms on the other side, the "constituted self" makes sense. But as an understanding of identity, it is meager. From the standpoint of Hawthorne's rich historical and psychological perspective on democracy, individuality, and community, we can see it as arid, remote from the reality of American political identity, and as an obstacle to understanding all that is interesting in elective community.

Notes

References to *Blithedale Romance* are to the W. W. Norton edition, New York, 1958, and to the New American Library edition of *The House of the Seven Gables*, New York, 1990. Unless otherwise noted, all other references are to the Modern Library edition of *The Novels and Tales of Nathaniel Hawthorne*, New York, 1937.

1. John Humphrey Noyes, *History of American Socialisms* (Hilary House, New York: 1961); Charles J. Erasmus, *In Search of the Common Good: Utopian Experiments Past and Future* (Free Press, New York: 1977); Frances Fitzgerald, *Cities on the Hill* (Simon and Shuster, New York: 1981); William McLaughlin, *Revivals, Awakenings, and Reforms* (University of Chicago Press: 1978). For an account of communitarianism in Great Britain since 1960, see Philip Abrams and Andrew McCulloch, *Communes, Sociology and Society* (Cambridge University Press, Cambridge: 1976), which sets communitarianism in the larger context of "modernity" as an attempt to repair the separation of self from the social.

2. John Humphrey Noyes, *Mutual Criticism* (Syracuse University Press: 1975); Erasmus, *In Search of the Common Good*.

3. Historians have shown that waves of community-building correspond to periods of social dislocation when problems of political unity and identity are especially acute. Noyes's *Mutual Criticism* discusses his techniques as a response to the failure of social institutions (88). See McLaughlin ("Great awakenings [and the revivals that are part of them] are the results, not of depressions, wars, or epidemics but of critical disjunctions in our self-understanding"), *Revivals, Awakenings, and Reforms*, 2. Fitzgerald summarizes the historical literature and surveys the sociological concepts used to capture these periods: "identity politics," "liminality," "revitalization," among them; see especially 40–46.

4. Even the categories developed by philosophers for elective or utopian communities are inadequate. For example, Robert Paul Wolff's typology of affective/productive/rational communities seems inclusive. But it turns out that his scheme does not encompass a community of friends like Brook Farm, since Wolff's most promising category—affective community—is defined as "a feelingful, nonrational natural community of men *bound together by tradition and culture*." Robert Paul Wolff, *The Poverty of Liberalism* (Beacon Press, Boston: 1968), 185, 189 (my italics).

5. R. M. Kanter quoted in Stanley Benn, "Individuality, Autonomy, and Community," in Eugene Kamenka, *Community as a Social Ideal* (St. Martins, 1982), 53. Stanley Benn provides the best typology of communities: total/mutuality/comradeship and a systematic account of their instability. Benn

discusses the tension between personal involvement and ideological consensus in each of these types.

6. Abrams and McCulloch, 5–6. They describe communitarians' "antisociological" desire to assert relationships between the self and the social that deny the validity of dualism, 9.

7. *Hegel and Modern Society* (Cambridge University Press, Cambridge: 1979), 90.

8. Herman Melville first noted Hawthorne's allegorical titles, commenting on "The Intelligence Office" as symbolizing the secret workings of men's minds, in "Hawthorne and His Mosses," ed. Edmund Wilson, *The Shock of Recognition* (Farrar, Strauss and Cudahy, New York: 1943), 187–204.

9. *The House of the Seven Gables*, ix. Hawthorne's political opinions and experience separate him from the transcendentalists despite Henry James's claim that life was uneventful for him and that he had few points of contact with "the world": Hawthorne, in Wilson, *The Shock of Recognition*, 427. He worked in the Custom House, wrote for *The Democratic Review*, held a consular post, wrote a campaign biography of his friend Franklin Pierce, held definite views on John Brown and slavery, lived and traveled abroad, and stayed at Brook Farm. All of this raises questions about the adequacy of interpretations of Hawthorne and his work that have him focused narrowly on the theme of the artist in retreat. Hawthorne was capable of privatization; he spent several years after college as a recluse in a garret; but his adult life was a mix of private and official public engagements, albeit out of necessity. For the isolationist interpretation see Irving Howe, who treats Hawthorne as what he takes to be the characteristic American novelist whose heroes are "wounded intelligences trying to transform isolation into the composure of solitude," see *Politics and the Novel* (Horizon Press, New York: 1957), 200. Similarly, F. O. Matthiessen sees Hawthorne's heroes as artist types, exceptional individuals in a centrifugal society who have no common ground for meeting, in *American Renaissance* (Oxford University Press, New York: 1941), 227–28. Hyatt Waggoner sees alienation as Hawthorne's most powerful theme; he speaks of "insulation," which is not only isolation but imperviousness, in *The Presence of Hawthorne* (Louisiana State University Press, Baton Rouge: 1979).

10. See the author's *Another Liberalism: Romanticism and the Reconstruction of Political Thought* (Harvard University Press, Cambridge, Mass.: 1987).

11. Allegory has long been associated with transcendentalist metaphysics. Larzer Ziff argues for the ethical dimension, but not the peculiarly democratic dimension of Hawthorne's essay in "The Ethical Dimension of 'The Custom House,'" in *Hawthorne: A Collection of Critical Essays*, ed. A. N. Kaul (Prentice-Hall, Inc., Englewood Cliffs, N.J. 1966).

12. I have not been able to take up here the difficult question of the relation between the real life of the author, the authorial voice in the text, and the narrator's voice. This problem is particularly difficult in Hawthorne's case, because of the introductions he wrote to his major works in which he appears

to speak in his own voice about his own life. I have tried to avoid the obvious pitfalls of confusing Hawthorne with his characters.

13. John P. Diggins discusses the Calvinist origins of this expansivism in *The Lost Soul of American Politics* (Basic Books, New York: 1984); Judith Shklar interprets Emerson in these terms in "Emerson and the Inhibitions of Democracy," *Political Theory*, 18, no. 4 (1990): 601–14.

14. See Nancy L. Rosenblum, "Strange Attractors: How Individualists Connect to Form Democratic Unity," in *Political Theory*, 18, no. 4 (1990): 576–86, a response to George Kateb, "Walt Whitman and the Culture of Democracy," ibid., 545–71.

15. Henry James, *Hawthorne*, 491.

16. Perry Miller, *The Life of the Mind in America from the Revolution to the Civil War* (Harcourt, Brace, and World, New York: 1965). The link to elective communities is drawn directly by Fitzgerald where the term "evangelical style" is used to describe the whole range of intentional communities, religious and secular, that characterized American culture in the 1960s and 1970s.

17. See John O'Sullivan, "The Democratic Review," 28–30, in *Social Theories of Jacksonian Democracy*, ed. Joseph Blau (Bobbs-Merrill, New York: 1954).

18. Elizabeth Peabody, "The Original Constitution of Brook Farm," cited in Noyes, *History of American Socialisms*, 113–14.

19. Self-made identity involved a proposition about self and society, and not ontology or moral selfhood; it had nothing to do with systematic philosophical positions on the subject of autonomy or existential choice, determinism, or free will.

20. James, 460, 436. George Santayana, *The Genteel Tradition*, (Harvard University Press, Cambridge, Mass.: 1967), 44. Remarkably, neither these commentators on the lack of social distinctions nor Hawthorne speaks of slavery in this connection; they are not among the hereditary conditions America pretends to have thrown off. (Irving Howe, *Politics and the Novel*, 163; Lionel Trilling, *Sincerity and Authenticity* [Harvard University Press, Cambridge, Mass.: 1971], 113).

21. Stephen Simpson, "Political Economy and Workers," in Blau, 145, 156.

22. "To be useful was to be degraded," Simpson, 143.

23. "Chiefly About War Matters," in *The Complete Writings of Nathaniel Hawthorne*, Vol. XVII (Houghton Mifflin, Boston: 1900), 366–67.

24. "Hints to Young Ambition," in *The Complete Writings*, Vol. XVII, 241–41.

25. "Chiefly About War Matters," 418.

26. Compare Henry James's misreading when he says of Brook Farm that "relations of the sexes there were neither more nor less than what they usually are in American life, excellent" (488).

27. For a critical discussion of the Foucaultian association of subjectivity, secrecy, and sexuality in reference to Hawthorne, see J. Hillis Miller, *Hawthorne and History* (Basil Blackwell, Oxford: 1991).

28. Fitzgerald, 141.
29. Herbert Schneider cited by Mattheissen, 199.
30. Other reformers are less harsh, but just as deluded in their denial of the conflict between the severe demands of perfectionism and happiness; in "The Celestial Railroad," Hawthorne heaps scorn on his contemporaries' easy accommodation of virtue and happiness: you can travel on the celestial railroad all your lifetime of a thousand years, he wrote, and never get beyond the limits of Vanity Fair (1080).
31. Bernard Williams, "The Idea of Equality" in eds. Peter Laslett and W. G. Runcima, *Philosophy, Politics and Society* (Blackwell, Oxford: 1972), 110–31.
32. *Mutual Criticism*, 22. The introduction to *Mutual Criticism* by Murray Levin and Barbara Benedict Bunker is a gloss, characterizing it as "mutual feedback" and as a method of "helping individual members to achieve goals of personal development," vii.
33. D. H. Lawrence, "Nathaniel Hawthorne and the Scarlet Letter," in Wilson, *The Shock of Recognition*, 1007.
34. This reading of ambivalence is quite different from J. Hillis Miller's claim, which challenges those who would put an end to hermeneutic suspension by explaining "The Minister's Veil." Since there is nothing definite behind the veil, our business as readers cannot be to identify what it is (*Hawthorne and History*, 104). Literary analysts since Matthiessen have focused on Hawthorne's "ambiguity device," and psychoanalytically inclined interpreters focus on ambiguity as the key to Hawthorne's temperament and beliefs (cf. Hyatt Waggoner commenting on Mattheissen in *The Presence of Hawthorne*, 60).
35. Frederick C. Crews, *the Sins of the Fathers: Hawthorne's Psychological Themes* (Oxford University Press, New York: 1966), 195.
36. See J. Hillis Miller (101) for an interpretation that turns on the incommensurability between solitary consciousness and language.
37. "Hints to Young Ambition," 243.
38. James Fenimore Cooper was explicit about the benign effects of political fluctuation, in "On Representation," in Blau, ed., 57.
39. "Chiefly About War Matters," 367. Hawthorne did not have much good to say about politicians: "I want nothing to do with politicians. Their hearts wither away and die out of their bodies. Their consciences are turned to india-rubber, or to some substance as black as that and which will stretch as much." Knowledge of politicians was one thing he took from his Custom House experience: "it is a knowledge which no previous thought or power of sympathy could have taught me; because the animal, or machine rather, is not in nature." See his account of America's "true representatives" at Willard's Hotel in Washington, in "Chiefly About War Matters," 414.
40. James, 482.
41. See Rosenblum, "Strange Attractors" (579), on Whitman's American Hegelianism. Irving Howe wrote that "in an age blazing with certainty, he had to make his way on doubt," *Politics and the Novel*, 165.

42. D. H. Lawrence, "Nathaniel Hawthorne and the Scarlet Letter," in Wilson, 985.
43. "Chiefly About War Matters," 402, 419.
44. "Chiefly About War Matters," 374.
45. James, 447. Matthiessen's characterization is right: Hawthorne was "as far from despair as optimism," 180.

5

Some Comparisons between Liberalism and an Eccentric Communitarianism

Thomas Moody

Much of the current debate between liberals and the suddenly fashionable communitarians has consisted of each side charging the other with criticizing straw versions of liberalism or communitarianism, respectively. In an intellectual context where even such familiar theories as liberalism and socialism fail to have an uncontroversial content, it should not be surprising that a theory as embryonic as communitarianism doesn't.

I propose that we not worry overly about labels. I shall describe some features that I take to be necessary for an adequate social ideal, which I call "communitarianism." I shall contrast it with some points that I take to be characteristic of liberalism. Given the lack of a canonical account of liberalism and communitarianism, this task is unavoidably somewhat arbitrary. Thus, not everyone will agree that these features are necessary for an acceptable social theory, or that they constitute communitarianism, and some, unlike me, will believe that these ideas are compatible with liberalism. James Sterba, for one, thinks that communitarianism simply brings out the latent possibilities of liberalism.[1] Others think that once the excessive individualism of classic liberalism has been rejected, there is such a thing as com-

---

This chapter originally appeared in *Communitarianism, Liberalism and Social Responsibility*, (eds). C. Peden and Y. Hadson. Lewiston, N.Y.: Edwin Mellen Press, 1992.

munitarian liberalism. This is Terry Pinkard's view.[2] Others think that communitarianism is a brand of socialism and thus fundamentally at odds with any liberal theory.[3]

As I construe communitarianism, its hallmark is its metaphysics of the state, the individual, and their relationship. Communitarianism, whatever else it may hold, rejects liberal atomism. It rejects, that is, the notion characteristic of contractarianism that it makes sense to conceive of individuals as in some way predating society, even if this sense is only metaphysical. It also rejects the characteristic liberal Hobbesian moral individualism, which posits antagonism between humans as the basis of society. Communitarians believe that the fundamental relationship between individuals and society is not Hobbesian antagonism, but Kropotkinite mutual aid.[4]

Communitarianism, as I see it, draws heavily on classic communist anarchism. The heart of anarchism's complaint against the deployment of power is a deepfelt moral intuition similar to Immanuel Kant's: no one should be used simply as an instrument of other people's will. The vision of Peter Kropotkin is one of the inviolability of the projects and interests of humans and of the concomitant obligation of society to respect those projects and interests. In the Kantian tradition, the persons we are to respect are not the everyday people that we meet on the street, but hypothetical selves representing an abstract rationality. Communitarians insist that at all levels of political analysis the self must be the actual self, embedded in culture and with corrigible desires and beliefs. So a Kantian notion of respect for persons won't do for communitarians. Nonetheless, Terry Pinkard suggests that principles that describes respect for persons can be generated from a communitarian basis. If Pinkard is right, communitarians can have the full-blown respect for persons that they desire as the anchor of their political theory, while not having to construe those persons in the atomistic style favored by liberalism. There is no space here for a discussion of what a relationally based concept of respect for persons would look like. But we can see at work here a central feature of communitarian methodology: retrievalism. Karl Marx thought liberal ideals were important but incomplete, and communitarians agree. That is, communitarians attempt to reconstruct important liberal political ideals such as respect for persons, liberty, and justice on a more acceptable metaphysical basis, that is, based on a relational self and a nonfoundationalist epistemology.

It is respect for persons that anchors communitarianism against collectivism. This sense of respect encourages individuality, tolerance, pluralism, and the politics of difference. It mitigates against conformism, homogeneity, or repression. Liberty and, if Pinkard is right, justice become derivative notions from this sense of respect for persons.

There is another side, however, to Kropotkin's anarchism, which emphasizes mutual aid and cooperation. While liberal constructions of respect for persons are usually couched in terms of duties of noninterference, communitarian respect also means that one attempts to aid others in their attempts to achieve their version of a good life, that one is not simply passively approving of those attempts. This sense of respect implies caring and solidarity, and knits individuals into a community of mutual respect and mutual aid.

Thus, the second major moral value underlying communitarianism is civic friendship. We can see the matter this way. Consider three types of social bonds. First, those of self-interest, wherein people cooperate only because cooperation makes their own private profit possible, as in the market. Marx claimed that this "cash nexus" eventually perverted and subsumed all other human relationships under capitalism. Then there are bonds of obligation wherein one acts properly but impartially toward another simply because that other is a moral agent like oneself. And there are communal and mutual bonds such as friendship, in which the bond is a good in itself, not a mere instrument or obligation. Such bonds have been the topic of much recent feminist discussion. Given this rough taxonomy, communitarianism holds that liberal theory relies much too heavily on bonds of the first two types, and has little theoretical space for bonds of mutuality. Whereas liberal theory has tended to relegate communal bonds to the private realm of friendship and the family and to see the public realm as characterized by self-interest and obligation, communitarians believe that public relationships must be seen as, to some extent, mutual and not exclusively instrumental or impartially obligatory. These mutualistic public relations must be seen as a constitutive element of who we are, the public analog to such private relationships as friendship and love. Communitarians see progress in the movement from the rule of paternalism to the rule of law and finally to civic friendship.

These twin ideas, then—solidarity and respect for persons—operate in an uneasy tension that allows communitarianism to avoid collectivism on the one hand and radical individualism on the other. A strong respect for persons prevents solidaristic goals from leading to the depreciation of individual interests in favor of the interests of the whole, while solidarity prevents respect for persons from degenerating into radical individualism with its inadequate conception of the public good and citizenship.

At the heart of these issues is individualism, whose several varieties must be made clear, if we are to understand the nature of the differences between communitarianism and liberalism.

Marilyn Friedman and other feminists have criticized liberalism for holding the view that human beings are able to become fully human, independent of any society or human relationships.[5] Call this "psychological individualism." In one of its incarnations, it is the descriptive half of "rugged individualism," the myth of the self-made person. Friedman is right to emphasize the importance of others for psychological development, but wrong to suggest that liberalism has no room for such a view. John Locke, for example, was quite aware of the importance of society to human development.

This mistaken criticism results from confusing psychological individualism with metaphysical individualism.[6] Metaphysical individualism, or "atomism," holds that it makes sense to conceptualize human beings in isolation from a society, and that a human being can be successfully described without reference to others. Contractarian liberalism is committed to metaphysical individualism. Contractarianism is the view that we can adequately describe a presocial human being and from this description derive certain political principles. In contrast, communitarianism insists on an "embedded" or "relational" self, which cannot be adequately delineated without reference to others.[7] Communitarians insist that some though not all of one's social affiliations and relations are at least partly definitive of one's identity. One cannot be successfully described in purely self-referential or presocial terms. This is not psychological individualism, for it has nothing to do with the conditions under which humans thrive or mature. Like most liberals, one can hold that others are necessary to human growth without holding that others are necessary for human definition or identity. Communitarians insist that both psychological and metaphysical individualism are incorrect.

Another point of disagreement between liberalism and communitarianism involves political individualism: the view that the relationship between the society and the individual is one of necessary antagonism.

The liberal picture of the society-individual relationship can be seen in an analogy. We speak sometimes of the "community of nations." It is, of course, no such thing. It is an assemblage of sovereign nations who act in their own self-interest in the international realm. A certain order is maintained by alliances made out of national interest and by a vague international morality enshrined in such ideas as the law of nations or the Good Samaritanism that Michael Walzer sees as appropriate among strangers.[8] Countries thus see the international realm as one of instrumental self-interest or impartial obligation. Such a community resembles the liberal state of nature.

Now, if nations could agree to hand over some of their sovereignty to a world government, we would have the perfect analog of liberal society. Nations would jealously guard their remaining sovereignty and regard other nations as potential aggressors, dealing with them from self-interest or obligation. The world government would be seen solely as a guarantor of security, a "night watchman."

The liberal picture of society sees the relationship between individuals and the state as like the relationship of states to a world government. Individuals come together out of self-interest and for protection, seeing association with others as simply a necessary evil and a potential violator of their natural liberties. Liberal states are not communities. They are founded on the wrong conceptions, and reinforce the wrong attitudes and relationships. To be sure, over time, individuals in real states relax a little, learn not to fear everyone, build some friendships. But those are erosions on the edges of the core of self-interested alliance. They do not disturb the fundamental outlook of political individualism, which consists of seeing others as potential aggressors and competitors, viewing the public as a mechanism for wringing out private advantage, and treating relationships with others as deals to achieve self-interest. A community founded on such notions cannot have a satisfying public life or mutualistic relationships. At best, it can create relationships of mutual self-interest and enforce a minimal public morality.

We can now see the source of one of the deep divisions between communitarianism and classic liberalism. The classic liberal picture of society was that it was rule governed and process oriented. The point of liberal society was to set out neutral rules that governed the interactions between individuals trying to achieve their own particular life plans. If the rules were legitimate, whatever outcomes resulted were justified.

To illustrate this, consider the laws governing contracts in Anglo-American societies. At one high point of pure liberal legal theory in the early nineteenth century, there were essentially no limitations on the outcomes of contracts. Whatever individuals agreed upon was legally binding. The point of law was simply to create the kind of orderly background against which rational individuals could bargain with other rational individuals in pursuit of their private goals. To get there, the law had to set aside some older notions of equity and fairness, which had for a long time provided that a contract that was unfair in its outcome was not valid. Principles of equity and the common good constrained the operation of the rules of contract. Liberal legal theory abolished such constraints for the sake of an untrammeled right to contract. We have since returned to such principles to constrain contracts because the social good has demanded it.

Here we have an illustration of the kind of tension that I think a communitarian theory requires. We must recognize that liberal neutrality is a myth—any social order will favor some forms of life over others. Capitalism favors the competitive, and aggressive, and liberal governments enforce capitalism with laws defining and defending property rights. But this does not mean that governments cannot go too far in favoring a form of life. Clearly they can and they ought not to. But it does mean that the issue cannot be posed as if communitarianism were threatening liberty by favoring a form of life while liberalism had the reassuring virtue of being neutral among them. Once it is recognized that liberalism too favors some forms of life over others, then the question becomes: to what extent should a polity favor a form of life and what form of life should a polity favor?

On the one hand we have respect for persons generating a demand that individuals be given as much freedom as possible to create their lives as they wish. But such an ideal, if unqualified, can lead to a view that society is nothing but a mechanism for permitting contracts and that it has no business interfering with their outcomes. That is, it leads directly to the liberal view that society is simply an instrument for the satisfaction of individual desires. Mutuality, solidarity, and the common good serve to temper this rabid individualism. If mutuality requires that elementary fairness, and decency be observed, then contracts that violate such fundamental notions are not justifiable. Now, liberalism too recognizes that there are limits on contractual liberty, and that the common good must be recognized. But it does so very grudgingly and only on the grounds that this common good is really the disguised private good of individuals. One infringes on contract liberty only to reserve the very possibility of continued contract liberty.

Communitarianism, while valuing human liberty as a derivative of respect for persons, has a more robust notion of the common good and its part in human life. There is a great difference between seeing society as simply an instrument for achieving the desires of autonomous choosers, and seeing society as constitutive of those individuals. One cannot ignore or destroy the common social world except at the peril of defeating the possibility of having a worthwhile private life. If I use water as a commercial fisher, I have a very different view of the importance of water than if I'm a fish. I may, since my livelihood depends on it, value water a great deal. Even so, that water can be polluted fairly severely without impinging on my private instrumental use of it. But if I am a fish, the character of the water is crucial to my happiness and well-being as a fish, and the good of the water will be a major constituent of my own good. This does not mean, as critics of liberalism have sometimes suggested, that private fishers cannot cooperate to keep the water clean; it means only that the viewpoint from which they assess their water policy will be quite different from that of one whose well-being is interdependent with the water. I suspect that such instrumentalism will, in fact, tend to lead to desecration of the commons, but that's another issue.

The communitarian complaint is not that people as conceived of by liberalism will not cooperate or act for the common good, but rather that they do so for the wrong reasons, simply from self-interest or as a matter of obligation. But communitarianism sees public life as a constitutive feature of human identity, and thus a necessary part of a good life and valuable for its own sake, not simply as an instrument for purely private ends. Liberalism has few, if any, conceptual tools to describe or justify such a view of the public realm.

Karl Marx once remarked that the problem with empiricists is that they first sever the knower from the known and then wonder why they have such problems with skepticism. Liberalism has an analogous problem. Having first abstractly and artificially severed the human being from society, liberals then wonder why they have such trouble justifying community. The answer in both cases is to refuse to make the initial split. Knowers live in a world, so do political animals.

Kathy Ferguson argues that liberalism also dessicates private life by depriving it of contrast with a healthy public arena.[9] Public activism is a crucial part of the formation of a communitarian self, presumably a richer self than the individual of liberalism, searching the rubble of an increasingly destitute private life for the bones of enrichment. That private life, in turn, is weakened, because individuals have little to bring to it, since they have no satisfying public life to enrich them.

This allows us to position communitarianism in the debate among competing political theories over the relative moral weight given to the society or to the individual. Using this question as a scale, one gets collectivism on one end and individualism on the other. When Terry Pinkard claims that he has a brand of liberalism that is communitarian because it is not "radically individualist," what he is saying is that he does not see that liberalism need endorse the kind of radical primacy of the individual that characterizes libertarianism, for example, nor that it must see society, and most particularly government, simply as a mechanism for the satisfaction of purely individual desires.

There are two communitarian responses here. The first is to emphasize that an acceptable communitarianism must be able to avoid radical individualism and forge robust notions of common good and public welfare without collapsing into the opposite error of subsuming the welfare of individuals entirely into the social good. But second, communitarianism insists that there is something skewed about the terms of this debate. To see the issue as the individual "versus" the society is to endorse a particular Hobbesian-liberal world view about the relationship between individuals and their societies. It is to endorse the belief that this relationship must be a zero-sum game where what one party gains the other loses. Communitarians would insist that this need not be so, that it isn't the fish "versus" the water, anymore than the good of a friendship is antagonistic to the good of the individuals in it. It shows a misunderstanding of friendship to think of it only or primarily in terms of what one gets out of it. Communitarians argue that it is a similar misunderstanding of the proper relationship between individuals and society to see society as an antagonistic or merely instrumental device.

Here arises an argument over political justification. Utilitarian liberalism has always presumed the sovereignty and authenticity of individual desire, and has used those desires as a test of the legitimacy of state power. A good state is an instrument for the satisfaction of people's desires, and this has been held both with respect to the actual desires of people and of the hypothetical desires of atomistic selves. The state and the market are parallel in this respect: individuals come to both with desires and the state and market are ultimately simply devices to satisfy those desires.

While the satisfaction of desire in some broad sense is an acceptable test of social legitimacy, communitarians reject the notion that desires can be taken at face value. We have too many analyses of how potent modern forms of domination work by affecting our desires and beliefs to be naive about the formation of such beliefs. Liberals such as Mill recognize these possibilities (at least in some embryonic form) but believe that it is simply safer and wiser policy for government to act as if desires were authentic, that any other policy leads to Rousseauistic "forcing people to be free." But the rejection of the authenticity of human desires leaves us in a quandary. If public institutions, like the market and the state, can shape our desires, as they clearly do, then how can we use the desires we have as a test of those institutions? Communitarianism, in rejecting the necessary authenticity of actual human desires, must provide an answer here.

Contractarian liberalism takes a different tack: it attempts to represent legitimate societies as the result of choices made by ahistorical hypothetical individuals. Atomism represents an attempt to have a universal objective presocial test for the legitimacy of a society, whether that test is found in natural rights or in the precontractual musings of a presocial individual. Communitarianism, in rejecting this view of the self as useful for political theory, must then have some other mode of justification.

This is a long story. Very briefly, that mode is immanent critique, examples of which lie in the work of Michael Walzer, for example. We abstract from a given culture its primary principles and use those to reflect upon the actual practices of that society. Values are context bound, rather than transcendental, and can be discovered by a process of ideological archeology. This epistemology is of course controversial and needs elucidation and defense, which is beyond the focus of this discussion. But it seems to me that communitarianism must construct a successful nonfoundationalist political epistemology, which can serve to sort out legitimate from illegitimate institutions. I think the kind of immanent critique suggested by Walzer holds promise of doing that. Respect for persons demands that any such justifications meet charges by critics that communitarianism would require homogeneity and a passive acceptance of a moral authoritarianism. An acceptable communitarianism is not a call for homogeneity or conformity or, in any fashion, the repression of individuality, but is simply an expression of a belief that genuine individuality is only possible within a good community.

A final brief remark: whereas liberalism sees property rights as necessary for liberty and is thus devoted to a defense of a strong system of individual property rights, communitarianism rejects the analysis and thus the defense. Property rights are inimical to community. Plato noted that in the *Republic* and Karl Marx points it out in his discussion of how capitalism replaces social relations among people with the cash nexus. Liberalism is the celebration and distillation of the kind of society in which the cash nexus prevails. But communitarians wish to foster other kinds of relations among people and thus strong property rights of the sort necessary to justify capitalism are unacceptable.

Capitalism breeds self-interest, the destruction of social ties, a vision of society as a tool of self-interest, and vast inequalities of wealth and power, all of which make community very difficult to achieve. Thus we have the astonishing phenomenon of ethicists seriously debating egoism: whether we ever act out of any motive but self-interest, and worse, whether we should ever do so. In any good community, the answer to this question would be so self-evident that the question wouldn't be worth asking. But in a culture that has enthroned self-interest as the moral and psychological mainspring of human action, this question tends to arise. There is no space here to discuss this in any detail but I refer you to the work of David Miller, among others.[10] This issue, if no other, sharply delineates any form of communitarianism from any form of liberalism.

It seems to me, then, that communitarianism is differentiated from liberalism on a number of important grounds. To sum up: liberalism has liberty as its chief value, whereas communitarianism has respect for persons and mutual aid. Liberalism endorses a metaphysical atomism, and in many of its forms, a political individualism, both of which communitarianism rejects. And liberalism sees a strong defense of property rights as a necessary condition for liberty, whereas communitarianism does not, but rather takes a strong socialist position on property rights. Finally, liberalism has traditionally been based on some form of foundationalism, usually in the form of contractarianism, which communitarianism rejects in favor of some version of immanent critique. It should then be clear that at least the possibly idiosyncratic communitarianism that I endorse cannot be a form of liberalism, much less compatible with liberal beliefs. The best statement of their relationship is that communitarianism is the fulfillment of liberal ideals in a retrievalist fashion, but in fulfilling those ideals, communitarianism transforms itself into quite a different political animal.

Notes

1. In his talk to the North American Society for Social Philosophy, August 12, 1990, in Burlington, Vermont.

2. Terry Pinkard, *Democratic Liberalism and Social Union* (Philadelphia: Temple University Press, 1987). I also interpret Michael Sandel in *Liberalism and the Limits of Justice* (Cambridge: Cambridge University Press, 1982) in this fashion.

3. This is my view and that of Carol Gould in *Rethinking Democracy: Freedom and Social Cooperation in Politics, Economy, and Society* (New York: Cambridge University Press, 1988).

4. See Porter Kropotkin, "Anarchist Communism: Its Basis and Principles"

in Roger Baldwin, ed., *Kropotkin's Revolutionary Pamphlets* (New York: Dover Publications, 1970), 44-79.

5. Marilyn Friedman, "Self-Rule in Social Context: Autonomy from a Feminist Perspective," in Creighton Peden and James P. Sterba, eds., *Freedom, Equality, and Social Change* (Lewiston, N.Y.: The Edwin Mellen Press, 1989), 158-69.

6. See Thomas Moody, "Liberal Conceptions of the Self and Autonomy," in Peden and Sterba, 109-20.

7. See, among others, Sandel, *Liberalism and the Limits of Justice*.

8. Michael Walzer, *Spheres of Justice* (New York: Basic Books, 1983).

9. Kathy Ferguson, "Toward a New Anarchism," *Contemporary Crises*, 7 (January 1983): 39-57. See also Ferguson, *The Feminist Case against Bureaucracy* (Philadelphia: Temple University Press, 1984).

10. David Miller, *Market, State and Community: Theoretical Foundations of Market Socialism* (Oxford: Clarendon Press, 1989).

6

The Theoretical Marginalization of the Disadvantaged: A Liberal/ Communitarian Failing

Thomas W. Simon

People exist and barely subsist at the margins of society. The concept of "the margins" reflects the role of the marginalized as outsiders; they eke out an existence at the periphery, far from the mainstream, away from the central core of society. The metaphors of margin and center help form a fairly accurate picture of social reality. The metaphors play a similar role in theory. Certain principles and concepts form the theoretical core, while others play a more derivative role in theory construction. Unraveling the interconnections between social and theoretical marginalization occupies the central core of this paper. My central thesis is that mainstream political theory has relegated disadvantaged groups, a particularly important constituent of the marginalized, to the theoretical margins.

The marginalization of the disadvantaged occurs within a wide variety of theoretical contexts. I have chosen to focus on the debate between liberals and communitarians as a particularly interesting theoretical context. Someday I hope that somebody will write a social history explaining why certain theoretical controversies gain prominence. In any event, I shall test the marginalization thesis within a currently raging theoretical dispute between liberals and communitarians. The only social history of ideas that I will undertake in this pa-

---

An earlier version of this chapter appeared in *Communitarianism, Liberalism and Social Responsibility*, (eds.) C. Peden and Y. Hudson. Lewiston, N.Y.: Edwin Mellen Press, 1992.

per is to note that the liberal/communitarian debate is not confined to one discipline. It emerges in philosophy, political science, and law. While glossing over some important distinctions between the debates in the varied fields, I shall focus on the common elements of the disputes.

The liberal/communitarian debate flares up around different issues within each of the disciplines. Philosophers of liberal and communitarian persuasions draw the battle lines upon the turf of justice. Political scientists wage their liberal/communitarian debate over the territory of democracy. In contrast, most of the controversy between liberals and communitarians in law appears in debates about constitutional interpretation, where communitarianism goes under the heading of republicanism.

The liberal/communitarian dispute has certainly generated considerable controversy. Despite the attention it has received, the debate has failed to address itself directly to a critical issue, namely, the plight of the disadvantaged. The lack of attention given to disadvantaged groups within liberalism and communitarianism creates problems for these theories for a number of reasons.

The first difficulty centers around the importance of the disadvantaged issue. Minimally, any worthwhile political theory should address the alleviation of suffering. A particularly pernicious form of suffering occurs when people suffer because of their group identity (often involuntary). The injustices associated with the disadvantaged loom large in our society. However, the problem goes beyond the failure of these theories to address an important problem in a direct manner. The disadvantaged pose theoretical conundrums for each theory. I shall briefly outline the discussions of each theory that occur in more detail in the main part of the text.

To take some examples from philosophy, charging liberal and communitarian philosophers with theoretically marginalizing the disadvantaged should be particularly troublesome to the liberalism of John Rawls and the communitarianism of Michael Sandel. Rawls should find the attack troublesome because concern for the least advantaged seems to lie at the heart of his project. Also, Sandel, one of Rawls's most adamant critics, has put forth specific policy recommendations that seem to favor the disadvantaged. Sandel's theories seem to lead him to policies that favor the disadvantaged. Yet, it remains unclear how Sandel gets from theory to policy. I have chosen Rawls and Sandel as representatives of liberalism and communitarianism not only because they are arguably the leading proponents of their respective positions, but also because they seem to offer solutions for remedying the problems of the disadvantaged. My goal is to demonstrate that the disadvantaged need not rejoice over the theories of Rawls and Sandel, even though Rawls and Sandel appear as their allies.

The case of democratic theorists within political science poses a slightly different challenge. The theorists chosen, Joseph Schumpeter and Benjamin Barber, operate at opposite ends of the democratic spectrum, which makes them good examples. Schumpeter offers one of the most restrictive forms of liberal democratic theory, while Barber, one of the most vociferous critics of liberalism, presents a very expansive version of communitarianism. Despite the vast theoretical divide separating Schumpeter and Barber, they both almost completely ignore any problems having to do with the disadvantaged. They bypass consideration of the disadvantaged despite the fact that their respective theories call for them to take a stand on the status of disadvantaged groups. Theoretically marginalizing the disadvantaged to the background becomes understandable once we see that the disadvantaged create challenging tensions for each theory—challenging to a point of undermining the respective theories.

Constitutional theory provides yet another fertile ground to view the theoretical marginalization of the disadvantaged within the liberal/communitarian debate. John Ely, a leading constitutional theorist, explicitly addresses himself to the status of disadvantaged groups, but he very narrowly confines his concerns by opting for form over substance in his process model for interpreting the Equal Protection Clause of the Fourteenth Amendment of the Constitution. Cass Sunstein's communitarianism, or republicanism, as he prefers to call it, explicitly tries to link abstract premises with concrete concern for the disadvantaged. Yet, the concrete concerns of the disadvantaged enter at a higher theoretical level than Sunstein seems willing to admit. Unfortunately, despite Sunstein's predilections, his abstract constructions do not mesh with his policy formulations.

To see how the marginalization process takes place at the theoretical level, let us return to the social sphere for illumination. Marginalization at the social level occurs in a number of different ways. Some more obvious ways include the following: the dominant group can directly perpetuate the marginalization process by taking action against the marginalized; or the dominant group can simply ignore the marginalized, thereby helping to make the marginalized invisible. Overt marginalization occurs where the theoretician takes on the role of the dominant social group, explicitly favoring principles and policies that clearly undermine the status of the disadvantaged. More covert forms happen where the theoretician employs principles and policies that exclude the disadvantaged from consideration, even where this is not intended.

However, a more subtle version of marginalization can also take place. Disadvantaged groups may find their social position worsened by their associations and alliances with dominant social groups who genuinely befriend and defend them but who nonetheless do not put the welfare of the disadvantaged at the center of their concern. This subtle variation of marginalization operates within the liberal/communitarian debate. Liberals and communitarians neither openly attack nor ignore the plight of disadvantaged groups. In fact, at least in the versions considered in this chapter, they support certain efforts on behalf of the disadvantaged. The theoretical marginalization occurs through the process of making the support efforts and their theoretical underpinnings a secondary concern. Just as I do not know of any easy way to uncover the more subtle forms of the social marginalization of the disadvantaged, I do not have a straightforward way of distinguishing primary from secondary theoretical concerns, short of unravelling a particular theory. However, some general things can be said.

A number of theoretical moves contribute to the secondary treatment of problems of the disadvantaged. The premises may not contain any specific reference to the disadvantaged, or if they do, then the notion of the disadvantaged (or its cognate) is left without any clear interpretation or without any rules of interpretation being provided. Lower ordered policies about the disadvantaged may or may not connect with higher order principles, which do not make reference to the disadvantaged. Similarly, those higher ordered principles containing a reference to the disadvantaged can be left uninterpreted or left to play a secondary role within the theory. Moreover, other priorities, such as form over substance and theoretical principle over concrete policy, can marginalize the disadvantaged.

Who are the disadvantaged? I can only provide a sketch of what a normative theory of the disadvantaged would look like. A good place to find an initial list of candidates for disadvantaged group status is those groups the Supreme Court has considered for special judicial protection under the Fourteenth Amendment Equal Protection Clause. The groups more or less accepted by the Court as suspect classes include: race, gender, alienage, and illegitimacy. These groups qualify for special judicial protection. The Court has also considered and unjustifiably rejected the following groups for suspect class status: the mentally retarded, the poor, homosexuals, the aged, and the children of illegal aliens.[1] When I refer to disadvantaged groups throughout this chapter, I have in mind the types of groups listed above. Although it would take considerable argumentation to defend this, disadvantaged groups can be identified in terms of a complex interplay of three factors: negative group identity, group harm, and powerlessness—all of which would require assessment and documentation within an historical narrative. For the purposes of this paper, I shall assume an agreement over the existence of disadvantaged social groups and a rough consensus about whether certain groups, such as African Americans, qualify as disadvantaged.

I shall also assume some agreement over what constitutes a normative theory of the disadvantaged. Within Supreme Court jurisprudence, the normative theory centers around the acceptance of the claim that courts ought to overturn laws that adversely and disproportionately affect groups satisfying certain conditions. In this paper I do not intend to defend judicial review. I use it here only as an illustration. My more limited purpose is to demonstrate the need for a normative theory of the disadvantaged.

Claims about the disadvantaged do not play a central role in the liberal/communitarian debate. They have played a crucial role in other debates. The late-nineteenth-century debate between social anarchists, led by Michael Bakunin, and Marxists provides an example of the status of the disadvantaged playing a key role in a debate within political theory. Bakunin claimed that Marx ignored the Lumpenproletariat, which "included all the submerged classes: unskilled, unemployed, and poor workers, poor peasant proprietors, landless agricultural laborers, oppressed racial minorities, alienated and idealistic youth, declasse intellectuals, and bandits."[2] Bakunin saw the Lumpenproletariat and not Marx's working class as the critical agents of social revolution. So, theorists within socialism did engage in a debate that roughly coincided with the dispute over the theoretical centrality of the disadvantaged. Marxism won, and anarchism lost. Class emerged victorious over all other forms of being disadvantaged.

I do not know of a similar debate within liberalism or communitarianism. The liberal/communitarian debate says something important about the quality of academic political discourse in the United States today. The status of disadvantaged groups poses a severe political challenge, which much of mainstream political theory has ignored.

The next two sections look at Rawls's liberalism and Sandel's communitarianism in more detail.

Political Philosophy

Rawlsian liberalism

Let's first take up the liberal case. Some concern for the disadvantaged generally comes out of liberal thought as a consequence of adopting a higher ordered principle such as equal opportunity, and not as result of building a theory around the injustices of the disadvantaged. However, John Rawls's *A Theory of Justice* seems to refute that contention since the disadvantaged lie at the very center of the theory. So, Rawls poses a formidable challenge to the theoretical marginalization claim.

The Rawlsian framework presents a complex case, and I can only indicate the direction of analysis rather than undertake a complete assessment, which would divert from the main topic. Rawls defends two principles of justice as those a rational person would adopt in the original position, having no knowledge of their own position in the society. These are:

First Principle
Each person is to have an equal right to the most extensive total system of equal basic liberties compatible with as a similar system of liberty for all.

Second Principle
Social and economic inequalities are to be arranged so that they are both:
(a) to the greatest benefit of the least advantaged, consistent with the just savings principle, and
(b) attached to offices and positions open to all under conditions of fair equal opportunity.[3]

Allowing for the unequal distribution of primary goods (liberty and opportunity, income and wealth, and bases of self-respect) only when it would not be to the advantage of the least favored sounds like a fairly strong endorsement of the centrality of the disadvantaged.

However, upon closer examination of the theory, the centrality of the disadvantaged begins to diminish. At each stage of the Rawlsian analysis uncertainty over the status of the disadvantaged arises. Just as no one set of acts might constitute marginalizing a social group in the real world, so no one set of questions fully marginalizes the disadvantaged at a theoretical level. However, when taken together, the acts and the questions make a case for marginalization, both social and theoretical.

To begin with, Rawls remains unclear about the representation of the disadvantaged in the original position. The original position requires the participants to be rational adults, who are able to manage their own affairs. That is not to say that the mentally infirm, children, etc., could not be represented in that "once the ideal conception is chosen," those in the original position "will want to insure themselves against the possibility that their powers are undeveloped and they cannot rationally advance their interests, as in the case of children; or that through some misfortune or accident they are unable to make decisions for their good, as in the case of those seriously injured or mentally disturbed."[4] Children and the mentally infirm do not get to speak for themselves. Their interests may be inadequately represented by rational, self-interested, sane adults dealing with the possibility of being a child or becoming mentally infirm. Moreover, Rawls injects a particular view of children and the mentally infirm into the idealized structure. For Rawls, children have undeveloped rational powers, and the mentally infirm cannot make decisions for their good. At the very minimum, the situation regarding children and the mentally infirm appears far more complicated, with considerable rational powers being displayed by both groups.[5]

Rawls places the participants in the original position under a veil of ignorance, unable to exploit any particular knowledge to their own advantage but equipped with general knowledge. Rawls never spells out exactly what he means by particular and general knowledge. Although the veil of ignorance is meant to assure neutrality in choosing the principles of justice, the degree and kind of general knowledge available to the participants in the original position might also affect not only the types of principles chosen but also their formulation. Does general knowledge include general facts about disadvantaged groups? The way of identifying disadvantaged groups may affect how readily participants in the original position are to separate liberties from power and wealth. Those in the original position might know general facts about how intertwined questions of liberty, power, and wealth are, thereby making them less likely to accept the formulations of principles of justice that give priority to some principles over others. Rawls does not provide any guidance as to whether or not knowledge about, let us say, the inextricable link between liberty and wealth could be a general piece of knowledge available to those in the original position.

Let us now turn to the principles themselves. Some protection for disadvantaged groups may come from the first principle of liberty. The basic liberties at stake in the first principle include the "freedom of the person,"[6] which could provide, for example, the basis for a Rawlsian rejection of *Bowers v. Hardwick*, where the Supreme Court upheld a Georgia anti-sodomy law. It appears that the Georgia legislature, had deprived homosexuals of their "freedom of the person." Yet, Rawls has very little to say about freedom of the person. So, it remains unclear how much protection homosexuals can get from the claim that a law violates their freedom of person. Admittedly, Rawls cannot conceive of any race or recognized group of human beings that lack the capacity for moral personhood, but he leaves the door slightly ajar by admitting that there are a few scattered individuals, who could form a certain type of group, without the capacity to have a conception of their good and a sense of justice.[7] We need to know more about the characteristics these few scattered individuals have that other groups do not. So far I have uncovered only some minor problems for the Rawlsian framework. Let us now turn to some more troublesome matters.

Rawls grants priority to the first principle of liberty over the second, difference principle. Political liberties can only be traded for other fundamental liberties and not for any greater economic or social welfare. Given the priority of political liberties, Rawls must accept that political liberties for the advantaged can come at the expense of social/economic welfare for the least advantaged.[8] The priority of the political does not mean that Rawls does not recognize the interplay between political liberties and economic welfare. An individual may not be able to exercise her political liberties because of her economic status. One way Rawls avoids the problem of the economic basis of political liberties is to distinguish between freedom as equal liberty, which is the same for all, and the worth of liberty, which is not the same for all.[9] The distinction between liberty and the worth of liberty seems simply to restate the problem rather than undermine the claim that "the inability to take advantage of one's rights and opportunities as a result of poverty and ignorance, a lack of means generally . . . [counts] among the constraints of liberty."[10] Rawls offers some solace to the less fortunate members of society since their capacity "to achieve their aims would be even less were they not to accept the existing inequalities whenever the difference principle is satisfied."[11] Yet, the question remains, is this really adequate compensation for having the lesser worth of liberty?

Failures to meet the ideals of the first principle must be dealt with prior to departures from the second principle. We must first remove the injustices related to political liberties before those associated with the inequalities addressed by the difference principle.[12] To put this in terms of a concrete example, a law school, then, would have to give priority to proposed regulations dealing with hate speech, given that freedom of speech is a primary good with priority, before addressing attempts to dismantle a loan forgiveness program, which rewards those students, minority and otherwise, practicing public interest areas of the law such as poverty law. Although I am not prepared to make a complete case here, it seems that a strong argument could be made that liberty issues often divert scarce resources away from more critical distributional issues.[13] Again, Rawls leaves the reader not quite certain.

The lexical ordering between the first and second principles has a counterpart within the second principle, wherein fair equality of opportunity has lexical priority over the difference principle. An example of a violation of the priority occurs in the situation, noted by Keynes, where "the immense accumulations of capital built up before the First World War" violated the principle of fair equality of opportunity.[14] It appears that Rawls has provided a further device for disadvantaged groups to employ against the implementation of social hierarchies. However, it is not altogether clear how this would come to pass. The fair opportunity principle applies to "offices and positions," which clearly includes government offices. It remains unclear what other offices and positions are included. Wealth accumulation may adversely affect the social position of a group. The strongest force of many caste systems is not the denial of opportunity to hold governmental offices but rather social ostracism.

Finally, the difference principle seems to allow for a fairly substantial amount of inequality: "self-interested individuals will be able to benefit from the possession of scarce skills, differentials which bring small increases in resources to the worst off may bring much larger benefits to other groups."[15] Furthermore, Rawls tends to characterize the worst off in terms of those having lower wages than the others and not in other terms. Please note that I have used the phrase "tends to characterize," for it is not as easy as some commentators of Rawls have thought to pin a purely economic interpretation of the disadvantaged on Rawls.[16]

When Rawls briefly addresses himself to "the serious difficulty of how to define the least fortunate group,"[17] he entertains two methods, one which employs social position, such as unskilled worker, and another that does not. So, Rawls at least considers the social position of the group members in defining the least advantaged. In fact, Rawls explicitly considers inequalities due to sex, race, ethnicity, and culture. He dismisses the social dimensions of group membership for two reasons. First of all, including race and the like in the definition of the least favored poses practical and not philosophical problems with the definition. Secondly, and more importantly, Rawls has difficulty imagining a just society where social iniquities, unlike economic inequalities, are ever to the advantage of the least favored.[18] Later Rawls proclaims that considering explicit racist doctrines in the initial situation would be not only unjust but also irrational.[19] Through these and other passages, Rawls clearly manifests a concern for the socially disadvantaged.

However, a subtle marginalization takes place within the Rawlsian system. The injustices inflicted upon disadvantaged groups appear to be easily managed within the Rawlsian framework. Racial inequalities would seldom (Rawls's hedge) be countenanced in a Rawlsian just society, and explicitly racist doctrines do not even qualify as rational. Yet, this position handles the easy cases—the instances of explicit, overt racism and other obvious forms of group injustice. Rawls leads us to believe that the problem of group injustice does not present any philosophical challenges.

Take a society where a housing project places a quota on the percentage of minority, namely, African American and Hispanic, tenants. If anything seems overtly racist, restricting opportunities for housing seems to qualify. Nothing in the Rawlsian framework tells the policy maker to look any further. In fact, anti-discrimination exemplifies our considered moral judgment. Yet, upon closer examination we might find, as you would in the case of Starrett City, that the seemingly racist policy in fact promotes rather than stifles the interest of the disadvantaged groups.[20]

No doubt someone could attempt to remedy these and the other defects in Rawls's system noted above in order to place the disadvantaged more centrally within the Rawlsian scheme. However, the teasing-out phenomenon represents the problem and not the solution. If a commitment to halt injustice inflicted on the disadvantaged is something that needs to be wrenched from a theory, then it shows, minimally, that the disadvantaged do not occupy a central place within the theory. The disadvantaged have, in effect, been theoretically marginalized. A theory of justice cannot escape the problem of the disadvantaged. The treatment of the most deprived people in a community needs to be placed at the very central core of any theory of justice. Thomas Pogge's recent work, *Realizing Rawls*, marks an attempt to uncover a radical core of concrete political proposals from Rawls's works. Rawls does say something about the disadvantaged, especially with respect to his second principle of justice. Yet, even after twenty years of development and criticisms of Rawls's liberal theory, no analysis of just who constitutes the least advantaged has fully emerged. Pogge attributes the conservative direction that Rawls's theory has taken to the abstract character of Rawls's system and to Rawls's refusal to take definitive stands on concrete political issues. However, the abstract character of the system does not fully account for the problem. Rather, as I have tried to show, the problem is more subtle and more complex. Rawls seems to provide a theory that is sensitive to the least advantaged. Yet, upon closer examination it remains unclear exactly where disadvantaged groups fit into the system. In short, the plight of disadvantaged groups is kept at bay by not centrally addressing them.[21]

In fact, it is not altogether clear whether Rawls could easily incorporate a normative theory of the disadvantaged into his theory without a serious disruption of primary claims within the theory. If a definition of disadvantaged groups inextricably intertwines liberties and other primary goods, then those in the original position should not choose principles of justice that neatly divide liberties from other primary goods, because the priority of liberties over primary goods might work to the detriment of the least advantaged.

Rawls leaves open crucial considerations regarding the disadvantaged. The issue of the disadvantaged becomes marginalized by the theorist's either not raising questions central to the issue or by leaving the issue in an uneasy state of flux. In a sense, Rawls places the disadvantaged at the theoretical core. Yet, the power of the central positioning remains untapped.

Sandel's Communitarianism

Communitarianism contains the ambiguous term "community." The core concept of community can be used in a way that severely lessens the plight of the disadvantaged or, alternatively, to stifle action on behalf of the disadvantaged. Communitarianism has a more conservative wing, represented through the works of MacIntyre, and a more democratically socialist oriented version, represented by the works of Michael Sandel. MacIntyre bemoans the incoherence of modern liberalism and longs for a return to an inculcation of the virtues through an immersion in the ethical tradition. Given the minor role played by the marginalized in the formation of that tradition, the fear that the tradition would yield an interpretation that favored the dominant groups seems well founded.[22]

Sandel's version of communitarianism poses a far different problem and leads to a different analysis of the disadvantaged than MacIntyre's. However, not all commentators agree on distinguishing MacIntyre from Sandel, painting them with the same critical brush. Just as we can ask "whose tradition?" of MacIntyre, so we can ask "which community?" of Sandel.

Sandel has been charged with promoting an overly generalized conception of the community that favors the dominant majority over the minority.[23] Sandel places great emphasis on those senses of community that describe "not a relationship they choose (as in a voluntary association) but an attachment they discover, not merely an attribute but a constituent of their identity."[24] So, Sandel's communitarianism gives priority to involuntary as opposed to voluntary communities.[25]

Involuntary communities such as the nation state we are born into and the neighborhood in which we reside have their own built-in social hierarchies and biases in favor of one social group over another. Appeals to involuntary communities would seem to replicate the problems inherent in their social hierarchies. If the dominant community of heterosexuals subordinates the interests of homosexuals, then the communitarian project marginalizes the marginalized even further. According to some critics of communitarianism, "the problem of the exclusion of the historically marginalized groups is endemic to the communitarian project."[26] Sandel's position on homosexuality shows how many of his critics have missed the mark. One of Sandel's most ardent critics, Will Kymlicka, baldly stated that "Nothing in Sandel's argument gives members of marginalized groups the power to reject the identity that others have historically defined for them."[27] But soon after Kymlicka chided Sandel for being incapable of defending homosexuality on communitarian grounds Sandel provided a communitarian defense of homosexuality.[28]

Sandel not only has a defense of homosexuals but his concrete examples evidence a concern for other marginalized groups. He notes that communitarians would justify the civil rights movement of the 1960s "in the name of recognizing the full membership of fellow citizens wrongly excluded from the common life of the nation."[29] Sandel also favors the regulation of pornography by the local community "on the grounds that pornography offends its way of life."[30] Finally, unlike many liberals, Sandel has advocated that states pass laws regulating plant closing in order to protect the local community. So, Sandel's communitarianism shows notable concern for the disadvantaged: African Americans, women, homosexuals, and workers.

However, Sandel's communitarianism is susceptible to the interpretation that he still marginalizes the disadvantaged. In the hands of a communitarian less sympathetic to the plight of the disadvantaged, the disadvantaged would not gain as much protection. The "common life of the nation" might exclude (rightfully, according to its dictates) disadvantaged groups, such as aliens. A local community might find pornography inoffensive to its way of life to a point where it promotes pornography. And perhaps at the level of the national community, regulating plant closing at a local level has dire effects. Protection for the disadvantaged seems to depend upon a fluid interpretation of community.

The fluidity of the notion of community becomes apparent when Sandel conveniently vacillates between the national and the local community. On the one hand, he resorts to the local community in agreeing to keep the neo-Nazis from marching in Skokie, where many Holocaust survivors live. On the other hand, he argues that segregation should be opposed because it excludes certain groups "from the common life of the nation."[31] And then again, he promotes the development of local communities and argues that "the nation is too vast to sustain more than a minimal communality."[32] Nothing in the communitarian premises guides us in forming a set of principles and policies for dealing with the disadvantaged. Communitarians construct their systems around a substantive conception of the good life which defines a community's way of life. We are left to our own, non-communitarian devices if we want to develop a position on the disadvantaged. At the critical juncture of providing a normative theory of social groups, communitarians leave us in a void. The problem is not what communitarians say about the disadvantaged at the more concrete policy level but rather how little they say about the disadvantaged within their central theoretical tenets.

The disadvantaged are theoretically marginalized by communitarians in their failure to place concern for the disadvantaged in the theoretical core. It will not do simply to append some rules for interpreting the notion of community so as to take into account the plight of the disadvantaged. To construct a normative theory of the disadvantaged would, in the end, radically change communitarianism into a theory of social groups instead of a theory of community. The problem is that the notion of community is too vague to do the theoretical work that Sandel wants it to do in order to place communitarian limits on certain forms of injustice. To put the point more dramatically, the marginalized find support in the communitarian framework; yet, the communitarian theoretical structure does not provide firm support for the marginalized.

Democratic Theory

All democratic theories seem to have common components. In sum, these components consist of: a reference to the people in general, a commitment to having the people participate in governance, and a refusal to tolerate a wide disparity among social groups in the society. Let us look at each of these in turn.

First of all, the democratic theory must make some reference to the "the people." Every democratic theory takes the etymology of the word "democracy" seriously and has at least some reference to the *demos,* or people, in its definition. Reference to the people needs to have a considerable degree of undifferentiation. In other words, "the people" is a general term; it does not mean certain people or certain types of people. This does not entail that some types of people cannot be excluded. It does mean that strong independent grounds must be given for the exclusion of a group. Convicted criminals, for example, are denied aspects of democratic citizenship because they have given up part of their citizenship by their criminal activity. Beyond categories like convicted criminals, the term "the people" cannot be further socially stratified. It would be an odd democratic theory that excluded large numbers of social groups.

Secondly, every democratic theory promotes some degree of participation in governance on the part of the people. Passive citizenship would be an oxymoron for any democratic theory. The debate, of course, is over the extensiveness of the participation. Should citizen participation be limited largely to voting or should it extend much more widely to active debate over, for example, conditions in the workplace?

Finally, every democratic theory should include a claim that prescribes a degree of levelling among the people that does not undermine their participation. If, for example, the society tolerates a wide disparity between individuals such that it precludes a large proportion of individuals from participating by voting, then the system fails to qualify as democratic. As a critical corollary to the levelling claim, certain types of disparity are especially antithetical to democracy. A particularly devastating type of stratification is a kind of group stratification. A democratic theory can countenance disparity among individuals who, for whatever reason, may not participate in the democratic governance. In fact, some democratic theorists such as Samuel Huntington in his report to the Trilateral Commission have advocated a certain degree of apathy among the populace as necessary to effective democratic governance. However, a democratic theory cannot tolerate wide disparities among social groups due to group subjugation, because that would undermine citizen participation. So, it is one thing to advocate that a certain percentage of the electorate should not vote and quite another to tolerate a de facto situation where all or most members of a social group, such as African Americans, cannot vote.

For the latter undermines any meaningful reference to the *demos*. Wide disparity between social groups in terms of the distribution of power can have similar, although not as dramatic, effects as the explicit exclusion of a social group.

The group-levelling desideratum has important ramifications for structuring debates over democratic theory. It means that constructing a social analysis through the prescription of a type of levelling among social groups takes high priority in developing an adequate democratic theory. However, a surprisingly high number of democratic theorists give scant attention to the problem of group disparity. Again, the disadvantaged become marginalized due to scant attention paid to their plight.

I want to turn now to an evaluation of how a representative sampling of democratic theorists fare in light of the above requirements, particularly with respect to the group-levelling requirement. Rather than engaging in an exhaustive survey of the array of democratic theories in political science, I will discuss the ends of the spectrum, starting with Joseph Schumpeter's competitive elitism and ending with Benjamin Barber's participatory version. Schumpeter represents a version of liberalism, while Barber represents communitarianism. The analysis of these will show their incompleteness, because each fails to prescribe a theory of disadvantaged groups. A consideration of the ends of the democratic theory spectrum provides at least some grounds for thinking that those democratic theories situated between Schumpeter's and Barber's will be similarly infected, at least in so far as the problem of marginalizing the disadvantaged is concerned.

Schumpeter's Competitive Elitism

Schumpeter, born in Austria, published *Capitalism, Socialism and Democracy*[33] in 1942. The work became a classic following the Second World War, and its popularity and notoriety persist to this day. Schumpeter defined democracy as "that institutional arrangement for arriving at political decisions in which individuals acquire power to decide by means of a competing struggle for the people's vote."[34] Schumpeter carved out a very narrow ground for citizen participation, thereby placing him at one end of the democratic theory spectrum. Citizens can vote for, or, minimally, vote out, the well-trained technocratic rulers needed to manage a large, complex modern state. In sum, Schumpeter proposed a "democracy for the politicians."

Schumpeter devised a narrow view of democracy in response to what he saw as the excesses of the classical view of democracy. The classical view has strong affinities to contemporary versions of communitarianism. Schumpeter took a sobering view of democracy, a perspective he thought would undermine the classical democrats' faith in rule by the people. Schumpeter reminded the classical believer that rule by the people often failed to achieve rule for the people. Overall, Schumpeter found appeals within the classical doctrine to the common good dangerous and appeals to the will of the people illusory. In contrast to the so-called myths underlying the classical doctrine, Schumpeter offered a realistic account of democracy, one that went beneath the rhetoric and platitudes and grounded itself in reality.

Basically, Schumpeter limited citizen involvement to the choosing of the leaders to follow. Leaders, and not citizens, formally debated issues and made major policy decisions. Democracy became a competitive business, dealing in the commodity of voting: Schumpeter's approval of the following statement from a politician says a great deal about how he saw democracy: "What businessmen do not understand is that exactly as they are dealing in oil so I am dealing in votes."[35] Schumpeter saw democracy as a business.

Schumpeter's definition of democracy is minimalist in a number of ways: First of all, the formal, mechanistic conception of democracy does not commit him to any substantive values, or, at least, that is what he thought. "Democracy is a political method," pure and simple. Substantive values, ends, and ideals are something entirely separate from democracy. The substantive condemnation of racial restrictions on the franchise, to take just one illustration, operated outside the purview of Schumpeter's democracy.

Secondly, Schumpeter's democracy required a minimal level of participation in governance on the part of the people. Schumpeter limited the general public's participation to voting. Voters voted for leaders, not for issues. To the extent that voting gave the electorate power, it did so largely in the negative. The electorate exerted power not so much in electing the leaders to office but rather in refusing to elect them.

Finally, Schumpeter, in keeping with the minimalist's agenda, drew sharp lines not only around democracy as a method but also around the spheres to which the democratic method applied. The democratic method should not extend its horizontal reach beyond the realm of politics into economics, forming odd hybrids such as industrial democracy, or into any other nonpolitical sphere. The democratic method prevailed within the narrow confines of government, and it had no business extending itself into any other areas of life.[36]

By confining democracy to the formal and governmental realms and by limiting citizen participation, Schumpeter devised a very minimalist version of democracy. So, "Democracy means only that the people have the opportunity of accepting or refusing to accept the men [sic] who are to rule them. . . ."[37] Once the voters have chosen the leader, "they must refrain from instructing him about what he is to do."[38] In fact, Schumpeter even recommended banning the practice of bombarding politicians with letters and telegrams.[39]

Schumpeter made only passing reference to different social groups when he addressed what he called "the tectonic principles of the social fabric":

> . . . democracy cannot be expected to function satisfactorily unless the vast majority of the people in all classes are resolved to abide by the rules of the democratic game and this in turn implies that they are substantially agreed on the fundamentals of their institutional structure.[40]

So, Schumpeter at least acknowledges the need to avoid disparity between social groups with regard to their common understanding and acceptance of the ground rules of the system.

However, Schumpeter's program presupposes claims that he refused to incorporate, centrally, into his system or even to consider. For example, Schumpeter assumed that citizens exhibit at least a modicum of intelligence in choosing their political leaders. Schumpeter recognized that "democracy thrives in social patterns that display certain characteristics,"[41] including the condition that "electorates and parliaments must be on an intellectual and moral level high enough to be proof against the offerings of the crook and the crank."[42] Participatory disparity can seriously undermine an informed citizenry, and it can make a mockery of the idea of choice in these circumstances. Participatory disparity could prevent the disadvantaged social groups from choosing their own leaders, render their participation effectively meaningless, or seriously distort the quality of their participation. Schumpeter remained silent on the need to protect the rights of members of disadvantaged groups to vote in a way that they too could protect themselves from the devices of unscrupulous politicians. Yet, the logic of his theory should have led him to incorporate centrally or, minimally, to consider the status of disadvantaged groups.

Take another implication of Schumpeter's theory. According to one commentator, "Democracy entails, in his [Schumpeter's] view, a state in which everyone is, in principle, free to compete for political leadership."[43] "Effective participation depends upon political will and upon having the actual capacity (the resources and skills) to pursue different courses of action."[44] Disadvantaged group status infects both the people's choice of leaders and undermines the conditions of participation needed for Schumpeter's elitist model to work. So, Schumpeter's version of democracy presupposes a commitment to overcoming disparity between groups. Otherwise, Schumpeter's version of democracy cannot work, even on its own terms.

In Schumpeter's system the disadvantaged become theoretically marginalized in that consideration of the status of disadvantaged groups serves as a background problem that need not be addressed. Putting the problem in the background effectively silences a potential threat to the theoretical structure. The more educated and enlightened the electorate, the more chance the electorate has of challenging the rule of the professional politicians. It would be difficult to provide the electorate with education and the like without conceding some resources and, ultimately, political power, to them. For Schumpeter an uninformed and immoral or amoral electorate would destroy the competitiveness of the political leadership race. Improving the lot of the disadvantaged segment of the electorate, by helping them to become better informed, etc., would begin to level the playing field of competition. However, while the leadership would benefit at first from the levelling, in the long run, levelling would threaten the status of an elite.

The label "competitive elitism" exposes the tension in Schumpeter's democratic theory. Competitively, the theory calls for a central role for a prescriptive stand on the status of the disadvantaged. True competitiveness, however, would start to erode the elitism.

Barber's Strong Democracy

Benjamin Barber in *Strong Democracy: Participatory Politics for a New Age,* published in 1984, contrasted three types of democracy: thin (liberal), unitary, and strong (participatory). He focused his wrath on the liberal form of representative democracy, which he found "incompatible with equality"[45] and producing "distrustful, passive"[46] citizens. Undoubtedly, Barber would have placed Schumpeter's competitive elitist version of democracy in the thin category. Barber used unitary democracy, with its citizens bound together by blood ties, as a danger area for strong democracy to avoid, because he recognized the ease with which strong democracy could fall into the unitary trap.

While Schumpeter represents a strand of liberal democracy, Barber exemplifies the communitarian wing. Barber depicts liberal versions of democracy as thin and his own as strong (not thick or fat!). Barber proposes the following strong, participatory, communitarian sense of democracy:

> Democracy is politics in the participatory mode where conflict is resolved in the absence of an independent ground through a participatory process of ongoing, proximate self-legislation and the creation of a political community capable of transforming dependent, private individuals into free citizens and the partial and private interests into public goods.[47]

Barber would object to Schumpeter's confining democratic participation to voting. On Barber's account, the Schumpeter version would stifle the development of citizens as full participants in the political process. Schumpeter emphasized procedures and carefully avoided promoting any particular interpretation of the public good. Schumpeter would have denied, quite vehemently, the claim that democracy should promote citizenship, except to the extent that citizenship involved voting for the leaders.

In contrast, citizenship lies at the heart of Barber's strong democracy. Schumpeter's citizens participate to a minimum degree in democratic governance, whereas Barber's citizens become fully engaged in every aspect of the governing structure. Schumpeter's citizens occasionally perform their democratic duties by voting for their leaders. For Barber, democratic citizenship constitutes a way of living and not simply an occasional civic act.[48] In fact, for Barber, political participation serves as a measure of citizenship.[49]

Despite their differences, Schumpeter and Barber do find common ground in their emphasis on the procedural aspects of democracy. Barber portrays democracy as largely a procedural device by which citizens come to agreement over moral issues such as social justice. Strong democracy does not rest on any particular moral foundation, but rather it provides the forum for constructing morality. Indeed, according to Barber, "democracy may exist entirely without moral foundation."[50] So, on Barber's account, morality and democracy have no necessary connection.

Barber's dichotomy between democracy and morals leads him to proclaim:

> If we wish to make such central values as freedom and equality the measure of democracy, then we must regard them as the products rather than the conditions of the political process—which is to say that politics precedes economics and therefore creates the central values of economy and society.[51]

Accordingly, substantive value judgments flow from, rather than precede, the participatory political process of a strong democracy. Citizens discuss value questions, seeking ways to establish equality and justice. Equality and justice are not the conditions of democracy; democracy is the condition for equality and justice.[52] Strong democracy creates equality and justice.

Thus, Barber maintains two related claims: (1) Strong democracy leads to equality and justice; and (2) Equality and justice are not conditions of democracy. Let us examine each of these in turn.

First of all, Barber may assume that allowing each citizen to participate would make the worst forms of inequality disappear. However, if the neighborhood assemblies he advocates do not presuppose a level playing field, then they could perpetuate these injustices even with the full participation of those afflicted. Barber contends that appeals to the reasonableness of citizens may prevent lynching and other reprehensible forms of mob rule. Yet, the neighborhood assembly could easily rationalize actions that, while not reaching the level of lynching, would have a disproportional negative impact on disadvantaged groups.

Barber thinks that he can avoid highly inequalitarian actions resulting from political deliberation by tying political deliberation to the public good: "Strong democratic talk always involves listening as well as speaking, feeling as well as thinking, and acting as well as reflecting."[53] Strong democrats deliberate in order to create public interests, common goods, and active citizens. Whatever the virtues of encouraging more democratic talk, it provides only a thin shield against the promulgation of injustices. Talking may or may not unleash the benign aspects of human nature (or, of human interaction). Democratic talk may even persuade the disadvantaged that they deserve their plight. So, contrary to Barber's wishes, strong democracy could lead to injustices. In fact, without built-in protections for disadvantaged groups, it seems highly likely that strong democracy would not benefit the disadvantaged, since they do not enter the democratic discussion on roughly an equal footing with the dominant groups.

Secondly, because of the unjust consequences potentially stemming from strong democracy it would behoove Barber to recognize the level playing field as a presupposition of strong democracy and not simply as a possible (or, what he thinks to be, a probable) consequence of it. Barber's strong democracy, apparently unbeknownst to him, presupposes a level playing field among its citizens. Participatory disparity undermines strong democracy. The public talk that Barber finds so crucial to strong democracy requires some levelling among the groups of citizens. Meaningful democratic discourse requires a certain social status among those engaged in the talk. Groups engaging in behavior, such as race riots, in all probability have not been made parties to the dominant political discourse. Racial unrest is symptomatic of participatory disparity. Strong democracy, in order to be effective, requires the eradication of those participatory disparities that impede the conditions needed for citizens to engage in political discourse. Participatory disparity saps the strength from strong democracy.

Occasionally, Barber lapses into making a connection between democracy and equality: "When the ideals of . . . public over private are deployed without their indispensable strong democratic concomitants—equality, autonomy, pluralism, tolerance, and the separation of the private from the public—then to be sure democracy can become unitary and collectivistic."[54] Barber allows values such as equality into strong democracy as a means of preventing strong democracy from turning into its totalitarian kin, unitary democracy. However, the level playing field symbolizes more than the brakes needed to prevent strong democracy from skidding into the abyss of a repressive unitary form. A strong democracy, to operate at all, presupposes a level playing field. Democratic talk, in its quest for the common good, presupposes a certain degree of levelling among the talkers. Given the importance of democratic talk to uncovering the common good for Barber, disadvantaged groups must be brought into the discussion on a roughly equal footing. Otherwise, the disadvantaged cannot contribute effectively to the type of discussion encouraged by strong democracy.

Despite an occasional reference to inequality, Barber's swipes at injustice cannot be very serious. Barber does not realize how critical a social theory of the disadvantaged is to his own. For at times, Barber leans toward an acceptance, if not a promotion, of participatory disparity. In a section on leadership, Barber admits that: "The talents and capabilities that generate the sort of political skills needed by founders or by conscientious facilitators in a direct democracy are unequally distributed among citizens."[55] Barber seems to advocate a vanguard of the self-governing elite. Presumably, however, the unequal distribution represents only a temporary state that can be remedied through civic education. Yet, if disadvantaged groups cannot be brought within earshot of democratic talk, then Barber's proposal is as thin and weak as the liberalism that he attacks. Part of what it means to be disadvantaged is to lack the tools needed to engage in the political discourse. Barber largely ignores the problems relating to the status of disadvantaged groups, to his own peril, for it considerably weakens his theory.

All that has been established thus far is that Barber's strong democracy calls for giving the status of the disadvantaged a more central theoretical role. Drawing a link between the problem of participatory disparity and democracy deserves a hearing, particularly since democratic theorists like Barber operate under the quite mistaken assumption that democracy can be easily separated from questions of injustice, such as the existence of disadvantaged groups. Without giving the problem of the disadvantaged a more central place, strong democracy could perpetuate the injustices inflicted upon disadvantaged groups by not challenging the participatory disparities embedded in the status quo. In Barber's case, theoretical marginalization of the disadvantaged takes place through largely ignoring an issue central to the theory.

Iris Young, for example, contends that strong democracy "will suppress difference, and tend to exclude some voices and perspectives from the public, because their greater privilege and dominant position allows some groups to articulate the 'common good' in terms influenced by their particular perspectives and interests."[56] If Barber fails to address the problem of the disadvantaged, then Young's point holds true.[57] Promoting participatory democracy without addressing the differential power relationships among the participants will reproduce, at best, the injustices, particularly the inequities of participatory disparity, of the status quo. Barber's strong democracy would then enhance the strength of the few, contrary to its goal of increasing participation among the people. Barber has done nothing, theoretically, to block the formation of a participatory elite. At least Schumpeter's electorate could "throw the bums out," whereas Barber's citizens seem condemned to continuous talk with little hope of levelling the conditions for the talk.

Barber's failure to develop the anti-inequalitarian presuppositions of strong democracy leads him to endorse teledemocracy projects enthusiastically without a serious critique. Electronic town meetings held via interactive television systems do little to stimulate participatory debate if the problem of inequitable resource allocation does not take priority. If Barber were truly interested in promoting participation for all citizens, he would pay attention to effective means of participation for disadvantaged groups. Allowing the homeless access to Santa Monica, California's electronic network does little more than let the technology drive the participation rather than have the participation guide the choice of technology.[58]

In closing, let us return to Barber's definition of strong democracy. Participation plays the key role in strong democracy; everything else revolves around it. Conflicts, in the absence of independent grounds (as Barber puts it), get resolved; citizens formed; and the public good promoted—all through participation. Yet, none of these things could take place without presupposing a level playing field, without addressing the status of the disadvantaged. For example, strong democracy can only have hopes of effecting Barber's vision of having participation transform conflict into cooperation within the context of a level playing field. If Barber wants to bring the human sources of the conflict into participatory politics, then effective participation of the antagonists depends on having previously addressed those conditions that effect their participatory status. In short, the problem of disadvantaged social groups needs to be centrally confronted.

Democratic Theories Compared

Schumpeter and Barber paid little attention, in general, to the level playing field desideratum of their respective definitions of democracy and, in particular, to disadvantaged groups. There is good reason for their bypassing critical issues of injustice, particularly the problem of participatory disparity caused by the unequal status of social groups. If Schumpeter and Barber had explicitly addressed the problem, then they may have had to face the formidable task of radically altering their respective theories.

A theory that directly confronts the problem of disadvantaged groups poses problems for Barber's strong democracy. To spread citizenship far and wide, strong democracy presupposes a levelling of the relative statuses of social groups. To have the wherewithal to enter into the political dialogue, injustices that impede the formation of participatory citizens need to be remedied. However, a serious effort to alleviate participatory disparity would run counter to Barber's reformist agenda.[59] Barber wants more talk to take place among the citizens without seriously disrupting the status quo. Yet, having too many citizens deliberating and deciding about too many important issues would either clog the communication networks, no matter how technocratic the political vision, or it would pose a serious threat to those who already dominate the participatory airwaves. In the final analysis, Barber's proposal, contrary to its own claims, would strengthen democracy for a relatively few social groups, primarily those already politically articulate.

Schumpeter's competitive elitism and Barber's strong democracy differ in terms of basic theoretical commitments. One difference centers around which groups the theorists conceive of as the central political actors. For Schumpeter, elites rule and voters elect. Whatever their role, distinct (atomic) individuals constitute the primary political actors in Schumpeter's democracy. Barber's strong democrats are in one sense individual participants, but in another sense they take on a general, rather abstract quality. Barber's *homo politicus* transcend their individuality. Strong democracy forces them to think and act in common. Self-interested individuals are transformed into citizens concerned with the general welfare in a strong democracy.

Groups are not easily accommodated with Schumpeter's individuals nor with Barber's general citizens. Schumpeter's "rule by the professional politician" and Barber's "citizen self-government" do not fit readily with groups, to say nothing of disadvantaged groups. Neither Schumpeter nor Barber takes problems associated with social stratification very seriously. For Schumpeter, the electorate are an undifferentiated blob "incapable of action other than a stampede."[60] Social class plays a role in Schumpeter's democracy only insofar as it serves as a breeding ground for politicians and for bureaucrats. Unlike Schumpeter, Barber, who advocates a strong political role for the people, wants to break down the barriers between rulers and the people. However, Barber's citizens have allegiances that transcend ties to kin, interest groups, or social groups. Barber's citizens have a general citizenship consciousness and not a group one.

The analysis provided here has challenged some cherished predilections. From competitive elitism one would not have expected disadvantaged groups to play any role whatsoever, but a levelling with respect to all social groups creates a concern for even elitist versions of democracy. Participatory theories of democracy have most often been associated with equalitarian proposals. Yet, in at least one prominent example, the anti-inequalitarian implications of strong democracy prove troublesome.

Both of these versions of democratic theory conveniently ignore the group levelling issue in democracy. Schumpeter must acknowledge a levelling with respect to the social groups involved in the democratic process of electing rulers into and out of office. The people do not choose or reject their technocratic rulers, as advocated by the theory, if some social groups, such as the homeless, remain completely misinformed or uninformed largely because of their group status. Schumpeter does not rule out a concern for disadvantaged social groups, but neither does he make explicit allowances for them.

When we turn from the liberal versions of democracy proposed by

Schumpeter to the communitarian version promoted by Barber, we find a similar pattern. Promoting the welfare of disadvantaged groups does not occupy the central core of his analysis. Democracy as participation by public-spirited citizens can be undermined if some citizens cannot effectively participate because of their group membership, but Barber devotes little attention to this phenomenon.

The debates over the nature of democracy, reflecting liberal and communitarian strands, show few signs of placing disadvantaged groups at the center.

Constitutional Interpretation

Legal scholarship, the third type of discourse considered, proves to be an excellent place to end the discussion since it includes the liberal/communitarian philosophical debate and the controversy over democratic theory. Legal scholars have argued that there are competing strands of liberal and republican constitutional interpretation throughout our history. For purposes of this discussion, I shall take republicanism as equivalent to communitarianism, even though I recognize differences. (I shall continue to use the latter designation.)

The history of how disadvantaged groups were treated within constitutional theory proves highly illuminating. Scholars place the critical juncture at the adoption of Footnote Four in a case called Carolene Products.[61] Former Supreme Court Justice Lewis Powell called it the "the most celebrated footnote in constitutional law."[62] Paragraph Two of Footnote Four proposed a more exacting form of judicial scrutiny when legislation directly impeded the political process. Paragraph Three took the analysis one step further by proclaiming the strict scrutiny of legislation that affected "discrete and insular minorities." The problem, which has obvious parallels in defining the disadvantaged for Rawls and community for Sandel, is how to interpret the phrase "discrete and insular minorities."

Robert Cover claimed that prior to the adoption of Footnote Four in 1938, a sense of quantitative minorities predominated judicial thinking, whereby minorities did not possess, at least in the eyes of the judiciary, any qualities indicative of disadvantaged groups.[63] The history of attempts to interpret "discrete and insular minorities" shows that the most narrow road was taken. Only a few disadvantaged social groups ended up qualifying as "discrete and insular minorities" worthy of judicial protection.

As mentioned in my introduction, one place where the Court talks about disadvantaged groups is in cases brought under the Equal Protection Clause of the Fourteenth Amendment. The Amendment states that "nor shall any State . . . deny to any person within its jurisdiction the equal protection of the laws." While the clause refers only to persons, the Court has found a way of analyzing the clause in terms of disadvantaged groups. It calls these disadvantaged groups suspect classes. The term "suspect class" has nothing to do with criminal suspects, nor does it refer to a Marxian or some other related sense of class. The Court uses suspect class analysis to indicate its suspicion of legislation about or cast in terms of disadvantaged groups. If someone can convince the Court that the case involves a suspect class, then the Court will engage in what it calls heightened scrutiny. The Court's scrutiny comes in various degrees. Heightened scrutiny means that the legislation about or in terms of the suspect class has little chance of passing constitutional muster. The Court will strictly scrutinize race and, to some extent, aliens. The Court will be slightly less sensitive to gender and illegitimacy classifications. Most other group designations will not pass the constitutional test as long as there is evidence of a rational link between the classification and legitimate governmental ends.

Ely's Process Model

The best way to illustrate the road of narrow interpretation is with the work of John Ely, a constitutional theorist. I chose Ely because his process interpretation of Footnote Four has become the most widely cited both inside and outside of the judiciary.

In *Democracy and Distrust*, Ely has presented the most complete theory of judicial interpretation in terms of what he calls the Process Model.[64] Basically, the role of judiciary is to keep the democratic processes open. The judiciary in some sense must serve as a surrogate representative for those groups denied the vote or the ability to form interest groups. If a governmental unit redraws its voting boundaries so as to dilute almost completely the voting power of black residents, that serves as reason enough for judicial intervention to protect the disadvantaged group. Similarly, aliens, by definition, have no direct representation in the legislature and thereby merit special judicial protection from abuse within the legislative process.

Ely's system has most of the earmarks of liberalism in its rough form. The judiciary embodies the neutrality characteristic of the neutral state. The judiciary assiduously avoids imposing any particular conception of the good on the participants in the legal system. The judiciary primarily concerns itself with fair process and not with substantive values; hence the name, Process Model. The individual, in contrast to the group, stands supreme in the Process Model. The judiciary focuses on individual fairness, although Ely urges that some attention be given to group fairness. A good way to see the individual/group contrast at work in the law is to note that many European countries have group libel laws while, except for one isolated case,[65] this is almost unheard of in American legal circles. Finally, Ely interprets the public/political realm rather narrowly. For Ely, like Schumpeter, the public engagement in politics consists largely in voting for representatives of the legislature.

Although Ely manifests some concern for the inequities between groups, he places severe restrictions on that concern. The judiciary acts on behalf of disadvantaged groups only when the pipelines of the legislative process get clogged with the debris of intentional discrimination on the part of the legislators and/or the legislature cannot have "plumbers" representing a group. So, for Ely, blacks (victims of intentional discrimination on the part of legislators) and aliens (unrepresented) clearly qualify for heightened judicial concern.

However, only a few disadvantaged groups qualify for heightened judicial protection in the Process Model. Furthermore, once a disadvantaged group squeezes itself into the political process, judicial protection gets lifted. Women had their access to the political process blocked in the past, but, given their current political clout, they now qualify for very limited judicial protection.[66]

The Process Model can be expanded to include more disadvantaged groups by making a number of moves. If greater emphasis were placed on the effect of subjugation on a disadvantaged group rather than on intentional discrimination, more disadvantaged groups would come under the aegis of the Process Model. Intentional discrimination sets a standard of proof that is very difficult to meet. Employment discrimination cases provide a good illustration of the differences between what the Court calls disparate treatment and disparate impact.

Moreover, the concept of political process could be more broadly construed so as to expand beyond the confines of the legislative process. Women, in a certain sense, may have the legislative process opened to them, but many other forms of subjugation operate against women that effectively cut off the legislative arena as a power base. The violence inflicted upon women takes its toll in more subtle ways than many males are willing to admit. Misogyny may not directly prevent women from running for political office; in fact, it may stimulate some towards a political career. Nevertheless, misogyny may well deplete the force needed by women to break down the old boy networks necessary for maintaining the male stranglehold on the political process.

The road for providing a broad interpretation of Footnote Four has been open to constitutional theorists. For the most part, scholars and the Court have opted for the narrow road. According to one scholar, Bruce Ackerman, only African Americans qualify as discrete and insular minorities.[67] Chief Justice William Rehnquist has led the charge to construe narrowly the bounds of suspect classes since his dissent in *Sugarman v. Dougall*, 413 U.S. 634 (1973), where he raised the specter of arbitrariness in the reading of "discrete and insular minorities." He stated that "It would hardly take extraordinary ingenuity for lawyers to find 'discrete and insular' minorities at every turn in the road."[68] The Court has followed suit in denying special protection to all but a narrow range of disadvantaged groups, particularly racial groups.

So, a strand of liberal constitutional interpretation has theoretically marginalized the disadvantaged by narrowly interpreting "discrete and insular minorities."

Sunstein's Republicanism

Liberals, of which defenders of the Process Model represent only one sect, have engaged in a heated debate with rival communitarians within legal scholarship. The contrast between the two can be made in the following terms. Liberals defend neutrality, individualism, and a narrow conception of the political. Communitarians advocate substantive conceptions of the good, community, and a broad conception of the political/public realm. Communitarians have not produced a definitive statement or a refined defense of their position. A great deal of the vitality of communitarianism comes from its opposition to liberalism.

Communitarians are quite well aware of their sordid past. Cass Sunstein, in promoting a republican version of communitarianism, notes that:

> . . . much in traditional republican thought gives little cause for celebration. Various strategies of exclusion—of the nonpropertied, blacks, and women—were built into the republican tradition. The republican belief in deliberation about the common good was closely tied to these practices of exclusion; it cannot be neatly separated from them. In some of its manifestations, moreover, the republican tradition has been highly militaristic, indeed heroic-exalting, as the model for

public life, the fraternity of soldiers during wartime. Equally important, the republican belief in the subordination of private interests to the public good carries a risk of tyranny and even mysticism. The belief is also threatening to those who reject the existence of unitary public good, and who emphasize that conceptions of the good are plural, and dependent on perspective and power.[69]

How can communitarianism/republicanism free itself from its past? More importantly, how can communitarianism block problematic inferences drawn from its premises?

Sunstein proposes four premises of republicanism: deliberation (the primary republican value), political equality ("all individuals and groups have access to the political process; large disparities in political influence are disfavored")[70]; universalism ("the possibility of mediating different approaches to politics, or different conceptions of the public good, troupe discussion and dialogue")[71]; and citizenship. Armed with these basic building blocks, Sunstein wants to employ republicanism on behalf of disadvantaged groups: "Republican premises might eventually serve as the foundation of a theory of social subordination to undergird constitutional hostility to discrimination against various social groups."[72]

Sunstein is surely correct: wide disparity of wealth and power might undermine deliberation and political equality. Yet, Sunstein's use of the word "might" presents a problem. While republicanism might lead to equalitarian results, it need not. Concern for disadvantaged groups may result from adopting republicanism, but nothing in republicanism compels any form of equalitarianism. Sunstein even toys with proportional representation for disadvantaged groups, but in the hands of a less sympathetic republican those sentiments could just as easily go by the wayside. The basic primitive notions of any communitarian system are far too flexible, making them highly vulnerable to inequalitarian and other problematic interpretations.

Since I have covered much of the same ground in the discussions of Sandel and Barber, I will not rehearse them here. Suffice it to say, it seems that irrespective of the context, the liberal/communitarian debate marginalizes, in some fashion or other, the disadvantaged.

Conclusion

Theoretical marginalization of the disadvantaged, like its counterpart in the social world, takes place under a variety of guises—some quite overt and others highly subtle. The more subtle means of marginalization have dominated this discussion. I quite consciously chose theorists who, for the most part, make positive claims on behalf of disadvantaged groups. They do not exhibit any overt hostility towards disadvantaged groups. In fact, many of them have publicly supported policy measures that favor disadvantaged groups.

The marginalization process, at the theoretical level, takes hold in indirect ways. The theorist may leave key concepts such as "the least advantaged" or "community" largely undefined, thereby creating an illusion that disadvantaged groups play a key role in the theory. The illusion becomes slowly dispelled once we enter the intricacies of the theory. From within the complexities of the theory it no longer appears obvious that the theory yields policies that favor or, in some cases, even deal with disadvantaged groups. Nor do the theorists provide rules of interpretation for the highly generalized concepts that might begin to resolve the issue of the status of the disadvantaged. Still other theorists who provide interpretations of cognate terms for the disadvantaged narrowly interpret the terms.

To meet the objections posed here, it may seem that liberal and communitarian theorists need to be more explicit in their formulations so as to define clearly disadvantaged groups. Yet, it is not altogether clear that, for at least those theorists considered here, more explicit formulations would resolve the problem of figuring out just where disadvantaged groups stand and how they would fare within the theory. Certain construals of disadvantaged groups would, for example with Rawls, begin to challenge some of the priority claims that Rawls holds as central to his theory. In fact, the real problem lies with the issue of centrality, with the central versus the peripheral role played by the disadvantaged. Placing disadvantaged groups at the theoretical core poses grave challenges for liberals and communitarians. Consider the following changes that centralizing the disadvantaged, so to speak, would have on liberalism and communitarianism: liberals of certain persuasions would have to reconsider the peripheral status of economics, to abandon the largely proceduralist sense of democratic rule, and to consider a much more expansive role for the judiciary in protecting disadvantaged groups. Appeals to abstract notions of community, so central to communitarianism, would no longer take center stage, thereby taking a great deal of the bite out of communitarianism.

Placing the disadvantaged at the theoretical core does not present any insuperable problems to theory construction. The theory would begin with some basic principles concerning suffering which, in turn, would have to be tied to previously defined social groups, in general, and disadvantaged groups, in particular. Then the theorist would have to provide an historically informed analysis of the criteria for disadvantaged groups, status, determining which social groups qualify and which ones do not qualify for disadvantaged status. The final steps would involve devising institutional arrangements that would alleviate group suffering. Constructing a theory that places disadvantaged groups at the theoretical core seems rather straightforward.

Placing the problem of disadvantaged groups at the center stage of academic political debate not only would help to turn the discussion to a critical problem but also it would generate far more robust debates.

Notes

1. Thomas W. Simon, "Suspect Class Democracy," *University of Miami Law Review* 45 (September 1990): 107.
2. Sam Dolgoff, "Introduction," *Bakunin on Anarchism* (Montreal: Black Rose Books, 1980), 14. "Marx speaks disdainfully of this Lumpenproletariat . . . but in them, and only in them—and not in the bourgeois-minded strata of the working class—is crystallized the whole power and intelligence of the Social Revolution." Michael Bakunin, *Statism and Anarchy* (New York: Cambridge University Press, 1990).
3. John Rawls, *A Theory of Justice* (Cambridge: Harvard University Press, 1971), 302.
4. Rawls, *A Theory of Justice*, 248–49. Rawls admits that "those more or less permanently deprived of moral personality may present a difficulty." *Ibid*, 510.
5. Martha Minow, *Making All the Difference* (Ithaca: Cornell University Press, 1990), 153–56.
6. John Rawls, *A Theory of Justice*, 61.
7. Rawls, *A Theory of Justice*, 505–6.
8. Thomas Pogge, *Realizing Rawls* (Ithaca, New York: Cornell University Press, 1989), 11, 126.
9. Rawls, *A Theory of Justice*, 204.
10. Rawls, *A Theory of Justice*, 204.
11. Rawls, *A Theory of Justice*, 204.
12. Rawls, *A Theory of Justice*, 246.
13. Thomas W. Simon, "Fighting Racism: The Hate Speech Detour," *Indiana Law Review* 26 (1993): 411.
14. Rawls, *A Theory of Justice*, 298.
15. Tom Campbell, *Justice* (Atlantic Highlands, New Jersey: Humanities Press International, 1988), 90.
16. Cf. Roy C. Weatherford, "Discussions Defining the Least Advantaged," *Equality and Liberty: Analyzing Rawls and Nozick*, J. Angelo Corlett, editor,

(New York: St. Martin's Press, 1991), 38.

17. Rawls, *A Theory of Justice*, 98.
18. Rawls, *A Theory of Justice*, 98.
19. Rawls, *A Theory of Justice*, 149.
20. See Thomas W. Simon, "Double Reverse Discrimination in Housing," *Buffalo Law Review* 39 (1991): 803.
21. Michael Sandel, *Liberalism and the Limits of Justice* (New York: Cambridge University Press, 1982), 12. Sandel notes that "altruism and benevolence . . . are wholly compatible with liberalism, and there is nothing in its assumptions to discourage their cultivation." True enough. However, alternatively, there is nothing in the assumptions of liberalism to compel the adoption of policies in favor of altruism and benevolence towards the disadvantaged.
22. For a critique that asks MacIntyre "Whose traditions?" see Susan Moller Okin, *Justice, Gender, and the Family* (New York: Basic Books, 1989), 43–62.
23. Will Kymlicka, *Liberalism, Community and Culture* (Oxford: Clarendon Press, 1989), 85–96.
24. Sandel, *Liberalism and the Limits of Justice*, 150.
25. Marilyn Friedman, "Feminism and Modern Friendship: Dislocating the Community," *Ethics* 99 (1989): 275-90.
26. Kymlicka, *Liberalism, Community, and Culture*, 87.
27. Kymlicka, *Liberalism, Community, and Culture*, 89.
28. Michael Sandel, "Moral Arguments and Liberal Toleration: Abortion and Homosexuality," *California Law Review* 77 (1989): 521.
29. Michael Sandel, *Liberalism and Its Critics* (New York: New York University Press, 1984), 6.
30. Michael Sandel, "Morality and the Liberal Ideal," *New Republic* 190 (May 7, 1984): 17.
31. Sandel, *Liberalism and Its Critics*, 6.
32. Sandel, "Democrats and Community: A Public Philosophy for our Times," *New Republic* (February 22, 1988), 22.
33. Joseph A. Schumpeter, *Capitalism, Socialism, and Democracy*, 5th edition (London: Allen and Unwin, 1976).
34. Schumpeter, *Capitalism, Socialism, and Democracy*, 284–85.
35. Schumpeter, *Capitalism, Socialism, and Democracy*, 285.
36. Schumpeter, *Capitalism, Socialism, and Democracy*, 242.
37. Schumpeter, *Capitalism, Socialism, and Democracy*, 284–85.
38. Schumpeter, *Capitalism, Socialism, and Democracy*, 295.
39. Schumpeter, *Capitalism, Socialism, and Democracy*, 295.
40. Schumpeter, *Capitalism, Socialism, and Democracy*, 301.
41. Schumpeter, *Capitalism, Socialism, and Democracy*, 290.
42. Schumpeter, *Capitalism, Socialism, and Democracy*, 294.
43. David Held, *Models of Democracy* (Stanford: Stanford University Press, 1987), 180.
44. Held, *Models of Democracy*, 183.

45. Benjamin Barber, *Strong Democracy* (Berkeley: University of California Press, 1984), 146.
46. Barber, *Strong Democracy*, 219.
47. Barber, *Strong Democracy*, 132.
48. Barber, *Strong Democracy*, 118.
49. Barber, *Strong Democracy*, 225–29.
50. Barber, *Strong Democracy*, 65.
51. Barber, *Strong Democracy*, 252.
52. Barber, *Strong Democracy*, xv.
53. Barber, *Strong Democracy*, 178.
54. Barber, *Strong Democracy*, 159.
55. Barber, *Strong Democracy*, 239.
56. Iris Young, "The Idea of Impartiality," *Justice and the Politics of Difference* (Princeton, N.J.: Princeton University Press, 1990), 118.
57. Barber does devote some attention to the problem of exclusion in defining citizenship: "The scope of citizenship itself becomes a subject for ongoing democratic discussion and review, and one's participation in such discussion becomes a brief for inclusion" (Barber, *Strong Democracy*, 227). To become a citizen, a person, even if she is a criminal or an immigrant, only needs to enter into the democratic discussion.
58. Mark Kahn, *Middle Class Radicals in Santa Monica* (Philadelphia: Temple University Press, 1986).
59. See, for example, Barber, *Strong Democracy*, 309, where Barber describes his concrete proposals.
60. Schumpeter, *Capitalism, Socialism and Democracy*, 283.
61. *Carolene Products*, 304 U.S. 144, 152 n.4 (1938).
62. Lewis Powell, "Carolene Products Revisited," *Columbia Law Review* 82 (1982): 1087.
63. Robert Cover, "The Origins of Judicial Activism in the Protection of Minorities," *Yale Law Journal* 91 (1982): 1287, 1294–97.
64. John Ely, *Democracy and Distrust* (Cambridge: Harvard University Press, 1980).
65. *Beauharnais v. Illinois*, 343 U.S. 250 (1952).
66. For an analysis along these lines see Bruce Ackerman, "Beyond Carolene Products," *Harvard Law Review* 98 (1985), 713.
67. Ackerman, "Beyond Carolene Products", 713, 729.
68. *Sugarman v. Dougall* 413 U.S. 634, 657 (1973), Rehnquist dissenting.
69. Cass Sunstein, "Beyond Revival," *Yale Law Journal* 97 (1988): 1539, 1539–40.
70. Sunstein, 1552.
71. Sunstein, 1554.
72. Sunstein, 1581.

7

Rawlsian Constructivism: A Version of Liberalism

C. F. Delaney

Since rights-based liberalism has captured center stage in political philosophy, it has been subject to many and varied criticisms. Some charge that its neutrality with regard to substantive views of the good life can only support a fragmented society with little or no communal identity. Others challenge the alleged neutrality, charging liberalism with smuggling in its own substantive theory of the good life, which, being impoverished, also underwrites the same fragmented society. Other critiques are more generally epistemological and metaphysical. Liberalism was charged with having a subjectivist or antirealist view of the status of moral values resulting in an inadequate grounding for our basic obligations and aspirations.

Rawlsian liberalism, since it is the dominant version, has been the primary focus of criticism. Both its substantive view of justice and its methodology have been subject to myriad different and often contrary critiques. On the one hand, the substantive view of justice embodied in the two principles has been seen as inimical to the social values necessary for a genuine moral community. On the other hand, the constructivist methodology and, in particular, the employment of the original position has been viewed in its neutrality as manifesting a pervasive skeptical attitude toward the ontological status and/or epistemic availability of moral values, and also criticized as being in no way neutral but rather as masking some deep moral and political commitments. In order to enable us better to come to grips with these critiques, I propose to delineate an understanding of the Rawlsian project with specific attention to its constructivist methodology as it bears on those features of the view relevant to these criticisms.

This chapter has three parts. In the first part, I discuss some quite general presuppositions of the Rawlsian project, which, being far from uncontroversial, would ideally require far more "motivation" than I am prepared to give them here. My purpose here is to exhibit them as background commitments against which the more specific features of the Rawlsian version of constructivism can be appreciated. In the second part, I attempt to clarify what I regard as the essential features of the constructivist strategy in general and Rawls's own "Kantian constructivism" in particular. Finally, in the third part, I discuss the senses in which such a constructivist view is or is not an "objective" account of the moral sphere, and the sense in which it can ground a genuine political community.

I

The first presupposition of the Rawlsian project to which I want to call attention is what I designate a *general antifoundational orientation*. The pragmatic tradition, in which I believe it is helpful to situate Rawls, is motivated by the anti-Cartesian conviction that there is no Archimedean starting point for any human inquiry, philosophizing included. You simply start "where you are." One formulates one's approach to the questionable against the background of what at the moment there seems to be no good reason to question. Given that there is no absolutely firm ground on which to build, you build on what seems firmest at the moment and hope for the best. Bootstrapping strategies are obviously part of the picture, and firm guarantees, whether in the form of self-evidence, incorrigibility, necessity, or infallibility, are viewed as snares and delusions. The pragmatist simply sees this as part of the human condition: every human inquiry is an inquiry with presuppositions. He or she views the difference between himself or herself and others on this point as simply the difference between acknowledging this essential feature of the human condition or attempting to mask one's presuppositions under honorific designations such as self-evidence, necessary truth, absolute presupposition, or other distinctions of merit in that family.

The second presupposition of the project is its commitment to *piecemeal* or *bottom-up theory construction*. Not only is the articulation of constructivism restricted to the sphere of political philosophy, but even more specifically to the concept of justice. It may or may not be the case that one is committed to a more general moral constructivism "all the way down." The project at hand is that of motivating and delineating the construction of certain principles of justice against the background of some general moral views about persons and societies. The status of these moral views is not in question and we are bracketing the general issue—should we be constructivists about moral views all the way down?—for the moment. It is enough, for now, that we agree on certain general moral attitudes and, on the basis of that agreement, can compellingly construct and motivate certain principles of justice. The theoretical project begins with a narrow wedge; and, as I will now go on to delineate, there is more to the venture at hand than a merely theoretical (PNM, 224, n2).[1]

The third presupposition to which I want to call attention is Rawls's *practical conception of political philosophy*. About this he is quite explicit. Acknowledging that there are several different projects that have been and can be carried out under the rubric of political philosophy, Rawls singles out one which is his:

> There are periods, sometimes even long periods, in the history of any society during which certain basic questions give rise to sharp and divisive political controversy and it seems difficult if not impossible to find any shared basis of political agreement. Indeed, certain questions may prove intractable and may never be fully settled. One task of political philosophy in a democratic society is to focus on such questions and to examine whether, despite appearances, some underlying basis of agreement can be uncovered and a mutually acceptable way of resolving these questions publicly established. Or if these questions cannot be fully settled, as may well be the case, perhaps the divergence of opinion can at least be narrowed sufficiently so that political and social cooperation on the basis of mutual respect can still be maintained. (PNM, 226)

Hence, the aim is to work out principles we can live by both now and for the foreseeable future. Ours is not the theoretical aim of articulating the structure of the true political order but the practical one of articulating and motivating principles that can form the basis of the informed and willing cooperation of the citizenry in the public dimensions of social life. More specifically, what we are after is a regulative political conception of justice that can order in a principled way the political ideals and values of a democratic regime and that is formulated in such a way as to provide some hope of achieving an overlapping consensus in society (IOC, 1). In contrast to the classically philosophical and/or utopian projects of political philosophy, Rawls restricts himself to the practical task of providing principles that will ground and enhance social unity.

This leads to a fourth but closely related presupposition, namely, a *rhetorical as opposed to epistemological conception of justification* in political philosophy. From Rawls's perspective, moral "theory" is merely descriptive whereas moral "philosophy" concerns itself with justification; but justification itself can be construed either epistemologically or practically. He recommends that in this context, that is, the political sphere, justification be construed practically:

> On this view justification is *not* regarded simply as valid argument from listed premises, even should these premises be true. Rather justification is by definition addressed to others who disagree with us, and therefore it must always proceed from some consensus, that is, from premises that we and others publicly recognize as true; or better, publicly recognize as acceptable to us for the purposes of establishing a working agreement on the fundamental questions of political justice. (PNM, 229)

We are interested in rationally securing consensus in a contested area; a given view is justified to the degree that it is successful in accomplishing this practical task. Since the task is that of convincing rather than proving, the structure of justification will involve the appeal only to premises that all the contenders accept and then proceed by modes of reasoning acceptable to all to the identification of one of the proposals as the resolution of the problem at hand. "To justify" in this sense is a matter of rhetoric rather than epistemology.

The fifth presupposition of the project is the belief that *pluralism is an intractable feature of modern democratic society*. As Rawls puts it: "justice as fairness tries to construct a conception of justice that takes deep and unresolvable differences on matters of fundamental significance as a permanent condition of human life" (KC, 542). He thinks that it is unrealistic to suppose that our deepest differences are rooted solely in ignorance or perversity; diversity naturally arises from our limited powers and distinct perspectives such that *various* general and comprehensive views (whether religious, philosophical, or ideological) bearing on ourselves and our relations to our fellows can plausibly be maintained from different standpoints. This diversity of incommensurable comprehensive moral perspectives (where "incommensurability" simply means "no available political understanding to commensurate") is not seen as a mere historical condition that will pass but as a permanent feature of modern democracy (IOC, 4). Bracketing the oppressive use of state power, a convergence of opinion on a single comprehensive moral perspective is unlikely at best.

When these five presuppositions are conjoined, they force an answer to the question of how one should proceed with the philosophical investigation of the political sphere. If there is no Archimedean point, we have to start the project of articulating and defending public political principles either *within our own* comprehensive religious, philosophical, or ideological perspective *or* against the backdrop of some more surface consensus with regard to things general (e.g., what is common to our views of persons and fairness) and particular (e.g., certain modes of conduct we find intolerable). Second, given our practical conception of political philosophy and justification, the second as opposed to the first pole of the disjunct is to be preferred.

Accordingly, our conception of the project of political philosophy falls somewhere between the classically philosophical (to discover the truth) and the merely political (to work out a modus vivendi). It is neither "mere philosophy" nor "mere politics." In Rawls's terms, "in addressing the public culture it takes the longest view, looks to society's permanent historical and social conditions, and tries to mediate society's deepest conflicts; it hopes to uncover and to help to articulate a shared basis of consensus on a political conception of justice drawing upon citizens' fundamental intuitive ideas about their society and their place in it" (IOC, 24–25).

As I now take a closer look at Rawls's constructivism, it is important to bear in mind these five presuppositions: his general antifoundational orientation, the strategy of piecemeal theory construction, his practical conception of political philosophy, his rhetorical conception of justification, and his belief in the intractability of pluralism.

II

It should be reasonably clear, then, the *kind* of theory these presuppositions dictate; what I propose to do now is to look more specifically at "constructivism" in general and "Kantian constructivism" in particular in an attempt to discern the essential features of the constructivist strategy.

It seems to me that the most helpful first step in getting a grip on this notion is to examine the notion or notions with which it is contrasted. The basic contrast term for "constructivism" is what Rawls calls "rational intuitionism." In his mind, this latter is a very broad notion ranging over such diverse moral philosophies as the classical positions of Plato and Aristotle; the modern perspectives of Leibniz and Wolff; and the more recent views of Price, Sidgwick, Moore, and Ross. He sums up rational intuitionism in two theses:

> *First*, the basic moral concepts of the right and the good and the moral worth of persons are not analyzable in terms of non-moral concepts (although possibly analyzable in terms of one another); and, *second*, first principles of morals (whether one or many) when correctly stated are self-evident propositions about what kinds of considerations are good grounds for applying one of the three basic moral concepts, that is, for asserting that something is (intrinsically) good, or that a certain action is the right thing to do, or that a certain trait of character has moral worth. These two theses imply that the agreement in judgment which is essential for an effective public conception of justice is founded on the recognition of self-evident truths about good reasons. And what these reasons are is fixed by a moral order that is prior to and independent of *our* conception of the person and the social role of morality. This order is given by the nature of things and is known, not by sense, but by rational intuition. (KC, 557)

This being the characterization of rational intuitionism, its contrast with constructivism is twofold. The basic contrast seems to be this: the rational intuitionist maintains that there is a moral order prior to and independent of our concept of the person, which, given our ability to know this order by rational intuition, can fix the content of our first principles rendering them straightforwardly *true* and this grasp of their truth can be sufficient for moral motivation. In contrast, the constructivist, not acknowledging an independent moral order to which our judgments can correspond, views these principles as being *constructed* by persons under specified conditions. He/she operates on the assumption that apart from the procedure of constructing principles, there are no reasons for justice. This basic contrast involves differing notions of the person: given the robustness of his/her conception of the antecedent moral order, the rational intuitionist requires but a sparse notion of the person primarily as a knower or spectator; the constructivist, on the other hand, needs a somewhat richer notion of the person involving, in particular, some specification with regard to practical reason in which to ground his/her procedures of construction. (KC, 560)

The second (and related) contrast drawn bears on differing conceptions of the boundaries of moral deliberation and notions of closure under moral principles. The rational intuitionist is tempted to think that there are answers to all our moral questions, answers that we can at least verbally describe. The constructivist accepts that a moral conception establishes only a loose framework of deliberation, which, while drawing on our developing powers of reflection, may still fail to provide guidance to many of our moral questions. We hope that our principles, designed to deal with our most basic and pervasive questions, will provide a fruitful framework for deliberating about others. But due to the limitations of our moral capacities and the complexity of our circumstances, it may well be the case that many of our questions will elude resolution by any moral conception we can understand and apply. We have no guarantee that there is always an answer awaiting our discovery (KC, 563).

The pair of more familiar categories that comes to mind in exploring this contrast between rational intuitionism and constructivism is the realism/nonrealism characterization. Pursuing this contrast through these categories may shed further light on the issue. My reason for preferring "nonrealism" to "antirealism" will become clear as we proceed. Taking the notion of "truth" as central, we can designate as a *realist moral project* any project that (1) makes the search for moral truth central; (2) sees such moral truths as fixed by a prior and independent order of objects and relations; and (3) construes the meaning of a given claim to truth as involving its correspondence with or approximation to this order. There are naturalistic varieties of realism, which view moral truths as supervenient on certain metaphysical facts about human nature and the order of things; and nonnaturalistic varieties wherein moral truths are immediately self-evident.

All these are in sharp contrast with *nonrealist moral projects* where the aim is not the search for moral truth but for otherwise "appropriate" moral principles. Specifically in the case of the theory of justice, "it presents itself not as a conception of justice that is true, but one that can serve as the basis of informed and willing political agreement between citizens viewed as free and equal persons" (PNM, 230). On this kind of view, what would justify a given conception of justice "is not its being true to an order antecedent and given to us but its congruence with our deeper understanding of ourselves and our realization that, given our history and the traditions embedded in our public life, it is the most reasonable doctrine for us" (KC, 519). The principles constructed are to single out what facts citizens are to count as reasons for justice; and apart from the procedure of constructing the principles, there are no reasons of justice (KC, 565). From this perspective, it would seem to follow that with regard to many of our moral questions, there may be at the moment no fact of the matter, and with regard to some, there may never be a fact of the matter. In short, we are to view moral principles not as *in* the world to be discovered by us but as constituted "by us" under certain suitable or appropriate conditions. Obviously, if any such nonrealist view is going to have much to recommend it, tokens such as "suitable" and "appropriate" will have to be cashed in. The specifics of any procedure of construction that will answer to these requirements of suitability and appropriateness will have to be detailed.

Any fully specified constructivist view will involve a definite view of persons and a definite view of what a well-ordered society would be, with both of these conceptions constraining its delineation of the procedure of construction itself. Given this general characterization, any number of substantively different moral views (e.g., utilitarianism, perfectionism) could be represented via *its* constructivist model. That they themselves are not constructivist views does not prejudice their being represented via constructivist models. Rawls's own position, that is, Kantian constructivism (or what we less misleadingly could call "Rawlsian constructivism") is to be understood as a specific interpretation of these three elements in the model (KC, 560).

Kantian constructivism essentially involves a certain conception of persons characterized as rational agents of construction specifying through their agreements the first principles of justice for a democratic society under modern conditions. The two foci of the view, then, are what Rawls calls the model conception of the *well-ordered society* and the model conception of the *moral person* with the *original position* being the mediating model conception connecting the other two. If he can render plausible his model conceptions of the well-ordered society and the moral person, and represent these via suitable constraints on the parties in the original position, and then show that certain principles of justice would be chosen by these parties, he will thereby have constructed an argument for those principles.

The source of the plausibility of the model conceptions of the well-ordered society and the moral person (and indirectly, then, of the constraints on the parties in the original position) will lie in their derivation. Rawls proposes his model conceptions as explications of shared notions and principles already latent in common sense or at least congenial with its most essential convictions and traditions. He sees himself as addressing the public culture of a democratic society and sees Kantian constructivism as invoking a conception of society and the person implicitly affirmed in that culture or at least ones that would prove most congenial to it once properly presented and explained (KC, 518). Accordingly, Rawls does not propose his theory as neutral vis à vis all substantive views of the good life; any such substantive view will involve a specific conception of the person and of the society in which that person would flourish. What he does claim, however, is that his approach is neutral vis à vis the viable alternative visions of the good life for our present conditions since all of the viable candidates share his general characterization of the model conceptions of the moral person and the well-ordered society. Let me now turn to these model conceptions.

Our conception of a well-ordered society is most fundamentally that of a system of cooperation between free and equal persons. This system of cooperation is effectively regulated by a publicly recognized set of rules that everyone accepts and that everyone knows that others likewise accept, which rules actually satisfy and are believed to satisfy a public conception of justice. Moreover, each participant in the society can reasonably view the rules as mutually fair terms of cooperation for individuals, all of whom are free and equal moral persons. The participants are equal in that they are conceived as having an equal right to determine and assess the rules under which they live and an equal standing before them. They are free in that they are entitled to make claims on the design of their common institutions in the name of their own fundamental aims and are capable of revising these aims on reasonable grounds (KC, 521). As so generally conceived, the well-ordered society is neutral regarding such specific modes of production and distribution as capitalism and socialism.

Second, given the role of persons in the well-ordered society, Rawls formulates a political conception of the person "as one who can be a citizen, i.e., a fully participating member of society over a complete life" (PNM, 233). As capable of participating fully in society, persons are characterized by two moral powers: (1) the capacity for an effective sense of justice, and (2) the capacity to form and rationally pursue a conception of the good. In addition to these two moral powers, persons are characterized as having the intellectual and physical capacities necessary for normally cooperating members of a society. This political conception of the person is neutral with regard to deeper (and much more controversial) metaphysical views about the nature of persons and their conditions of identity.

This brings us to our third model conception, the original position. The intuitive idea is that the most appropriate concept of justice for a well-ordered democratic society would be one that its citizens would adopt or agree to under conditions that are fair between them and in which their status as free and equal moral persons is effectively represented (KC, 522). The original position is simply a device for vividly representing these conditions.

What would be the most appropriate way for the terms of co-operation among such individuals to be fixed? Since they are free and equal agents, it would seem that rather than being imposed on them from without, the terms should be established by undertakings among the individuals themselves, and the appropriate kind of undertaking would seem to be the attempt to come to agreement. Second, this attempt to come to agreement should be guided not only by principles of rational choice but also by even broader principles of reasonableness bearing on reciprocity and mutuality that derive from the kind of cooperative venture they are endeavoring to design. Third, it would further seem that this coming to agreement should be under conditions that would not allow some to have unfair bargaining advantages over others. And, fourth, as a final recognition of their being free and equal moral persons, it would seem that the agreement should be unanimous with each having an effective veto over the outcome.

The original position is simply a vivid way of representing the fact that the agreements that in fact constitute or construct the fundamental principles that bind us in the social sphere should be carried out under fair conditions and subject to certain restrictions on what are to count as acceptable reasons for justice. It models the way in which the citizens of a well-ordered society viewed as moral persons would *ideally select* first principles of justice for their society (KC, 520). It is simply a device, for representing what we regard as reasonable conditions for reaching a fair agreement. As a fictive device, it does not bind; it merely represents. What binds is the fact that its reasons are what we regard on reflection as appropriate reasons for justice (PNM, 236).

Now, it is very important to note that just as this constructivist strategy stands in sharp contrast to rational intuitionism at one end of the spectrum, it also stands in contrast to what could be called a radical Nietzschean constructivism at the other end. Far from being an irrational individualistic projection of value, Rawls's project involves "a suitably constructed social point of view" (KC, 519). Accordingly, it is a social constructivism, not an individual constructivism; and second, it is not an arbitrary or irrational social construction but one constrained by what most would recognize as rational and reasonable conditions. What remains is to specify in what sense or senses this kind of construction can be seen to be an objective account of the moral sphere.

III

What would count as an "objective" account of the moral sphere? Obviously, if as "objective" one would countenance only those rational intuitionist or realist strategies that involve principles "corresponding to" or "approximating to" independent moral facts, a constructivism however constrained would not as such result in an objective account. Rawls is quite clear about admitting that his view would not satisfy *this* criterion of objectivity:

> The idea of approximating to moral truth has no place in a constructivist doctrine: the parties in the original position do not recognize any principles of justice as true or correct and so as "antecedently given"; their aim is simply to select the conception most rational for them given their circumstances. This conception is not regarded as a workable approximation to the moral facts: there are no such moral facts to which the principles adopted could approximate. (KC, 564)

In constructivism, the principles generated are simply those that are most reasonable for those who conceive of their person and society as it is represented in the procedure of construction. The constructivist strategy is intended as an instance of pure procedural justice at the highest level. Its success does not have an external but only an internal measure. If "objective" necessarily means more than this, clearly a constructivist account is not an objective account. But there seems to be no good reason to restrict so severely the meaning of "objective."

Rawls puts forward his view as objective in a more modest but familiar sense of that term. As he puts it, Kantian constructivism "interprets the notion of objectivity in terms of a suitably constructed social point of view that is authoritative with respect to all individual and associational points of view" (KC, 554). The conception of the person that lies behind the construction and the notions of rational and reasonable that guide it are publicly available authoritative notions such that the principles that result will have an intersubjective authority. It does not seem inappropriate that a view presented under the label "Kantian" should avail itself of an understanding of objectivity in terms of intersubjective authority. After all, the rules of other admittedly less-pervasive human institutions have a much weaker version of precisely this kind of status and are seen to be uncontroversially objective.

There is an even stronger sense of "objective" compatible with constructivism; what we might call "unique constructibility." There may be only a few viable conceptions of the person for people situated as we are, and it may be that only *one* of these can generate a specific procedure of construction that will issue in acceptable and workable principles given the relevant general beliefs. Constructivism certainly does not presuppose that this is the case but it is certainly compatible with this possibility. If there were to be such a convergence on a unique construction, one might be tempted (in the spirit of Peirce) to define "truth" in terms of such convergence, but, for the moment, both Rawls and I will resist such a temptation (IOC, 15).

Furthermore, constructivism as I have characterized it, that is, as a nonrealism rather than antirealism, is not strictly incompatible with the much "stronger" aspiration to realist moral truth that motivates rational intuitionism. Although constructivism does not claim anything like this, it does not deny it either. It simply brackets the issue of moral truth as not being germane to the subject at hand. In Rawls's terms, "we try to avoid the problem of truth and the controversy between realism and subjectivism about the status of moral and political values; this form of constructivism neither asserts nor denies these doctrines" (PNM, 230). Rawls claims to be neither skeptical nor indifferent to the deep issues or comprehensive views bearing on moral truth. He certainly does not claim that the search for such truth is impossible (IOC, 13, n21). He is simply making the practical point that our justification of political first principles cannot and should not wait for the satisfactory resolution of those perennial philosophical questions. We need principles we can live by *now*. His claim is that the stronger realist notion of objectivity is not necessary for this project; the question remains—is Rawls's weaker notion sufficient? A contentious way of putting the question might be, what kind of political community can be built on such a shallow consensus where the contrast is between a deep consensus—one involving a shared commitment to a comprehensive view all the way down—and a shallow consensus—one (such as Rawls's proposal) that falls short of this?

Rawls's answer can best be appreciated by allowing for two levels of deviation from what we might designate "strong communitarianism"—the kind of political community built on a shared comprehensive view all the way down. Rawls might well agree that the strongest or closest kind of community would be one grounded in a consensus on a general and comprehensive moral view all the way down; whether or not such would be a desirable community is another and interesting question in its own right. However, this kind of community is ruled out by the fact of pluralism together with the rejection of the oppressive use of state power to overcome it. His point is that there are at least two alternatives to this strong communitarianism that should be distinguished: there is what he is urging, namely, an overlapping consensus on a reasonable political conception of justice; and, there is what he calls a mere modus vivendi (IOC, 10). The latter may well be unstable and humanly unfulfilling, but it is far from obvious that the former (what we might call "weak communitarianism") would fall short of any ideals of commitment that are appropriate for the modern world.

Rawls goes to great length to point out the significant differences between any community founded in this manner on his principles and a mere modus vivendi. A modus vivendi is not an inherently stable social arrangement. It would be a social unity constituted (as in a treaty) by a momentary equilibrium of different centers of self-interest. The conditions of the unity would be adhered to only because each knows that it is not in its self-interest to deviate from them. But this social unity is very shallow because its stability is contingent on circumstances remaining such as not to upset the favorable equilibrium point. Should conditions change, all parties would be ready to pursue their own goals at the expense of the others (IOC, 10–11). Rawls's overlapping consensus or weak communitarianism is not this kind of shallow or merely apparent unity but rather a genuine community of commitment. There are several important differences between a Rawlsian social order and a mere modus vivendi, and several reasons why he thinks that this kind of social order is realistically achievable.

The differences Rawls notes are that the object of his envisioned consensus, the political conception of justice, is itself a *moral conception*; it is *affirmed on moral grounds*; and it would have a much greater *stability* than a mere modus vivendi (IOC, 11). More specifically, the content of the consensus consists in certain ideals of the person and society and the principles and standards that follow from them; these ideals and principles are affirmed either on their own moral merits (the Rawlsian line of argumentation) or because they otherwise follow from or comport with a given individual's comprehensive moral view. Accordingly, given the moral pluralism of a society, there can be two quite different kinds of grounds for the relevant consensus. Many comprehensive moral views are incomplete and may have little or nothing to say about the morality of specific political arrangements. This looseness would permit the direct appreciation of and commitment to liberal political views in accordance with the Rawlsian argumentation. On the other hand, with regard to those comprehensive views that are not loose in this way, there may be reasons within these views for commitment to the same liberal values or, in the event of conflict rather than immediate fit, adaptations may be made to accommodate these liberal values. The fact that those who affirm the political conception may do so either directly or from within different comprehensive views does not make their affirmation of and commitment to their common ground any less real. It is the reality of this commitment that leads to the third difference, namely, degree of stability. Since the common aim of each is justice as articulated in the political conception, this can be sustained regardless of shifts in the distribution of political power and the balance of relative forces. Moreover, these various different roads to consensus are not mere abstract possibilities but have clear historical instantiations.

In addition to articulating these differences between a mere modus vivendi and the real moral community that would be generated by his overlapping consensus, Rawls even has a plausible story to tell about how the former could develop over time into the latter. Using as illustrative the notion of religious toleration in its development from being accepted as a mere modus vivendi by the various warring religious sects to its gradual embrace as a genuine value in its own right by these very sects, he tries to show how mere political accommodation can develop over time into genuine political value. Drawing on some general views from developmental moral psychology, he tells the story of how a structure initially only acquiesced in, if it allows for increasingly successful and fulfilling political cooperation, could actually create a new possibility, namely, the possibility of a reasonably harmonious and stable pluralist society (IOC, 22–23). The principles of justice once in place would ultimately generate their own support.

Notes

1. The references in this paper are to the writings of John Rawls. The abbreviations are as follows:

KC—"Kantian Constructivism in Moral Theory," *Journal of Philosophy*, 77 (1980): 515–72;

PNM—"Justice as Fairness: Political Not Metaphysical," *Philosophy and Public Affairs*, 14 (1985): 223–51;

IOC—"The Idea of an Overlapping Consensus," *Oxford Journal of Legal Studies*, 7 (1987): 1–25.

8

Should Political Philosophy Be Done Without Metaphysics?

Jean Hampton

> Most of the points I have made in support of my argument are not such as I can confidently assert; but that the belief in the duty of inquiring after what we do not know will make us better and braver and less helpless than the notion that there is not even a possibility of discovering what we do not know, nor any duty of inquiring after it—this is a point for which I am determined to do battle, as far as I am able, both in word and deed.
>
> —Plato, *Meno*

In *A Theory of Justice*, John Rawls engaged the interest of contemporary philosophers not only with his substantive conception of justice but also with his justification of it as the conception preferred by all parties fairly placed relative to one another in an "original position." But more recently he has defended his conception of justice with an argument that uses the idea of an original position in an unfamiliar, revisionary way.[1] He does not advance this new argument out of fear that the old one failed to justify his conclusions (which is not to say that he should not have abandoned it for that reason).[2] He con-

---

This chapter was originally published under the same title in *Ethics*, 99 (July 1991): 791–814. Reprinted with permission of the University of Chicago Press. For this volume, I have added a postscript, which discusses Rawls's recent response to the sorts of criticisms I made in the original article. The original article was written while I was supported by grants from the National Endowment for the Humanities (NEH), the American Council on Learned Societies, and an NEH Summer Stipend for research on constitutional issues. I am very grateful for this support.

tinues to endorse it as an argument in moral theory. But he no longer believes it offers the right kind of justification given what he now takes to be the aim of political philosophy, which is not the pursuit of the truth but the pursuit of "free agreement, reconciliation through public reason" (JFPM, 230). He proposes that political philosophers in modern pluralist societies with constitutional democracies must make reference to our history and the shared experiences of our community to forge what he calls an "overlapping consensus" on a conception of justice.

In this article I want to examine Rawls's new, more community-minded, deliberately nonuniversal and nonmetaphysical justificatory method, which he calls "political." I want first to explore what this method is; second, to show that it is new and hence not the method used in *A Theory of Justice*; third, to better understand why Rawls felt compelled to adopt this kind of justification; and finally, to evaluate it. Despite my fascination with and partial endorsement of Rawls's proposal, I want to argue that we should reject his recommendation to do only political and not metaphysical theorizing about the structuring of our political institutions in constitutional democracies.

The New Method

In *A Theory of Justice*, there are many passages in which Rawls offers characterizations of his method of justification in that book; how they all hang together (if they do) is an intriguing question. Some of the passages—for example, those on reflective equilibrium—might be interpreted such that they are at least consistent with Rawls's new political method (as he himself suggests, e.g., in IOC, 5, n. 8). But other passages, particularly section 40 of the book, suggest a very Kantian way of understanding the contract argument; for example: "The description of the original position interprets the point of view of noumenal selves, or what it means to be a free and equal rational being. Our nature as such beings is displayed when we act from the principles we would choose when this nature is reflected in the conditions determining choice. Thus men exhibit their freedom, their independence from the contingencies of nature and society, by acting in ways they would acknowledge in the original position."[3]

The idea seems to be that in the same way Kant's moral law tests a plan of action by considering what it would be like for him if all people acted that way, the original position procedure tests conceptions of justice by forcing the deliberator who uses it to consider what

Should Political Philosophy Be Done without Metaphysics? 153

society would be like for him or her if he or she were anyone in that society. The results of both tests are supposed to be authoritative and universal ("independent of the contingencies of nature and society") because they are supposed to represent the correct operation of our practical reason. The idea is that each test's endorsement constitutes the endorsement of reason.

This kind of justification has recently come under heavy attack from certain "Hegelian" critics. For example, Alasdair MacIntyre argues that a conception of justice must be rooted in "a community whose primary bond is a shared understanding both of the good for man and the good for that community,"[4] and Michael Sandel argues that Rawls's contention that justice is the first virtue of social institutions involves the dubious metaethical claim that the foundations of justice must also be independent of all social and historical contingencies (without being transcendental). Sandel contends that the original position procedure presents the self as a chooser of its ends and thus "as independent from social convention—separate and individual."[5] In contrast, Sandel characterizes Rawls's communitarian critics as proposing that the self is not independent of its aims and attachments but is always "situated" in a social life "embedded in a history which locates [it] among others, and implicates [its] good in the good of the communities whose stories [it] shares."[6] Thus Sandel sees "political discourse as proceeding within the common meanings and traditions of a political community, not appealing to a critical standpoint wholly external to those meanings."[7]

The descriptive language of this last quotation may puzzle some readers. Is Sandel saying that, in fact, people who are arguing over substantive issues in a political society never try to appeal to some extrasocietal critical standpoint in order to establish what position is right? Surely not, for such a descriptive claim is clearly wrong. He must therefore be saying that even when people think that they are appealing to some extrasocietal standpoint, in fact they are using the shared ideas and traditions of their community. In other words, Sandel is describing not what they intend to be doing, but what they can in fact do, based upon what he takes to be the metaethical facts. Thus, fundamental to this communitarian's position is a metaethical commitment to the community as the source of value.[8] And this commitment motivates a methodological criticism of those philosophers such as Rawls who persist in attempting to gain access to some extrasocietal source of moral truth. Such philosophers should know better, Sandel is arguing, and were they to embrace the proper metaethics, they would embrace a different methodology, one which justified political conclusions by reference to the shared beliefs and traditions of their community.

In his recent articles, Rawls is simultaneously hostile toward these critics' substantive recommendations for charting the direction of our political community and sensitive to their charge that his justification of the two principles presupposes a controversial metaethics and an overly individualistic conception of persons. His response is one of partial capitulation—not substantively, and not metaethically (nowhere does Rawls suggest that he is drawn to the idea that the community is the source of all value), but *methodologically*. Although he never repudiates the Kantian style of justification used in the book, he now argues that this way of defending the two principles makes it part of a "comprehensive moral theory," and that a different, nonmoral and nonmetaphysical defense of those principles is required of him as a political philosopher.

This view leads him in his most recent papers to develop a new kind of justification for his conception of justice, which he calls "political," that makes reference only to the histories and traditions of our democratic culture—presumably in just the way that at least some of his Hegelian critics would want a conception of justice defended. However, his motivation for presenting this argument does not derive from any decision to embrace the communitarians' metaethics but, rather, from a decision to avoid metaphysics altogether when engaged in the justification of political conceptions. Indeed, Rawls makes the remarkable claim that "the aims of political philosophy depend upon the society it addresses" (IOC, 1), and that in a modern constitutional democracy, its aim should be the development of an "overlapping consensus" on matters pertaining to justice without in any way relying on controversial metaphysics. Whereas political philosophy has traditionally been seen as a branch of moral philosophy, which builds upon and applies to social structures the results of moral theorizing (in the way that, e.g., Aristotle's *Politics* builds upon his *Nicomachean Ethics*), Rawls argues that political philosophy in our time and place should be free of controversial moral assumptions and indeed of all metaphysical foundations in order that it might "provide a shared public basis of the justification of political and social institutions" that will help "ensure stability from one generation to the next" (IOC, 1). The political philosopher who pursues this objective is looking for and/or striving to develop a shared fund of ideas that are latent in the culture of the community and that can be endorsed by people no matter what their metaphysical views.

Unfortunately, Rawls gives us no precise definition of what he

Should Political Philosophy Be Done without Metaphysics? 155

means by "metaphysical." From context, it doesn't seem that he can mean it in the positivists' sense as "nonsense to be dismissed" but, rather, in a more Hobbesian sense, as "doctrines for which an incontrovertible demonstration is not possible."[9] Such doctrines have the potential to arouse controversy and provoke conflict in the community. Note that Rawls might have to count even certain theories of science, such as the thesis that species have evolved, to be part of metaphysics so understood if they have been heavily contested in the community.

But whatever else falls into this category of metaphysics, certainly normative ethics and metaethics fall into it. Many political philosophers will be alarmed by the proposal that this sort of philosophizing should be excluded from political theorizing and will regard the sanitized product as too meager, too applied, too political. Rawls replies:

> Some may think that to ensure stable social unity in a constitutional regime by looking for an overlapping consensus detaches political philosophy from philosophy and makes it into politics. Yes and no: the politician, we say, looks to the next election, the statesman to the next generation, and philosophy to the indefinite future. Philosophy sees the political world as an on-going system of cooperation over time, in perpetuity practically speaking. Political philosophy is related to politics because it must be concerned, as moral philosophy need not be, with practical possibilities. . . .
>
> Thus political philosophy is not mere politics: in addressing the public culture it takes the longest view, looks to society's permanent historical and social conditions, and tries to mediate society's deepest conflicts. It hopes to uncover, and help to articulate, a shared basis of consensus on a political conception of justice drawing upon citizens' fundamental intuitive ideas about their society and their place in it. (IOC, 24–25)

So the man who is primarily responsible for breathing new life into the seemingly dead corpse of political philosophy after World War II is now challenging us to rethink what we are doing when we theorize about our political life.

Rawls does not believe this kind of theorizing is appropriate for just any time or place, but only for those societies in which the following five facts hold (all of which he takes to hold in modern democratic societies): the first fact is that the society is pluralistic. The second fact is that this pluralism is permanent, by which I take Rawls to mean that unless there were certain remarkable events or the use of extreme coercive measures, the divergence of moral and religious views in our society is highly likely to persist (IOC, 22; JFPM, 225). The third fact is that such pluralism could be overcome only by the "oppressive use of state power (which presupposes a control of the state no group possesses)." I am not quite sure of the force of the word "oppressive" in this passage; let us take it to mean a substantial degree of coercive power over one's life, which, given human nature, people find highly undesirable—and thus unacceptable. These three facts define, according to Rawls, a "common predicament" (IOC, 22). This predicament is worsened by the fourth fact: the existence of moderate scarcity of resources. So a workable conception of justice in any situation in which these facts hold is one that distributes scarce resources so as to "allow for a diversity of doctrines and the plurality of conflicting and incommensurable conceptions of the good affirmed by the members of existing democratic societies" (JFPM, 225).

The fifth fact allows for a kind of escape from the predicament: it is the existence of numerous possibilities for gain that come from well-organized social cooperation. In Rawls's discussion of this fact, it is an unstated assumption that the people in this society desire to realize this cooperative gain, and that a central ingredient of a well-organized scheme of social cooperation is that it be stable. The following is a reconstructed statement of the fifth fact which renders it more precise and complete: there are numerous possibilities for gain which everyone desires to realize and which can only come about when a well-organized and, in particular, stable system of social cooperation is established.

In "Justice as Fairness: Political Not Metaphysical," Rawls rests his argument on two additional "basic intuitive ideas" that he claims are latent in the political cultures of modern democratic societies. First is the idea that people should cooperate with one another in a "fair system of cooperation": "The overarching fundamental intuitive idea, within which other basic intuitive ideas are systematically connected, is that of a society as a fair system of cooperation between free and equal persons. Justice as fairness starts from this idea as one of the basic intuitive ideas which we take to be implicit in the public culture of a democratic society" (JFPM, 231). Second is the idea that human beings are free and equal: "Since we start within the tradition of modern democratic thought, we also think of citizens as free and equal moral persons. The basic intuitive idea is that in virtue of what we may call their moral powers, and their powers of reasoning, thought and judgement connected with those powers, we say that persons are free. And in virtue of their having these powers to the requisite degree to be fully cooperating members of society, we say that people are equal" (JFPM, 233). In part because these ideas are latent in our political culture, Rawls argues that in our society there is an overlapping consensus on a liberal conception of justice—in particular, on *his* conception of justice.

However, in "The Idea of an Overlapping Consensus," Rawls no longer insists that the bulk of society holds these two beliefs. Instead, the ideals of "fairness" and "equality" are taken to be instrumentally necessary to the achievement of a stable cooperative society (which, in turn, is taken to be universally desired). In particular, fairness is linked instrumentally to the achievement of cooperation and, thus, to the realization of cooperative gain.[10] And equal protection of every individual by rights that accord each one "basic liberties" is taken to be necessary for stability and harmony.[11] So in essence, fairness and equality are now included in the fifth fact, as follows: there are numerous possibilities, for gain which everyone desires to realize and which can come about only when a well-organized and, in particular, stable system of cooperation is established, and such a system can be established only if each party is treated fairly and accorded equal basic liberties.

In "The Idea of an Overlapping Consensus," Rawls goes on to argue that in any society in which these five facts hold—and that includes contemporary democracies—only a liberal conception of justice will "work" politically. Such a conception specifies certain basic rights, liberties, and opportunities; assigns a special priority to these rights; and assures to all citizens adequate means to make effective use of their basic rights, liberties, and opportunities (IOC, 18). By virtue of the pervasive and permanent pluralism in these societies and the need for fair and equal treatment in the distribution of scarce resources, Rawls argues that only this kind of conception will enable members to achieve the stability they need for cooperation without relying on oppressive state power. And given the fact that it makes the stable system of cooperation viable, citizens can embrace the liberal view "without being committed in other parts of their life to comprehensive moral ideas often associated with liberalism, for example the ideals of autonomy and individuality" (JFPM, 245). Hence, although a liberal conception of justice can be and generally is presented as a comprehensive moral doctrine (which is presumably how it is presented in *A Theory of Justice*), it can be successfully justified with an argument that is neutral between competing moral conceptions in just the way a theory must be if it is to serve as the theoretical arbiter in a pluralistic society.

Rawls believes that his two principles of justice ought to serve as that conception on which there is an overlapping consensus. However, he admits that it is "also likely that more than one political conception may be worked up from the fund of shared political ideas; indeed this is desirable, as these rival conceptions will then compete for citizens' allegiance and be gradually modified and deepened by the contest between them" (IOC, 3). Admitting the possibility of a contest allows Rawls to find a place in debates in political philosophy for the archrival of the Rawlsian theory, utilitarianism. But because utilitarianism in its purest (Benthamite) form guarantees neither political equality nor individual protection of liberties via rights, Rawls generously allows that there may be ways of "construing or revising utilitarian doctrine so that it can support a conception of justice appropriate for a constitutional regime" given the inescapable fact of pluralism in such a regime (IOC, 12). For reasons we shall discuss later, utilitarians may be apt to resist such generosity.

Thus far I have presented Rawls as saying that the overlapping consensus is defined either by looking at what principles are *instrumentally valuable* to the creation of a stable cooperative society, or by looking for values or principles that, as a matter of fact, everyone in the pluralist society *happens to accept*, albeit for different reasons. "The essential elements of the political conception, its principles, standards and ideals, are theorems, as it were, at which the comprehensive doctrines in the consensus intersect or converge" (IOC, 9). However, this process of constructing a convergence of ideas need not involve only discovery; it might be necessary for the philosopher to develop and extend, from any accepted fund of shared ideas, the principles upon which to decide new issues. But note that she would be doing so not by making reference to non-neutral moral or religious views, which some members of the pluralist society do not share, but by looking for and attempting to articulate shared values and principles on which these matters can be adjudicated.

In order for this process even to be possible, there must be a shared commitment to reasoned discussion. Rawls therefore argues that implicit in our public culture are shared guidelines for inquiry, and publicly recognized rules for assessing evidence. Otherwise there can be no way of interpreting, applying, or extending any conception of justice that is agreed upon. Rawls calls this part of the overlapping consensus the "conception of free public reason" (IOC, 8).

Finally, he proposes that there is even a shared endorsement of certain virtues by all parties in pluralist democracies, so that these too are part of the overlapping consensus. These "virtues of political cooperation" (IOC, 17) include such things as tolerance and reasonability in debate. Such virtues are presumably endorsed because they make possible fair social cooperation "on a footing of mutual respect" and are part of society's "political capital" (IOC, 17).

We can now summarize the justificatory methodology Rawls is urging political philosophers to follow whenever the five facts described above hold (e.g., in modern constitutional democracies):

> A political philosopher should justify any principle or doctrine to a pluralist community by finding or seeking to develop an "overlapping consensus," and she should do so while relying on the prevailing conception of free public reason and any shared virtues that encourage political cooperation, either by articulating the values or principles that are instrumentally necessary for the achievement of certain universally held objectives, or by looking for or else seeking to develop theoretical overlap among the disparate groups in the society, so as to define a fund of implicitly shared ideas and principles.

Rawls calls this the "method of avoidance" (JFPM, 231); by using it, one avoids argument on the basis of any contested premise and any controversial claim about what is true.

But where, the reader might want to know, is the original position procedure in this justification of the two principles? That procedure, according to Rawls, is a way of helping us to identify a kernel of overlapping consensus. The fact of pluralism indicates that an acceptable conception of justice for our society is one that is perceived as setting out fair terms of cooperation and one that recognizes that people are free and equal. The original position procedure is a device allowing us to pick out that conception of justice that would be fair, and that would treat people as free and equal: "The original position [is] simply a device of representation: it describes the parties, each of whom are responsible for the essential interests of a free and equal person, as fairly situated and as reaching an agreement subject to appropriate restrictions on what are to count as good reasons" (JFPM, 237). By representing to ourselves an agreement situation in which there is a veil of ignorance that ensures that the bargainers are free and equal, we determine which conception of justice available to us is fair, and which treats people as free and equal (JFPM, 235–36). And while the veil excludes them from knowing their conception of the good, this does not mean that we should take it as resting on a metaphysical conception of the person in which the self is considered ontologically prior to such a conception. The veil is simply a useful means for arriving at a conception of justice that will ensure a stable cooperative society.

Finally, we should appreciate that Rawls's political justification for his two principles enables him to defend his conception of justice against Sandel's and MacIntyre's communitarian attacks with a style of argument they would have to respect insofar as it takes seriously the shared values, beliefs, and traditions of our society. And, remarkably, Rawls defends such an argument without in any way endorsing their metaethical views or their antiliberal conception of the state as a group of people bound by a shared conception of the good.[12]

Rawls and Hobbes

In the last section, I noted how one aspect of Rawls's methodology resembles that of Hobbes. But Hobbes's way of political theorizing is still too metaphysical for Rawls because it rests upon contested philosophical ideas that some members of contemporary pluralist societies could not accept.

Hobbes does not start from the fact of societal pluralism, but from an individualistic conception of human beings and what he takes to be the psychological fact that our highest goals (self-preservation and glory) are self-regarding, meaning that individuals' interests will inevitably diverge and generate conflict. Rawls does not endorse Hobbes's conception of the person, nor his facts of human nature, nor his determinism. So his reasons for insisting on defining a conception of justice that will realize a stable cooperative society are different from Hobbes's more metaphysical motivations. Rawls simply says, "Here are the circumstances which prevail in our society today; what must we do?" whereas Hobbes searches for a (universal) method for peace based upon (what we would see as contestable) theses in human psychology, philosophy of mind, and the theory of value.

Nonetheless, one might think that Rawls's political methodology is importantly Hobbesian in at least one respect: like Hobbes, he seems to be attempting to define a political modus vivendi for societies of people who are in conflict but who desire peace. It is interesting that Rawls rejects this Hobbesian characterization of his project. He does not deny that he is interested in defining a conception of justice that can serve as a modus vivendi, but he does strongly deny that the conception of justice which constitutes the overlapping consensus is *merely* a modus vivendi. A "mere" modus vivendi, according to Rawls, is one that would provide a way for conflicting factions of people to get along despite their conflict, but which would not be a way that either side would be disposed to carry on if the conflict disappeared. Only temporary social unity has been purchased by the modus vivendi: "Social unity is only apparent as its stability is contingent on circumstances remaining such as not to upset the fortunate convergence of interests" (IOC, 11). The parties perceive the modus vivendi as a necessary evil and not something that has any intrinsic value for them apart from its ability to secure peace in these circumstances. So if power relations changed and one party suddenly were in a position to enforce its particular viewpoint, that party would happily reject, and be correct to reject, the modus vivendi and use its power to coerce agreement from those who had previously opposed its viewpoint.

Can Rawls successfully accord his overlapping consensus the status of "right" and not merely "expedient"? I will take up this question in the next section. For now, however, I want to ask whether or not he is correct to argue that it is at least expedient (if not more than that). And the philosopher who would be most likely to be dubious about the overlapping consensus as instrumentally valuable in the pursuit of stable, cooperative societies is Hobbes.

Hobbes is, if anything, even more concerned than Rawls about the damage to societies that contestable human doctrines can cause. But his prescription for stability in a world of potential conflict is not the creation of an overlapping consensus but the institution of an absolute sovereign. It would be, in his eyes, a hopeless task to try to find any significant overlap of views in pluralist societies such as ours, and even if such overlap were possible, he would not believe it to be permanent or extensive enough to ensure peace in the face of the inevitable generation of conflicting ideas among human beings who have differing conceptions of the good. Stability, according to Hobbes, is something that we pursue via polity and not via consensus on ideas. Only a ruler with the power to have the last word is able to forestall conflict.

Rawls never explicitly discusses polity solutions to social discord (which is odd for a political philosopher). Of course, he might argue that there must be an overlapping consensus on a particular polity in order for it to be successful in retaining power and resolving conflict. And Hobbes would agree; this is one of the ideas I interpret him as trying to get across with his contract language.[13] It is what Kurt Baier would call a "constitutional consensus."[14] But this consensus is on structure, not substance. And Hobbes would argue that even if an agreement on substance could be reached, in fact the lion's share of the work in ensuring peace would have to be done by the political structure that had the power to resolve or prevent controversies, and not by the consensus on conceptions (perhaps vaguely or ambiguously stated) that could never, by themselves, effect the peaceful resolution of conflict.

Rawls need not, and I think does not, disagree with the idea that some political adjudicators (performing as judges, or legislators, or executives) are necessary for realizing peace in a pluralist society. But I believe he would insist that history shows us that peace can also be achieved in a less costly way through reliance on an overlapping consensus. Remember Rawls's third fact, that is, that pluralism in modern societies could be ended only by the unacceptably oppressive use of state power. Hobbes's solution for conflict would strike Rawls as unacceptable because of its reliance on potentially oppressive coercion rather than consensus. Now, Hobbes thought such reliance was necessary because it was the only means to peace, but Rawls believes history has confirmed "a new social possibility: the possibility of a reasonably harmonious and stable pluralist society. Before the successful and peaceful practise of toleration in societies with liberal political institutions there was no way of knowing of that possibility" (IOC, 23). Once people become tolerant of disagreements in metaphysical areas and come to share agreement on a conception of justice governing their interactions with one another, peace is secured without forcing any person to give up his or her deeply held views. Indeed, this solution respects the beliefs of everyone. In contrast, the decision of a political ruler to resolve conflict in a situation where there is no toleration of others' views and/or where there is no consensus on a conception of justice governing their interactions will invariably result in one or more parties to the conflict losing—and losing hurts. Now, Rawls would have to admit that in a pluralist society such as our own, even if we are all perfectly tolerant of others' conceptions of the good, the overlap of shared beliefs constituting the consensus on justice can never be large or explicit enough to decide all conflicts between the parties, so that some political adjudication will always be required for peace. He observes, "We appeal to a political conception of justice to distinguish between those questions that can be reasonably removed from the political agenda and those that cannot, all the while aiming for an overlapping consensus" (IOC, 13). Presumably, the arbiters will have to decide those issues that cannot be removed from the political agenda and placed into the core of consensus. Nonetheless, the larger the overlapping consensus, the less society will have to rely on them, and thus, the less will any party feel its beliefs are being trampled upon or disrespected by the state.

In the end, the principle of toleration, which is the substantive heart of liberalism, turns out to be the keystone of this new, low-cost approach to political stability. Commitment to this principle is a kind of background assumption of Rawls's non-Hobbesian way of pursuing stability.

But is not this too "moral" a principle for his nonmetaphysical method of philosophizing to rely upon? Rawls need not admit that it is. Instead, he can argue that the principle of toleration is really implicit in his third "fact," that only an unacceptable level of oppression could end the pluralism in our societies. If coercion designed to end discord is unacceptable, then that discord must be resolved through respect for others' differing views. And such respect is what the principle of toleration insists upon. So even if this principle can be endorsed for moral reasons, it is also necessary, according to Rawls, to endorse it for prudential reasons, because this principle (along with certain related virtues such as the willingness to listen to and not violently attack one's opponents) is what makes possible the new non-Hobbesian method for achieving peaceful cooperation in a community of people with differing conceptions of the good.

In essence, Rawls is arguing that in modern constitutional democracies, which reject the pursuit of peace through oppressive state power, the overlapping consensus includes the very principle that directs society to further define and expand that consensus.

More than a Modus Vivendi?

If this is how we are to understand the motivation behind the development of an overlapping consensus, how is that consensus more than a mere modus vivendi? Rawls argues that it is more than this when people have allegiance to it as right and not merely as instrumentally valuable (although each may have different moral, philosophical, or religious reasons for doing so): "First, the object of consensus, the political conception of justice, is itself a moral conception. And second, it is affirmed on moral grounds. . . . The fact that those who affirm the political conception start from within their own comprehensive view, and hence begin from different premises and grounds, does not make their affirmation any less religious, philosophical or moral, as the case may be" (IOC, 11).

But notice what Rawls has done: if this style of justification of a political conception (i.e., as part of an overlapping consensus) really makes sense, it would seem he has found a way of solving what might be called the "paradox" of liberalism.[15] On the one hand, liberalism is committed to tolerance and thus to the state's remaining impartial in its dealings with the clashing ideas of its citizens; yet, on the other hand, it demands partiality with respect to itself, and thus insists on the use of coercion against anyone who would challenge the principle of tolerance. It would seem that a liberal, to be consistent, would have to tolerate even those who would challenge (and use violence to attack) that principle, so that, to paraphrase Robert Frost, the liberal could not take his own side in this argument.[16] However, Rawls's justification of a political conception as part of an overlapping consensus allows him to argue, on everyone's behalf, that the substantive conception of justice included within it is right (and worthy of enforcement through state power) even while remaining tolerant of (and impartial toward) the disparate ideas, life-styles, religions, and moral views of the citizenry. Thus we see why Rawls says that formulating a "political" conception of justice is simply applying the principle of toleration to philosophy itself (JFPM, 223, 231; IOC, 15). His idea is that political philosophy is useful to a liberal society only if it rids itself of all metaphysical views so as to be properly tolerant of the diversity of ideas and practices in our political culture.

One may wonder whether or not this solution is too good to be true. The paradox only seems to be resolved in circumstances where there is a substantial degree of overlap between individuals' differing views and where there is no minority advocating intolerance toward beliefs other than their own. Suppose, however, that these circumstances don't hold. For example, suppose there is a group of religious fundamentalists whose premier objective is to make converts to their religion in order to achieve salvation for them, and who tolerate the views and practices of atheists and members of other religions only because they are not strong enough to use the power of the state to stamp out these heresies. Such people would see a central component of the overlapping consensus, the principle of toleration, as merely expedient in the circumstances. While it might allow them to forestall war in their dealings with the infidels, they would just as soon get rid of it if conditions allowed them to do so.

Could a political philosopher change the minds of these people if she eschewed metaphysics and used only Rawls's political method? If these fundamentalists were genuinely opposed to toleration, she could not argue for it as an idea in the overlap of divergent metaphysical conceptions—because it would not be in their overlap. Perhaps she might argue that toleration was henceforth always going to be necessary to achieve a cooperative stable society, and let us go so far as to suppose that this is true. Is this style of political argument sufficient to make the religious fundamentalists accept toleration as right? No; the fundamentalists' acceptance of it on these grounds would be acceptance of it as a mere modus vivendi; if only the world could be different, they would happily jettison it.

The upshot of this argument is that the creation of an overlapping consensus in a pluralistic society cannot guarantee, even if members of this society accept toleration, that they do so because they believe it to be intrinsically right. The only argument for its acceptance that a practitioner of Rawls' method can give to one whose metaphysical beliefs do not endorse it as right is that in the circumstances it is instrumentally valuable for achieving peaceful cooperation. So either the principle of toleration is endorsed by a person's comprehensive moral conception, or it is endorsed as a mere modus vivendi. There is no political method that will allow one to argue for its endorsement as more than the latter when the person's comprehensive moral conception opposes it. In these situations, Rawls can either keep his political methodology, in which case he has allowed political philosophy in pluralist societies only the job of articulating a modus vivendi; or he can give political philosophy the role of arguing in these societies that the principle of toleration is right, in which case he has committed the philosopher to doing metaphysics. There is no intermediate "third way."

But Rawls does not disagree with any of this. And the fact that he does not, enables us to get a better understanding of what he takes an overlapping consensus to be. In the situation I described, he would say that there was a modus vivendi but no overlapping consensus. This is, in fact, how he describes a similar political world: sixteenth-century Europe, where Catholics and Protestants vied for political dominance. Suppose they had decided to tolerate one another. Then, says Rawls, "we no longer have an overlapping consensus on the principle of toleration. At that time both faiths held that it was the duty of the ruler to uphold the true religion and to repress the spread of heresy and false doctrine. In this case the acceptance of the principle of toleration would indeed be a mere *modus vivendi*, because if either faith becomes dominant, the principle of toleration will no longer be followed. Stability with respect to the distribution of power no longer exists" (IOC, 11). If the agreement of Catholics and Protestants at that time could not count as the creation of an overlapping consensus on the principle of toleration, then Rawls essentially believes that in order for a genuine overlapping consensus to exist, the bulk of the population must endorse these ideas for a certain kind of reason, that is, a moral, religious, or philosophical reason that makes the citizens accept these ideas as right (in addition to any appreciation they may have of the instrumental value of accepting these ideas). Rawls wants this sort of reason to explain the citizenry's belief in these ideas because the stability of the community will thereby be enhanced. Indeed, that stability, he says, comes in degrees, depending upon the content of the religious, philosophical, or moral doctrines available to create the consensus (JFPM, 250). A consensus on the principle of toleration reached in a society in which people embrace it as Kantians, or as Millians, as Rawlsians, or as members of religions committed to it as intrinsically right, will be "far more stable than one founded on views that express skepticism and indifference to religious, philosophical or moral values, or that regard the acceptance of the principles of justice simply as a prudent *modus vivendi* given the existing balance of social forces" (JFPM, 250).[17]

I have three critical reactions to this Rawlsian argument. First, if that argument is right, then the primary task of a political philosopher is to find metaphysical reasons implicit in each party's belief system to support ideas as right in the consensus. If this is not possible, then either Rawls would have to say that the political philosopher must be content with stability arguments for endorsing these ideas, making them a mere modus vivendi, or he would have to hope that the philosopher could persuade people to "will to believe" in an idea's rightness (where they are not otherwise inclined to do so) for the sake of stability. The latter project, however, may be self-defeating,[18] in which case the generation of an overlapping consensus would depend upon sixth fact, namely, that each party (or, at any rate, the vast majority) has a metaphysics that supports the ideas in the shared fund as "right" and not merely as expedient. But one may wonder whether or not any existing constitutional democracy is one in which that sixth fact holds, and thus whether or not there is any society today in which Rawls's methodology could really be practiced.

The second critical reaction is that, contra Rawls, an overlapping consensus among Millians or Rawlsians is not more stable than one among moral skeptics or persons who only accept the principle of toleration as expedient. If the pluralism in the latter society really is permanent (because the parties reject the use of the kind of state power that would destroy it), then it would seem the relative power of the parties would always be such as to support this noncoercive means to peace. Remember that Rawls's entire argument for this way of philosophizing presupposed that his five facts held. To point out that the modus vivendi would not last if the society became relatively homogeneous (so that the first three facts don't hold) is to change the subject; Rawls should have nothing to say to a dominant group that suddenly finds itself able to enforce its conception of the good with minimal reliance on coercion (because few would resist). His entire justification of consensus-building philosophy presupposed that this was not so.

Finally, the third and (to my mind) most important critical reaction involves the rejection of Rawls's claim that an overlapping consensus is more than a modus vivendi. Because Rawls's justification of the project of developing an overlapping consensus is instrumental, then no matter what turns out to be required for stability, his project is, and will always be, Hobbesian. To see this, suppose he is right that only when citizens embrace the elements of the overlapping consensus as right (perhaps for one of the reasons he gave in the passage just quoted) can the pluralist society remain stable. Now, in this situation, each individual will not believe that the ideas he shares with his fellows constitute a mere modus vivendi, because each will believe that these ideas are correct in their own right. But what is the political philosopher's justification for his project of developing an overlapping consensus? Whatever the private metaphysical reasons, these cannot constitute the public justification of the project. It is useful to distinguish at this point between public and private philosophizing. The former is what one does when one theorizes about issues that are relevant to the construction of public institutions, especially institutions of government. The latter is what one does as an individual pursuing what one takes to be the truth about the world. Rawls is not against metaphysical speculation, theology, or moral theorizing; instead he sees them as appropriate only in the private realm. Public philosophizing, in his view, must not rely on metaphysics in constitutional democracies, which accept (for reasons of stability) the principle of toleration. It endorses no contestable thesis in its justification of ideas.

So Rawls must give a public argument for the philosophical project of developing an overlapping consensus that is neutral among the citizenry's competing metaphysical conceptions. And of course he mounts just this sort of argument in "Justice as Fairness" and "The Idea of an Overlapping Consensus": he argues that this project promotes the stability of (and prevents the degeneration of) modern constitutional democracies. Any political philosopher who accepts this argument will therefore believe herself obligated to contribute to the development of an overlapping consensus for instrumental reasons. And, as any Hobbesian would point out, this means that her public justification of her project is that of constructing a modus vivendi in a permanently pluralist world. Moreover, if Rawls's stability argument is right, we can see that the modus vivendi is not so much the set of beliefs constituting that overlapping consensus as it is both that set of beliefs and the citizenry's "I-accept-them-because-they-are-right" attitude toward them. Any Hobbesian intent on peace who could be persuaded by Rawls that this way of securing peace really works would want the citizenry to adopt both these beliefs and that attitude.

The point is that even if the ideas in the overlapping consensus are believed by the citizenry to be right as opposed to merely expedient, Rawls can offer only Hobbes-style expediency arguments for the generation of the overlapping consensus itself.

But, Rawls might protest, maybe these citizens have private metaphysical views that also allow them to endorse the generation of the overlapping consensus as right. Maybe. But the only thing that they can all agree that they are doing is creating a modus vivendi. The public, neutral justification of the project is one that makes it the creation of peace and stability at the lowest political cost, and this is a Hobbesian justification.

A Plea for Metaphysics

I am one philosopher who does not think that calling a methodology "Hobbesian" is an argument against it. What worries me is not Rawls's kinship with the man who began modern political philosophy; rather, it is his conception of what philosophy amounts to if his prescriptions for achieving stability in our world are right.

Consider my motives if I strive to develop an overlapping consensus. I cannot be interested in showing to all the parties involved that any idea I believe they all share is true, but only that they have reason to accept it, perhaps for (moral or religious) reasons that I myself think are bad or discredited. So I am after the idea's acceptance, not a proof of its truth. Am I not behaving as a (mere) politician? Politicians, after all, only want acceptance of ideas they (for whatever reason) are pushing; philosophers are supposed to want truth.

Indeed, because it is her acceptance of it which counts (even if it is on what I take to be wrongheaded religious or philosophical grounds), why stick to logical argumentation to persuade her? Why not use rhetoric, or emotional appeals, or socialization techniques that achieve peace by changing rather than coercing people? The maxim characterizing my practice might be: "Achieve political consensus on any given tenet by taking advantage of any ideology or device that could be used to gain others' acceptance of it, no matter how boneheaded or illogical." Perhaps there is nothing wrong with members of a pluralist society engaging in this undertaking, and I can certainly see how it is a "political" undertaking. But is it in any way a philosophical one?

These questions set the stage for a discussion of the most interesting aspect of Rawls's recent work: his challenge to us to think about what political philosophers ought to be doing in our place and time. But reflections on this topic inevitably drive one back to reflections on what any sort of philosophy ought to be doing at any time. Socrates, the founder of our discipline, characterized philosophy as the pursuit of the truth, and Plato's defense of that pursuit is quoted at the start of this essay. Rawls endorses what I will call "Socratic philosophizing" in fields such as ethics, or aesthetics, or philosophy of science, but he is asking us to replace it with something else when doing political philosophy in modern constitutional democracies. It is not merely that we are supposed to eschew metaphysics in this political realm; more fundamentally, we are supposed to eschew attempts at philosophical proof through argumentation that involves commitment to controversial metaphysical premises. Not truth, but noncoerced social agreement is to be our goal. And if that goal can be achieved via definitive demonstration, fine; but when it cannot, and controversy is inevitable, we are to strive for consensus rather than conversion, persuasion rather than proof.

In order to be sure we political philosophers ought to follow Rawls's advice, we need to be sure, first, that there is something about political philosophy in constitutional democracies that marks it as different both in aim and method from other kinds of philosophizing; and second, that the pursuit of consensus counts as a kind of philosophizing, even if it is not the Socratic kind. Rawls offers no explicit answer to these questions, but in order to pursue the issues they raise, let me start by offering, on his behalf, a (Socratic) argument for answering yes to them.

Consider, first, the worry that political theorizing may not be philosophy. Now, one of the central tasks of a philosophy professor is helping students to understand the logical implications of their beliefs. Accordingly, if she were to see two students arguing over some political issue and realized that they were in conflict only because one of them had drawn the wrong conclusion from his metaphysical premises, she would certainly be engaging in philosophy when she enabled the student to see this fact. Analogously, it would seem that a political philosopher who sought to show all parties involved in a social conflict how they shared political theses that followed logically from their differing metaphysical premises would be doing philosophy also.

Of course, philosophy professors correct their students so that the students' beliefs will be rationally held. A critic might worry that a political philosopher following Rawls's advice would be pursuing not this goal but the goal of consensus building, which, as I just proposed, might be better pursued with emotional or rhetorical appeals. However, whatever use these appeals may have initially, Rawls could argue that stability is best achieved and longest lasting only when the citizenry's shared beliefs are rationally, rather than irrationally, held. If this is right, then political philosophers who want successful and long-lived social cooperation must pursue an overlapping consensus of ideas using precisely the techniques of the philosophy professor, so that the ideas in this consensus are securely held by all parties in this pluralist society.

Moreover, if the philosopher were haunted by the fear (as Hobbes was) that the metaphysical theses upon which political theses rest in Socratic arguments can never be proven to be true or false, then the socially informed consensus building just described would be the only kind of political philosophizing that had any claim to being true. Although one could never say, "It is true that X is the correct conception of justice," nonetheless, one would be able to say, "It is true that if one accepts premises A, B, and C, then X is the correct conception of justice."

But Rawls is at pains to point out that his method of philosophizing does not presuppose such skepticism. Instead, the principle of toleration gives Rawls his intellectual motivation for this kind of philosophizing and provides him with an answer to the first question above, about how political philosophy differs in aim and method from other kinds of philosophizing. From Plato to the present, political philosophers have sought a remedy for social discord. But what if the Socratic practice of philosophy adds to that discord? Mustn't the political philosopher modify how she and others philosophize in order that the goal of social peace be achieved? If tolerance is the best (and most desirable) means to peace, must we not, as Rawls says, apply the principle of tolerance to the practice of political philosophy itself? Doing so means accepting a non-Socratic style of political theorizing. At one point in "Justice as Fairness," Rawls worries that liberalism, which rests on the principle of toleration, is in danger of becoming "just another sectarian doctrine" if it must be defended by arguments that rest on controversial metaphysical premises (JFPM, 246). Only if the philosopher applies the principle of toleration to philosophy itself as he theorizes politically does he seem properly tolerant of the diversity of ideas in his society and properly respectful of the fact that his own metaphysical beliefs may not be used to justify political coercion of others, any more than their beliefs may be used to justify political coercion of him. Such respect is demanded of him, at the very least, to ensure stability, and it may also be something that his moral or religious beliefs compel him to pay.

I find myself moved enough by these considerations to believe that, whatever else political philosophy ought to involve, it should sometimes be political. Indeed, I think we are in Rawls's debt for pointing out to us the valuable and unique intellectual role that political philosophers can play in contemporary constitutional democracies, namely, helping to create the intellectual ground rules upon which people of disparate views can peacefully interact. Such people would not even be able to present a claim for public adjudication if there were not a shared understanding of what a valid claim is, what the rules of assessing that claim are, and what "capital" the society ought to dispense in order to settle it. No matter what our religion, moral beliefs, or metaphysical commitments, if we are to work together in one system of cooperation, we have to have a "common currency" for the debating and settling of disputes or our society will be in ruins. Surely, the creation of such an intellectual common currency has been going on for years, perhaps more often in law schools than in philosophy departments (e.g., in discussions about what our constitutional tradition is). Its creation is an intellectual feat in which philosophers can usefully participate, given their training. To the extent that political philosophers engage in this enterprise, they are indeed doing something far more practical than philosophers who speculate about the truth in other fields of inquiry.

But I also want to argue, first, that this kind of practical aim is not unique to political philosophy, and second, that creating an overlapping consensus is not the only aim that political philosophy ought to have.

To make the first point, consider the fact that people who do applied ethics may also find it appropriate to refrain from advancing their own ideas about moral truth to the doctors, lawyers, or legislators who are consulting them, and to attempt instead to clarify the beliefs of their clients, draw out the conclusions implicit in these beliefs, and encourage reflection so as to enable these people to agree (and act) on a way to settle a dispute or a problem. Such "reflective consensus building" by these moral philosophers is not unlike the aim Rawls attributes to political philosophers. In general, it seems inappropriate for both moral and political philosophers to speculate about what is right when there are pressing problems that can be solved only when groups of people get philosophers' intellectual help to reach the agreement necessary to a solution.

However, I also want to argue that political philosophers must do more than simply engage in consensus building; they ought also to engage in Socratic philosophizing.

Suppose that conditions are as ripe for the practice of Rawls's method of philosophizing as they can be: the five facts prevail, everyone accepts the principle of toleration (albeit for different moral and religious reasons), the overlap of ideas is considerable enough that there is a consensus on a well-defined conception of justice and perhaps also a good (but limited) government able to decide questions on which there is no consensus. Nonetheless, there is still controversy, for example, about whether people should be accorded free health service supplied by the state or about whether a ban on pornography is a violation of freedom of speech. These are items upon which there is no consensus and which cannot be removed from the political agenda. Why not, Socrates might ask, engage in metaphysical political philosophy when publicly discussing these issues? Those who do so will not be contemptuous of their opponents' ideas, nor will they be prepared to call upon force to get the others to change their minds. Indeed, to the extent that they are committed as Socrates wishes them to be to the truth rather than to the particular belief they are presently endorsing, they ought to be prepared to argue under the assumption that they might be wrong and, thus, prepared to change their minds if their opponents offer them better arguments for the opposing view than they have for their own. Why should this spell trouble for a political community?

Rawls might argue that it spells trouble because the philosopher who insists that he is right and others wrong violates the principle of toleration, which we must all follow to insure long-lasting stability. But consider that there is a difference between tolerance of another's ideas and tolerance of another's holding of these ideas. Socrates would insist that the principle of toleration requires only the second kind of tolerance, not the first kind. Indeed, he would argue that as long as each disputant remains tolerant of and respects the fact that her opponent holds different ideas, she need not and should not be tolerant of the ideas themselves if she believes she is in possession of an argument that shows her opponents' ideas to be wrong or problematic. And if, as skeptics might claim, no such proofs are forthcoming, the disputants' discussion and speculation seem harmless enough as long as all parties respect each other as they participate in it.

Moreover, the public pursuit of the truth about these aspects of justice need not threaten the security of anyone in a pluralist society as long as there are universally shared (and enforced) guidelines for people's argumentative interaction with one another that insist, as Socrates did himself in his practice of philosophy, on respect for everyone's effort to construct his or her own belief system. Of course, people's beliefs might be threatened by the existence of an argument undermining them. But why should those who are committed to the truth sustain a tolerance of ideas when they believe they have an argument showing them to be false? Tolerance of others who hold what one takes to be false ideas is one thing; tolerance of the ideas themselves is quite another.

My point is that implicit in genuine philosophical argumentation is respect for one's opponent. One might not respect his ideas, but when one argues with him (as opposed to, say, fighting with him), one respects him and seeks to win him over to one's side not via coercion but by appeal to the truth, an appeal that might unexpectedly show one to be wrong and one's opponent to be right. A society that fostered such philosophizing would be a society that fostered such respect. Socrates himself tried to persuade the jury that eventually convicted him that philosophizing was neither a dangerous nor a divisive activity. And aren't we supposed to think that he was right that a society has nothing to fear from a group of people who are earnestly committed to working out what is true and who are respectful of one another's attempts to formulate answers—even if those answers are ones with which they disagree? Indeed, such respect seems to be what Mill argued that liberalism was all about.

Those communitarians who share MacIntyre's or Sandel's metaethics need not reject any of this. They would only want to argue that Socratic philosophizing is of necessity suffused with the shared values of the community in which the disputants participate. But even if they are right that one can search for truth only in a social framework, nonetheless, Socrates's point would be that when one engages in such a search, one is still doing metaphysics. Of course, communitarians such as Rorty would reject any enterprise characterized as the search for truth as a self-defeating search for an extrasocietal perspective that does not exist, and they would thereby reject the doing of philosophy as it has been classically understood. But other communitarians can endorse socially informed metaphysical theorizing as worth pursuing and as different from the pursuit of mere consensus.

Perhaps one thing that scared the Athenian jury about Socrates' activity was the fact that appeals to the truth are frequently invoked to justify intolerance. Perhaps, thought the jury, Socrates' young men would believe, armed by Socrates' arguments, that they knew better than the rest of the populace what ought to happen in Athens and so foist their views upon an unwilling city.

But such is the behavior of people who are not philosophers. These people are not committed to the truth; instead, they are true believers committed to their cause.[19] True believers not only attack opposing ideas but also those who hold opposing ideas. So they fail to be tolerant in both of the ways described above. They see their intellectual opponents as "enemies," "infidels," "heretics," "fascists"—to be fought, resisted, even killed if they get in the way of building their dream, be it the kingdom of heaven, or the perfect state of anarchy, or the ideal communist state. It is their blind faith, not their metaphysics, which results in discord and even war.

I would argue that the true believer is the one enemy the philosopher has—for two reasons. First, she would block reform justified by good argument. Those who are committed to the truth act as gadflies for their society, striving not merely for stability but for stability on just terms. They will be resisted by those whose faith prevents them from hearing the better argument. Since the death of Socrates, philosophers have believed that they owed it to their communities to fight such resistance and examine the theoretical foundations of society as much to overturn what is unjustifiable as to find shared bases of agreement.

Second, the true believer is the enemy of the philosopher because he will not respect his opponent's attempts to formulate and reflect on the opponent's ideas. Such respect is the foundation not only of philosophy but also of liberal society; it is that upon which we must insist if we wish to have either. One who is committed to philosophy must also be committed to remaining intolerant of others' intolerance. To attempt to reach consensus with intolerant true believers would be to betray one's belief in the respect that grounds one's very philosophizing.

Rawls himself comes very close to making this same point. In "The Idea of an Overlapping Consensus," he admits that "in affirming a political conception of justice we may eventually have to assert at least certain aspects of our own comprehensive (by no means necessarily fully comprehensive) religious or philosophical doctrine. This happens whenever someone insists, for example, that certain questions are so fundamental that to ensure their being rightly settled justifies civil strife. The religious salvation of those holding a particular religion may be thought to depend upon it. At this point we may have no alternative but to deny this, and to assert the kind of thing we had

Should Political Philosophy Be Done without Metaphysics? 175

hoped to avoid" (IOC, 14). Rawls seems to be endorsing the assertion of our moral conception in a public, political context. And what he believes we must assert—even with force—is toleration, respect for others' ideas. Here is an idea over which he is prepared to fight. And, of course, as a philosopher he must be so prepared because philosophers are true believers also—true believers in the value of pursuing truth through philosophical argumentation that respects equally the disputants who participate in it.

It may even be that this respect is the foundation of justice. Now, insofar as Rawls's conception of justice attempts to incorporate and give voice to that respect, then if there were an overlapping consensus on it (as he believes), our society would have the foundations necessary for genuine philosophizing rather than divisive argumentative clashes among intolerant opponents. But in my view, not only is there no consensus on Rawls's conception of justice in our society, but, more disturbingly, there is no consensus on the idea that all human beings deserve equal respect. The Bill of Rights is only part of our history; the persistence of racial discrimination, sexism, and exploitation betrays a commitment by many to the second-class status of some of their fellows. Because they have that status, such people are perceived as appropriate targets of coercion by those of higher status—who need not argue with their inferiors. In contrast, a person who is committed to philosophizing with another is rejecting the idea that she has a higher status that permits her to exercise control over the other's beliefs and is instead allowing and respecting her opponent's ability to formulate and decide on his own beliefs freely. Anyone committed to philosophizing with her opponent is thus committed to respecting him as a human being. That is, she is respecting him not necessarily as a virtuous person, or as a smart person, or as a person who satisfies any particular social ideal, but as a human being who can and ought to choose how to lead his own life. Hence, a society committed to philosophizing with all human beings would also be committed to the kind of respect for one another that is the foundation of justice. If a philosopher finds herself in a society that is committed neither to justice nor to reasoned debate, then she will indeed be a divisive force in the community as she strives for reform of practices that she cannot tolerate.

And now we have come to the crux of my argument for metaphysical political philosophizing. Given that modern constitutional democracies are still not societies in which there is widespread agreement that all people should be accorded the same rights and opportunities, we have an obligation as philosophers committed to arguing with, and thus respecting, our fellow human beings to persuade opponents of that idea and thus to change their minds. Arguing that they ought to do so because such respect promotes stability is one kind of Socratic argument (it is an argument that is supposed to assert a true causal connection). But even better in the eyes of those who have been denied such respect is an argument maintaining that disrespectful ideas and practices ought to be rejected because they are wrong.

These reflections are meant to suggest that the activity of philosophy is itself based upon substantive metaphysical beliefs about the nature of human beings. I would argue that those political philosophers who share Socrates' delight in the pursuit of knowledge with their fellow human beings should not want to give up that pursuit, or the fight for the conditions of free and equal respect that make it possible.

Postscript: The New Reliance on the "Reasonable"

After the preceding was written, Rawls published "The Domain of the Political and Overlapping Consensus,"[20] which attempts to allay the worries of critics such as myself that his most recent work constitutes a retreat from the moral objectivity that he seemed to embrace in his book. His arguments in this paper are highly interesting, but I shall argue that they are unsuccessful.

As he expounds his conception of the overlapping consensus in this article, he abandons the word "metaphysical" and instead relies on what he calls "the burdens of reason" argument. We disagree, he points out, for many reasons, and often those reasons reflect our prejudices, bad reasoning processes, or limited intellectual capacities. But even when we are properly open-minded, well-reasoning, and intelligent, we can still disagree (often intractably) because of "the many hazards involved in the correct (and conscientious) exercise of our powers of reason and judgment in the ordinary course of political life" (DPOC, 236).

He goes on to list six sources of such reasonable disagreement, including incomplete evidence, differing backgrounds that shape our judgement differently, and conflicting normative considerations that are difficult to weigh or assess. In situations where any of these conditions hold, each of us may arrive at very different conclusions, and we may be quite unable to resolve our disagreements. To put it another way, in such situations we are right to take our positions as reasonable, given what we can ascertain about the world, and thus we are reasonable to resist any claim made by those who disagree with us that we *must* be wrong.

How does a political society respond to the reasonable intractability of disagreement? Rawls argues that precisely because such disagreement is reasonable, a society would be unreasonable to use its power to resolve the disagreement in favor of one of the parties. In the course of explaining why a liberal political society could not tolerate the attempt by a religious constituency to enforce its religious views on the whole of the population, Rawls maintains:

> From the point of view of political liberalism, the appropriate reply is to say that the conclusion is unreasonable: it proposes to use the public's political power—a power in which citizens have an equal share—to enforce a view affecting constitutional essentials about which citizens as reasonable persons, given the burdens of reason, are bound to differ uncompromisingly in judgment.
>
> It is important to stress that this reply does not say that a doctrine *Extra ecclesiam nulla salus* is not true. Rather it says that its is unreasonable to use the public's political power to enforce it (DPOC, 243).

This passage suggests what Rawls goes on explicitly to articulate, namely, what I will call the "Reasonableness" Principle of Legitimate Political Coercion: "since political power is the coercive power of free and equal citizens as a corporate body, this power should be exercised, when constitutional essentials are at stake, only in ways that all citizens can reasonably be expected to endorse publicly in the light of their own common, human reason" (DPOC, 244). The principle says that it isn't the purported truth or falsity of a view, but rather the lack of decisive proof of its truth in the eyes of all reasonable human beings that makes it unenforceable.

On the basis of this principle, let me define, on Rawls's behalf, what I will call his "reasonableness test," setting out the criterion of admission for any normative belief proposed for membership in the set of such beliefs comprising the overlapping consensus. The Reasonableness Test for Admissable Beliefs in the Overlapping Consensus may be defined thus: the beliefs that constitute the overlapping consensus must be ones that all citizens can reasonably be expected to endorse publicly in the light of their own common, human reason.

Note that this test appears to allow two kinds of normative beliefs to be admitted: first, those for which there is either an incontrovertible proof or which can be taken to be self-evident; and second, those that, as it happens, everyone in the society rationally endorses given the (partial) evidence available to them, but that could be contested by anyone with differing evidence and/or experiences with life.

Rawls goes on to argue that in modern democratic societies, the admissible beliefs within the overlapping consensus include special "political" values that "give expression to the liberal political ideal" (DPOC, 244). And in addition to the principle of toleration, these include the idea that human beings are free and equal, although he does not go into very much detail about what these notoriously difficult concepts should mean.

But what justifies the inclusion of a belief in our freedom and equality in such a consensus, particularly if some members of the pluralist society do not accept them or have substantially different interpretations than Rawls of what these concepts mean? Where is your proof, they would ask, for our equality? And if you cannot give one, how can you insist that our public charter endorse this idea?

Perhaps Rawls might deny that he need say anything to them at all. Often in his recent work, Rawls stresses the fact that the content for the sort of overlapping consensus he is commending depends upon the political society being a modern Western democracy with certain fundamental beliefs (e.g., freedom and equality) that are part of the intellectual culture of that society. Hence, he might claim that it is beside the point to ask what kind of overlapping consensus should be created if the society changed so much that it was substantially different from the sort of society his theory assumes. If he took this position, Rawls's justification of his theory of justice is critically dependent upon the fact that certain contingent features hold in the society to be governed by that theory.

However, taking such a position will undermine the effectiveness of his defense of his theory of justice in the eyes of many philosophers. On this view, Rawls would be arguing: "If a society believes in x, y, and z, then the theory of justice I commend will be shared by all the members." The force of the "will" is interesting here: either it means that members of the society do in fact believe that theory, or it means that were the theory explained to them, and a deduction of that theory from the fundamental beliefs performed, they would have to accept it as long as they were fully reasonable and rational. Either position, however, makes the justification of his theory of justice entirely contingent on what fundamental beliefs people happen to have. And what is the moral status of these fundamental beliefs? "Okay," say the members of this society, "maybe you are right that we're logically required to hold this view and/or that we already do hold it (albeit, perhaps, unaware of our doing so) in virtue of the other ideas we embrace. But *ought* we to hold these other ideas? If they come under challenge by some of our members who begin to question them, are we required—and do we have the conceptual resources—to defend them, and if necessary to use the power of the state to enforce them? Or have we little or nothing to say as a way of establishing their reasonableness in the face of this challenge? And if the latter, do we eschew the use of force, and try to work out a new overlapping consensus that takes into account the fact that some of our members embrace fundamental beliefs that are substantially different from our own?"

The answer that I believe Rawls *wants* to give to such questions is that no society can be politically legitimate, much less "democratic and liberal," unless it is governed by the values of freedom and equality. Hence, the citizenry would be somehow justified in criticizing the nonliberal views of members of their society as unjust, opposing any proposals from them to use political power to enforce their views, and persisting in policies that adhere to and even enforce (using the state's coercive power) the idea of equality. On this view, to be politically legitimate, an overlapping consensus must have the *right* values.

But Rawls can only give this reply if he can explain how we can tell which values are right. A bit later in the article, Rawls says that the political values he endorses, which are implicit in his own conception of justice, are "reasonable," suggesting these values are ones that the proper exercise of reason will uncover:

> [A]s a liberal political conception, justice as fairness relies for its reasonableness in the first place upon generating its own support in a suitable way by addressing each citizen's reason, as explained within its own framework.
> Only in this manner is justice as fairness an account of political legitimacy. Only so does it escape being a mere account of how those who hold political power can satisfy themselves, in the light of their own convictions, whether political or fully comprehensive, that they are acting properly—satisfy themselves, that is, and not citizens generally. A conception of political legitimacy aims for a public basis of justification and appeals to free public reason, and hence to all citizens viewed as reasonable and rational. (DPOC, 247–48)

So Rawls appears to be saying that the values of freedom and equality are and should be part of the overlapping consensus of Western democracies not because they happen to be widely endorsed in these societies, but rather because these values would be endorsed by fully reasonable people. It is that fact that makes them the right ones to include in such a consensus, and since (only) belief in these values is reasonable, any political power used to enforce them is legitimate, and not an unfair exercise of coercion by a group of citizens based upon their particular disputable religious or philosophical views.

So this reply depends upon being able to call the use of political power to enforce the values of freedom and equality "reasonable." But when we do so, aren't we ruling out the "wrong" views (i.e., the intolerant, freedom-denying, equality-denying views) by covertly presupposing a particular controversial comprehensive moral view to do so? Rawls might argue that we are not as long as (1) it is not true that the only defense of these values presupposes a particular comprehensive or partially comprehensive view that, given the burdens of reasons, some people in the society could reasonably reject; and (2) the values of freedom and equality have a force or authority in and of themselves that is so powerful that the burdens of reason are not sufficient for us to allow that someone could reasonably dispute them. Is it possible for Rawls to establish both of these claims?

I take it that when Rawls says these values are "free-standing" (e.g., in DPOC, 245), he is insisting that claim 1 is true. It would seem that values could be free-standing so that claim 1 is true in one of two ways. First, such values can be embraced "on their own," without being derived from any larger philosophical or religious view.[21] I would think that this way of endorsing such values is common: the terrain of our moral life is complicated, and I doubt that either philosophy or religion is always or even usually important in explaining why we hold particular moral or political beliefs, or that those beliefs are always the logical conclusion of trains of deductive reasoning. Consequently, a citizen's perception of the necessity of insisting that her society foster freedom and equality for all may be a judgment to which she is committed independent of her commitments to other philosophical and religious views, and is in this sense, free-standing. (Indeed it may even be at odds with some of her other views, in a way that might be hard for her to reconcile.)

When values are free-standing, our fundamental commitments are to the values themselves, and not to the theoretical speculations we generate to explain them. Moreover, values can also be free-standing when individuals in a community come to develop differing comprehensive doctrines that incorporate the values, as long as their fundamental commitment is still to the values themselves and not to the differing philosophical or religious speculations in which they have embedded those values. For example, suppose that all of them hold the belief that we are free and equal, but some of them construct a religious justification for that belief, while others develop a secular, reason-based justification. As long as all of them are agreed that the belief is true, and admit that the comprehensive view in which they had embedded the belief might be the wrong justification for it, their commitment to the belief is still free-standing in the right sense. That is, all are committed to the idea *that* the belief is true, and not similarly committed to any particular explanation of *why* it is true.

I suspect that a lot of our beliefs are free-standing, forming a bedrock of ideas that we use to approach the world. Just as epistemological theories attempt to articulate and supply warrant for bedrock beliefs such as the existence of the material world, so too can political philosophy or religious theology involve, at least in part, the attempt to articulate and supply the warrant for bedrock political and religious beliefs that are part of the public charter. Such reflection cannot only deepen our appreciation of and commitment to these ideas, but also help to correct our understanding of them. But in such cases our reflection comes *after* the endorsement of the political or the religious values; our endorsement of them does not depend on these speculations being true.[22]

So I take claim 1 to be often—perhaps even usually—correct. I do not see how Rawls can establish that it is true for all such values, and for all citizens in democratic societies, and if he cannot, then the existence of the right kind of overlapping consensus in such societies is still a contingent matter. But this needn't be taken as a problem for his position as long as he has a way of defending the liberal values as inescapably correct, such that reasonable people would have to accept them. This is what claim 2 says is possible: so can Rawls defend claim 2?

To defend claim 2, Rawls must argue that it is unreasonable *not* to believe that we are free and equal. Now, I would find it easy to say such a thing, but I have a morally informed conception of reasonableness, making it, to use Rawls's terminology, a partially comprehensive conception. In contrast, Rawls tells us that his notion of reasonableness is meant to be deliberately uninformed by nonpolitical values. So how can he use it to criticize the rejection of freedom and equality?

Might he be able to do so if the notion were invested not with moral norms, but with epistemic ones? From this view, when Rawls calls someone unreasonable, he would be saying that this person rejects a view for which other fully reasonable and rational people believe a proof exists or which is reasonably taken to be self-evident. So if he would call those who reject the liberal ideas of human freedom and equality unreasonable, he would believe that reasonable and rational people would believe these ideas to be either self-evident or decisively proved. Such a position makes the ultimate defense of Rawls's theory of justice depend not on the authority of any particular moral theory, but on the authority of epistemic and logical norms. Instead of grounding his political theory on the shaky norms of morality, he would be grounding it on (what would be taken to be) the "incontrovertible" authority of the norms of epistemology and logic.

But even supposing this ground is "incontrovertible,"[23] is it plausible to suppose that there is a decisive proof for these ideas, and/or a way of showing that they are self-evident? Certainly, there is no universally accepted proof establishing their truth, and with apologies to Thomas Jefferson, I fear we cannot take them to be self-evident. Human history provides enormous evidence for their contestability; commitment to these beliefs has been (and remains) unusual rather than usual. Outside of the West, social hierarchies and restrictions of freedom are commonplace (and Western societies are derided for their commitments to liberty and equality); and even within Western democracies, beliefs that would limit liberty (e.g., within certain forms of fundamentalist religions) or challenge equality (such as racist or sexist views) are far more widespread than many would like to admit. If so many people can fail to see the warrant for these values, don't the burdens of reason argument force us to conclude (however much we may dislike to do so) that it is reasonable (albeit, in our view, incorrect and/or immoral) to believe otherwise? If Rawls were to persist in calling the rejection of these values unreasonable, wouldn't his use of that term be just as ill supported as, say, the claim made by a fervent religious believer that it would be unreasonable not to admit God's existence?

I must be careful to note that I like Rawls's rhetoric here; but this is because I have a morally informed notion of reason. If I were to say "Senator Jesse Helms is unreasonable to reject homosexuals' rights," I would understand "unreasonable" here to be informed by moral ideas that are surely contestable but in which I have great faith. If the admission of a belief into the overlapping consensus rests solely upon its lack of contestability by fully reasonable and rational people who have nonetheless had access to different evidence, and whose experience with life yields different ways of judging and evaluating the world, I do not see how the values of freedom and equality pass that test. On the other hand, if Rawls is prepared to accept that his notion of reasonableness is morally informed, then (at least in my view) he is right to argue that the rejection of human freedom and equality is unreasonable. But clearly this position is a theoretically partisan one, and if it were openly embraced by a liberal society, that society could not claim to be neutral with respect to a variety of different forms of religious or philosophical beliefs that exist not merely in the world, but within Western democratic societies themselves.

I suspect that the difficulties I am pointing to arise because, without realizing it, Rawls actually uses two notions of reason in his recent work. In the burdens of reason argument in "Domain of the Political and Overlapping Consensus," he asks, "Given who a person is and what he knows, what is it reasonable for him to conclude?" And he is surely right that there are all sorts of conclusions that individuals can reach, while adhering to standards of rational belief formation, about various religious, moral, and political issues in virtue of their differing background and evidence. (Even the most hardened atheist could not fairly call a woman raised in the Mennonite tradition in Pennsylvania "unreasonable" or "irrational" because she believed in God, although he could certainly consider her wrong to believe so.)

But Rawls is famous for asking a different kind of question in his earlier work, namely, "If a person could be placed in a moral Archimedean point, what would he be rational to conclude about moral matters?" Or (to use T. M. Scanlon's formulation), "what would a person be unreasonable to reject as the basis of informed, unforced general agreement?"[24] This sort of question does not ask whether the beliefs of real people satisfy standards of rational belief formation, but rather what beliefs would be rational if an individual had a morally ideal perspective. The beliefs about justice that a person on the street would hold might be perfectly rational beliefs given that person's upbringing, but they might not be the *right* beliefs as determined by that ideal reasoning procedure.

So, there is ideal reasoning, that is, reasoning in morally and epistemically ideal circumstances, and there is reasoning in real, less than ideal circumstances. When Rawls makes his burdens of reason argument, he is clearly talking about real reasoning, but when he insists that reason mandate a belief in human freedom and equality, he appears to have shifted (as one might predict a Kantian contractarian would do) to an appeal to the conclusions of (what he takes to be) ideal human reasoning. But clearly, conceptions of what ideal reasoning is like are informed by a whole variety of normative ideas that are eminently disputable by individuals who have grown up in a world that is not ideal. So, to the extent that Rawls's theory is informed by these ideals, it is, in his own terms, a partially comprehensive view, and were it to be used in a liberal society, that society would be theoretically partisan rather than neutral.

In the end, the middle ground Rawls sought to define doesn't exist. Either Rawls must defend his theory of justice in a way that is genuinely morally neutral by arguing that the ideas from which it is deduced are accepted by the populace—in which case the public charter of the society turns into a mere modus vivendi based on beliefs that happen to be held by the people today, which they might abandon tomorrow—or he must defend them as correct (and for that reason worthy of being accepted). In the latter case, his defense presupposes the truth of a comprehensive moral view that includes them, and implicitly rejects the idea that a liberal democratic society can take a neutral stand on every value-issue.

To conclude, let me return again to the way Rawls's new method of justifying his political views was an attempt to answer the communitarians' charge that his "Kantian" theory was insufficiently tied to the particularities of real political cultures and real political values. The ingenious idea he puts forward in his recent papers is that, in fact, his view is actually implicit in the societies of modern democracies: hence, communitarians who respect the values of their community must, says Rawls, be good liberals.

But although this might seem a lovely argumentative strategy to win support from his theoretical opponents, it ultimately sells out the position he wants to defend. Liberals are *not* those who submissively accept the ideas and principles that happen to be current in their society: they are and have been partisans for a certain understanding of individual liberty and human equality, who advocate toleration not only for its own sake but also because of the way a tolerant political climate allows each individual self-expression and self-development. Such liberals (and I am one of them) do not find unambiguous and wholehearted support for liberal values and toleration in Western societies. Not merely do many members of such societies support racist, sexist, and anti-Semitic positions, but many of them (including some who embrace what are supposed to be liberal positions) advocate silencing those whose views they take to be "obviously wrong." Right now, were members of Western societies to attempt to forge overlapping consensus reflecting the freestanding beliefs of their citizenry, liberals could well find they were outnumbered by those in their society who were not committed to human equality, and eager to constrain human freedom and human expression in certain areas.

Rawls's methodology assumes that liberal ideology has largely won over rival political conceptions; but reflection on the world in which

Should Political Philosophy Be Done without Metaphysics? 185

we live sadly shows that this is not so. Liberals are still fighting for the souls of even the most democratic of political societies. They endanger their cause if they pretend the fight is won.

Notes

1. In most of this chapter, I will refer to two of John Rawls's recent writings: "Justice as Fairness: Political not Metaphysical," in *Philosophy and Public Affairs*, 14 (1985): 223–51, and "The Idea of an Overlapping Consensus," *Oxford Journal of Legal Studies*, 7 (1987): 1–25. In the final section of the paper, I discuss Rawls's article "The Domain of the Political and Overlapping Consensus," which appeared in *New York Law Review*, 64, no. 2 (May 1989): 233–55. Hereafter, all references will appear in the body of the text with the articles abbreviated as JFPM, IOC, and DPOC, respectively.

2. For examples of criticisms of the argument's validity, see John Harsanyi, "Can the Maximin Principle Serve as the Basis for Morality? A Critique of John Rawls's Theory," in his *Essays on Ethics, Social Behavior and Scientific Explanation* (Dordrecht: Reidel, 1980), 37–63; and D. Clayton Hubin, "Minimizing Maximin," *Philosophical Studies* 37 (1980): 363–72.

3. John Rawls, *A Theory of Justice* (Cambridge: Harvard University Press, 1971): 255–56.

4. Alasdair MacIntyre, *After Virtue* (Notre Dame, Ind.: University of Notre Dame Press, 1981), 232–33, quoted by Amy Gutmann, "Communitarian Critics of Liberalism," *Philosophy and Public Affairs*, 14 (1985): 308.

5. Michael Sandel, "Introduction," *Liberalism and Its Critics*, ed. M. Sandel (London: Blackwell, 1984), 9.

6. Ibid.

7. Ibid., 10.

8. But not all communitarians need share, or do share, this metaethical thesis. See, e.g., Philip Selznick, "The Idea of a Communitarian Morality," *California Law Review*, 75 (1987). Michael Walzer is also prepared to endorse liberal values; see his *Spheres of Justice* (New York: Basic, 1983).

9. For Hobbes, any doctrine is part of "science" if it cannot be contested because there is a conclusive demonstration of it. Any thesis that cannot be so demonstrated is contestable and thus liable to disturb the peace of the commonwealth unless a sovereign is given authority to decide to matter. See his "Six Lessons to the Professors of Mathematics . . . in The University of Oxford" (1656), *Epistle Dedicatory*, in *English Works of Thomas Hobbes*, ed. W. Molesworth (London: John Bohn, 1840), 7: 183–84, and *De Homine*, chap. 10, iv–v, 41–43, in *Man and Citizen*, ed. B. Gert (New York: Humanities Press, 1972).

10. "When they believe that institutions or social practices are just (or fair) . . . they are ready and willing to do their part in those arrangements provided they have reasonable assurance that others will also do their part" (IOC, 22).

11. He writes, "Given the fact of pluralism—the fact that necessitates a liberal regime as a *modus vivendi* in the first place—a liberal conception meets the urgent requirement to fix, once and for all, the content of basic rights and liberties, and to assign them special priority. Doing this takes those guarantees off the political agenda and puts them beyond the calculus of social interests, thereby establishing clearly and firmly the terms of social cooperation on a footing of mutual respect. To regard the calculus as relevant in these matters leaves the status and content of those rights and liberties still unsettled; it subjects them to the shifting circumstances of time and place, and by greatly raising the stakes of political controversy, dangerously increases the insecurity and hostility of public life. Thus, the unwillingness to take these matters off the agenda perpetuates deep divisions latent in society; it betrays a readiness to revive antagonisms in the hope of gaining a more favourable position should later circumstances prove propitious. So, by contrast, securing the basic liberties and recognizing their priority achieves the work of reconciliation and mutual acceptance on a footing of equality" (19–20).

12. Rawls writes, "Justice as fairness assumes, as other liberal political views do, that the values of community are not only essential but realizable, first in the various associations that carry on life within the framework for the basic structure, and second, in those associations that extend across the boundaries of nation-states, such as churches and scientific societies. Liberalism rejects the state as a community because, among other things, it leads to a systematic denial of basic liberties and to the oppressive use of the state's monopoly of legal force" (TOC, 10, n. 17).

13. See my *Hobbes and the Social Contract Tradition* (Cambridge: Cambridge University Press, 1986), chap. 6.

14. See Kurt Baier, "Justice and the Aims of Political Philosophy," *Ethics*, 99 (July 1989), 771–90.

15. This paradox is nicely introduced by Thomas Nagel in "Moral Conflict and Political Legitimacy," *Philosophy and Public Affairs*, 16 (1987): 215–40.

16. Quoted in ibid., 215.

17. In his discussions of stability, Rawls leaves out one kind of reason why one might embrace the principle of toleration and the liberal conception of justice, namely, the utilitarian reason that doing so in those situations where Rawls's five facts hold will maximize the happiness of the community. This reason for adopting these principles as right still makes them instrumentally rather than intrinsically valuable. Is this moral reason good enough, or does the utilitarian's endorsement still seem too Hobbesian to ensure stability?

18. Bernard Williams has argued that trying to do this is self-defeating. See his "Deciding to Believe," in his *Problems of the Self* (Cambridge: Cambridge University Press, 1973).

19. The term "true believer" was coined by Eric Hoffer to characterize such people in his *The True Believer* (New York: New American Library, 1951).

20. DPOC, 233–55. This article is reprinted in *The Idea of Democracy*, eds. D. Copp, J. Hampton, and J. Roemer (Cambridge: Cambridge University Press, 1992), and it is followed by my paper, "The Moral Commitments of Liberalism," some of the arguments of which are presented in an abridged form here.

For another paper critical of Rawls's work whose arguments Rawls was concerned to answer, see Joseph Raz, "Facing Diversity: The Case of Epistemic Abstinence" *Philosophy and Public Affairs*, 19, no. 1 (Winter, 1990): 3–46.

21. Rawls suggests this idea when he notes: "It is left to citizens individually, as part of their liberty of conscience, to settle how they think the great values of the political domain relate to other values within their comprehensive doctrine" (DPOC, 245).

22. Consider, for example, Russell's puzzlement about how to reconcile his outright moral condemnation of cruelty toward animals with his moral skepticism, discussed by John Mackie in *Inventing Right and Wrong* (Harmondworth: Penguin, 1977): 34–35.

23. However, philosophers who are used to questioning the authority of these norms may believe that Rawls has made no great bargain trading moral norms for these norms if he wished thereby to purchase a more solid foundation for his theory.

24. T. M. Scanlon, "Contractualism and Utilitarianism," *Utilitarianism and Beyond*, eds. A. Sen and B. Williams (Cambridge: Cambridge University Press, 1982): 117.

9

Liberalism and the Political Character of Political Philosophy

Paul Weithman

I

John Rawls's insistence in recent years that justice as fairness is political and not metaphysical has attracted a great deal of attention.[1] It is by now commonplace to note how many of Rawls's readers see in this insistence a retreat from what seemed the much more ambitious project of *A Theory of Justice*. In that book, readers found a theory that was "part, perhaps the most significant part, of the theory of rational choice."[2] As such, it seemed to articulate principles that could, in the spirit of Kant, be justified to all rational agents who entered the original position. Those principles were, moreover, thought universal in their application, applicable to the basic structure of societies regardless of their time or place.

By contrast, Rawls now tells us that justice as fairness is developed from the "basic intuitive ideas" of fairness, freedom, and equality latent in the public culture of democratic societies.[3] These ideas provide what Joseph Raz has called "shallow foundations," for no attempt is made to ground the basic ideas on anything deeper.[4] Explicitly disavowed is any attempt to show that the foundations of justice as fairness are true to an "independent metaphysical and moral order" like God's law or moral facts implicit in the nature of rationality;[5] indeed Rawls refrains from speaking of justice as fairness or of his principles of justice as true at all.[6]

Political philosophy, Rawls now says, proceeds by "the method of avoidance": it leaves aside controversial topics in theology, philosophy of mind, epistemology, and moral philosophy.[7] Instead, the ideas from which justice as fairness are worked up are regarded as widely shared by those who live in a democratic culture. And political philosophy begins from widely shared ideas because this procedure affords the greatest chance of consensus on the conception of justice that results.[8] The justification of justice as fairness is complete, it seems, with the achievement of what Rawls calls an "overlapping consensus." Such a consensus obtains when adherents of diverse religious and moral conceptions accept justice as fairness on moral grounds, even if their moral grounds for consent are very different.[9] And justice as fairness is, Rawls now says, a conception appropriate to the basic structures of only a limited range of societies, those with a culture and tradition in which the basic intuitive ideas are found.

Some see a thinly veiled moral skepticism in Rawls's refusal to assert the truth of justice as fairness. Most see in his recent essays a de-emphasis of the Kantian elements so prominent in *A Theory of Justice* and a move toward the realpolitik of Hobbes[10] or the pragmatism of Dewey.[11] But what elicits the strongest reaction from both those who applaud and those who criticize Rawls's recent work is what seems to be his politicization of political philosophy. The importance Rawls attaches to the achievement of an overlapping consensus and the foundation of his theory in widely shared ideas have suggested to some that what Rawls really values are political and not philosophical results—in Jean Hampton's words, "peace and stability at the lowest political cost."[12] Moreover, Rawls seems uninterested in precisely the sort of justification philosophers have traditionally sought. His claim that ideas implicit in democratic culture are the appropriate starting point for political philosophy and his refusal to justify them by digging deeper strike some as inconsistent with the claim that Rawls is engaged in philosophy rather than practical politics.[13]

Rawls seems, in a slight paraphrase of Richard Rorty's description, to have accorded democracy priority over philosophy. Rorty argues that Rawls takes the moral worth of liberal democratic politics for granted. He then, Rorty says, develops a theory that "comports with the institutions he admires. . . . He is putting politics first and tailoring a philosophy to suit."[14] Rorty himself looks with favor on what he takes to be Rawls's moves away from the justificatory aspirations of traditional political philosophy. He sees in them vindication of his own animus towards metaphysics.[15] Critics, on the other hand, argue that Rawls's current conception of political philosophy is untenable,[16] inconsistent,[17] or unable to meet its stated aims.[18] They claim that political philosophy ought to be more metaphysical and far less political than Rawls's later essays suggest. Both Rorty and the critics operate with a sharp distinction between metaphysics and politics.[19] And all employ it to locate in Rawls's recent essays a fundamental challenge to traditional conceptions of political philosophy.

I want to use and interpret Rawls's recent work to consider the political character of political philosophy. I shall argue that Rawls is best read as dividing the labor of political philosophy into two tasks: (1) that of developing a theory of justice and (2) that of building an overlapping consensus on the conception of justice the theory presents. I shall reserve the term "political philosophy" for the enterprise that includes both of these tasks. For reasons that will become clear as we proceed, I shall call the former of the two tasks "political theory"; the latter I shall call "comprehensive public philosophy."

Corresponding to these two tasks are two very different sorts of justification. The political theorist justifies his or her conception of justice by showing that it is a reasonable conception for the society he or she addresses. The comprehensive public philosopher, on the other hand, argues not just that that conception is a reasonable one, but that those whom he or she addresses ought to accept it. He or she justifies the conception by working within one or another moral or philosophical tradition, availing himself or herself of the full range of its moral and metaphysical resources to help build consensus on the conception of justice in question.

Rawls, I shall argue, is engaged only in political theory as I have characterized it. His appeal to the shallow foundations provided by the basic intuitive ideas is meant only to provide the limited justification associated with political theory. It is meant only to show that justice as fairness is a reasonable conception of justice for the democratic and pluralistic societies to which Rawls's arguments are directed. The further arguments that Kantians, utilitarians, intuitionists, moral realists, Catholics, and Jews in those societies should accept justice as fairness all await the efforts of comprehensive public philosophy. But that is not an enterprise in which Rawls is engaged; we should not expect to find him presenting these further arguments.

Political theory and comprehensive public philosophy are tasks both political and traditionally philosophical. Distinguishing the two enterprises and analyzing the political and philosophical character of each refines our view of the relationship between politics and political philosophy generally. It also shows that Rawls's challenge to the traditional character of political philosophy has been exaggerated. Friends like Rorty and foes like Jean Hampton have overestimated the distance Rawls puts between metaphysics and political philosophy.

II

I want to begin by saying something more about the nature of political theory as I believe Rawls conceives it. The tasks of elaborating its nature and of arguing that Rawls is engaged in it are much facilitated by the fact that the distinction between political philosophy and political theory comports nicely with a distinction Rawls himself has drawn.

In "The Independence of Moral Theory," Rawls wrote:

> I distinguish between moral philosophy and moral theory; moral philosophy includes the latter as one of its main parts. Moral theory is the study of substantive moral conceptions, that is, the study of how the basic notions of the right, the good and moral worth may be arranged to form different moral structures. Moral theory tries to identify the chief similarities and differences between these structures and to characterize the way in which they are related to our moral sensibilities and natural attitudes.[20]

Rawls does not elucidate the notion of a moral structure but it is safe to assume, I believe, that moral theories like utilitarianism, perfectionism, and natural law theory are moral structures in his sense. So, too, is the theory in which Rawls embeds justice as fairness. That theory specifies principles of justice and a conception of justice, and connects these notions of the right with various ideas of the good and of moral worth. Thus, if moral theory is that part of moral philosophy that studies moral structures generally, political theory includes that part of moral theory that studies theories and conceptions of justice.

Rawls contributes to political theory, of course, not just by studying moral structures, but by developing the moral structure he inherited from the contract tradition of Locke, Rousseau, and Kant. Rawls's further developing of a moral structure handed down by one of the traditional schools of political thought is consistent with his remarks about the task of moral theory generally.[21] This suggests that political theory is the task in which he sees himself engaged.

But the detached, academic study and development of moral structures would not by itself advance the practical aims of Rawls's work.[22] The stated aim of *A Theory of Justice* was to develop a contractarian conception of justice that could be adopted as the moral basis for a democratic society.[23] At minimum, this practical task demands that Rawls show the conception he develops to be a workable one. And so Rawls did not merely develop and study a conception of justice in ignorance of prevailing conditions in the society he addressed. He developed a theory not premised on conditions, like limitless plenty, that do not obtain, but one that is premised on salient facts, like religious and moral pluralism, that do.

Moreover, the practical task demands that Rawls show that his conception would, if realized, be a stable one. It must be capable of generating its own moral support among citizens who live in a society well ordered by it. The political theorist, like the moral theorist, must therefore examine how his or her moral structure would influence the development of the virtues and would be related to natural human interests and motives. That is why the political theorist, like the moral theorist of Rawls's description, tries "to characterize the way in which [the moral structures he develops] are related to our moral sensibilities and natural attitudes." Rawls devotes much of the third part of *A Theory of Justice* to this task.

If Rawls's political theory is to realize the practical aims he entertains, he must develop a conception of justice that is not only a workable one but also a reasonable one for the society he addresses. That is, he must develop one that members of the society he addresses have prima facie moral reasons to adopt. That justice as fairness is reasonable in this sense is guaranteed by its foundation in basic intuitive ideas that are drawn from democratic culture and that members of democratic culture can be presumed to share. Let me elaborate.

The basic intuitive ideas of moral personality and society as a fair system of cooperation express values like freedom, equality, and fairness. These are values to which all who participate in the democratic culture from which the basic ideas are drawn are presumed to attach great importance. Freedom, equality, and fairness are, of course, moral values, which can be realized in many areas of human life. They can be taken as family values when aspired to or realized at home, or they can be taken as values aspired to and realized in a friendship. Freedom, equality, and fairness are political values when they are realized or promoted by basic social and political institutions or when citizens aspire so to order their political society that these moral values are realized by those institutions. These values are not as important in some spheres of life as in others. Freedom or autonomy might be valued far more highly in the arrangement of political institutions than in the arrangement of ecclesiastical ones, for example. It is only as political values that freedom, equality, and fairness can be presumed to be of such great importance to participants in democratic culture. It is as political values that they are expressed by the basic intuitive ideas with which Rawls begins.

But these political values and the basic intuitive ideas that express them, however important, are too abstract to provide political guidance. We cannot attempt to realize fair cooperation, for example, without knowing a great deal about fairness and how its demands are to be reconciled with those of liberty. Rawls therefore frames a conception of justice that further specifies those basic intuitive ideas and values to provide, in his words, "guidance where guidance is needed."[24] The idea of moral personality is specified to yield a conception of a citizen acting autonomously and possessing a sense of justice the content of which is given by Rawls's two principles. The idea of society as a fair cooperative scheme is specified to yield a conception of society the basic structure of which conforms to those two principles. So specified, the ideas are sufficiently concrete to serve as ideals, as objects of human aspiration. The basic intuitive ideas are thus shared resources from which Rawls develops his ideals of citizenship and of the well-ordered society. The specification of basic intuitive ideas into these ideals provides the political guidance that neither the basic intuitive ideas nor the values they express could furnish, for the ideals Rawls specifies provide detailed conceptions of a just society and of such a society's citizens.[25]

Much of the theory in which justice as fairness is located is designed to show that the well-ordered society is one in which our deeply held political values are realized. It is thus that our aspirations and desires to live in a society well ordered by justice as fairness are elicited. Consider, in this connection, the following passage from section 72 of *A Theory of Justice*:

> Best of all, a theory should present a description of an ideally just state of affairs, a conception of a well-ordered society such that the aspiration to realize this state of affairs, and to maintain it in being, answers to our good and is continuous with our natural sentiments. A perfectly just society should be part of an ideal that rational human beings could desire more than anything else once they had full knowledge and experience of what it was.[26]

Rawls's theory presents such a description of an ideally just society and elaborates it to provide us with full knowledge and experience—at least in thought—of how that well-ordered society realizes political values like freedom and equality. Rawls thinks that this knowledge will elicit in us "the aspiration to realize this state of affairs, and to maintain it in being" because we already have a strong moral interest in these political values. Description of an ideally just society, which realizes these values, therefore heightens and focuses our moral interest. Thus, arguments that show that the well-ordered society of justice as fairness realizes deeply held political values provide us with moral reasons to desire that justice as fairness regulate political society. They thereby show that justice as fairness is a reasonable conception for us.

That justice is fairness is rooted in the basic intuitive ideas of freedom, equality, and fairness found in the public culture of a democratic society is therefore crucial to its being a reasonable conception. It is the depth and prevalence of these basic ideas and the wide acceptance within democratic societies of the political values they express that gives us some reason to think that a conception of justice that specifies and combines them could gain acceptance.

How, then, do the basic ideas justify justice as fairness to Rawls's readers? Perfecting the moral structure found in the contract tradition of Locke, Rousseau, and Kant is an act of faith in the practical import of one's efforts, for it is an act of faith that members of democratic society will accept a contractarian moral structure once it is developed. It can be shown an act of reasonable faith if it can be shown that the structure itself is a reasonable one, one that members of democratic society have prima facie moral reason to adopt. Rawls's founding his conception on widely shared ideas and political values makes that faith in eventual consensus on justice as fairness a reasonable faith. Rawls's appeal to the basic intuitive ideas thus justifies or shows reasonable the act of faith in which his political theory consists. And Rawls says explicitly, in a paraphrase of Kant, that his philosophical task is that of defending reasonable faith in the possibility of a just democratic regime like the one he sketches.[27]

Once justice as fairness has been shown a reasonable conception of justice, one that members of a democratic society have prima facie moral reason to adopt, the question of what further justification it requires naturally suggests itself. For the reasonability of justice as fairness depends upon its foundation in the basic intuitive ideas and the political values they express. Acceptance of these political values gives citizens some reasons, prima facie reasons, for accepting justice as fairness. But citizens may hold other moral values and principles than those on which justice as fairness is founded, values and principles that may conflict or seem to conflict with the conception of justice Rawls outlines. To have ultima facie and not just prima facie reasons to accept that conception, citizens need to be assured that they hold no other moral values or principles that defeat it. Rawls's answer to this problem of ultima facie justification seems to challenge the traditional character of political philosophy.

Rawls explicitly denies, as I have already noted, that he tries to demonstrate the truth of justice as fairness. Rorty infers from this denial that Rawls thinks no further justification of the conception is required. The priority Rorty thinks Rawls assigns to democracy implies, Rorty thinks, that showing justice as fairness a reasonable conception is showing enough. In this, Rorty sees the politicization of political philosophy and the denial of political philosophy's traditional ambitions.

But Rawls's refusal to consider the question of truth does not have the strong implications Rorty believes. Rawls is engaged in what I have called "political theory," which is a part of moral theory. And it is characteristic of moral theory generally, Rawls says, to postpone questions about the truth of a moral structure.[28] Political theory thus takes from moral theory the more limited ambition of laying out and studying workable and reasonable conceptions. It does not limit its aims because there is no moral truth or because, as Rorty believes, "truth . . . is simply not relevant to democratic politics."[29] It does so because the tasks of political theory are difficult enough and because determining which conception of justice is true first requires determining which conceptions are workable and reasonable.[30] Metaphysical questions are not dismissed. They are, I will argue, left to those working within religious and philosophical traditions.

Hampton reads Rawls's politicization of political philosophy differently than does Rorty. She focuses on the arguments she thinks the Rawlsian political philosopher must offer to adherents of various religious and moral views if an overlapping consensus on justice as fairness is to be secured. And she focuses on the philosopher's motives for offering those arguments. The arguments must, she says, be political and not philosophical arguments. They must be political, she thinks, because the Rawlsian political philosopher builds consensus by appealing only to what Rawls calls "public reason," by appealing only to political values and principles without trying to found them on anything deeper.[31] They will be politically motivated, since the Rawlsian political philosopher must, she thinks, give publicly acceptable reasons for securing a consensus. The only such reason he can give, Hampton argues, is his interest in social stability.[32]

I believe both Rorty and Hampton are mistaken in their interpretations. Rorty, as I have indicated, is mistaken in thinking that Rawls claims no further justification is necessary beyond showing that justice as fairness is reasonable. Hampton is mistaken about the sort of justification she thinks is available to Rawlsian political philosophers. To show this, it is necessary to turn to the way in which Rawls thinks an overlapping consensus on justice as fairness would be secured. The task of securing consensus is, I suggested, a task that falls not to political theory, but to what I called "comprehensive public philosophy."

III

In an overlapping consensus, adherents of diverse philosophical and religious traditions accept justice as fairness, but for different moral reasons; each supports the conception for reasons drawn from his or her own more comprehensive moral views.[33] Thus, in an overlapping consensus, Kantians affirm justice as fairness for one set of reasons, utilitarians accept it for another, and Christians accept it for still another. Such an overlapping consensus is, of course, a political ideal. Even in societies where justice as fairness is accepted as the public conception of justice, an overlapping consensus may not obtain since some may accept it on purely prudential grounds. Even so, we can ask how an overlapping consensus could come about since it is the ideal case, Rorty and Hampton think, that reveals most about Rawls's conception of political philosophy's task.

Rawls uses consensus on the principle of toleration to illustrate the development of an overlapping consensus over time.[34] Catholics and Protestants overlap in their consensus on the principle since both accept it; their views of toleration are not congruent, however, since their moral and religious reasons for accepting the principle differ. The principle of religious tolerance, which was initially accepted to put an end to religious strife, gradually came to be accepted by Protestants and Catholics for moral reasons. An overlapping consensus on justice as fairness could, Rawls argues, develop similarly.

Rawls provides little historical detail about how consensus on the principle of toleration developed. It is, however, a history that I believe he intends us to take seriously. That history is, of course, long and complicated; I will focus only on a couple of its features that will prove useful for highlighting philosophy's role in building a consensus on justice as fairness. Careful attention to these features, which follow, shows that both Rorty and Hampton are mistaken about the way in which such a consensus is achieved.

1. The principle of toleration was known from experience to be workable even before it was accepted on moral grounds.

2. Theologians who developed, for example, Catholic arguments for the principle of toleration worked within the Catholic tradition to do so. In this, John Courtney Murray, who was largely responsible for

the Catholic church's principled acceptance of toleration, was exemplary. He drew upon all the moral and theological resources within his tradition to frame the arguments he addressed to other Catholics.[35] Those he addressed to Protestants drew on premises he thought that Catholics and Protestants shared. In neither case did he feel compelled to restrict himself to those premises that he thought would be accepted by political society at large.[36]

3. While many Catholics may long have accepted the principle on prudential grounds, Murray himself had already accepted it for moral and religious reasons when he framed his arguments. If asked by other Catholics to justify the project of constructing moral arguments for the principle he could reply that he was not simply trying to build a firmer peace with Protestants, but that he was also trying to convince his fellow Catholics of a moral principle in which he already believed.[37]

These three features of the development of consensus on religious tolerance would be mirrored in the development of an overlapping consensus on justice as fairness.

1. In the case of the principle of tolerance, experience proved the principle workable. In the case of conceptions of justice, the political theorist—Rawls—argues that the conception proposed is both workable and reasonable for the society he addresses. He does so by showing that the conception would be stable, would generate its own moral support, and is founded on that society's fundamental political ideas and values.

2. The process of building an overlapping consensus will be a long and complicated one, as was the process of building moral consensus on religious toleration. Those working to build a consensus need not address only members of their own tradition or school of thought. And arguments addressed to those outside one's own tradition need not, as Hampton claims, appeal only to a common desire for peace and stability. Instead, the basic intuitive ideas and political values on which justice as fairness is built provide moral common ground for these arguments. All in a democratic culture are presumed to share these ideas and to have at least some interest in realizing the values they express. In relying on moral common ground, these arguments will resemble those arguments for religious tolerance that Murray addressed to Protestants.

Philosophers and theologians will also address some arguments to members of the moral communities to which they belong. They will attempt to show how justice as fairness can be endorsed from within the comprehensive views of those communities, just as Murray did when he urged that Catholics should accept religious toleration on moral grounds. Like those who forged a consensus on the principle of toleration, those who argue for the moral acceptability of justice as fairness need not restrict themselves to arguments that rely on premises that would be acceptable to all. Hampton is mistaken in her suggestion that they must do so.

When Kantians, utilitarians, and moral theologians from various religions address members of their own traditions, they work within the tradition they are addressing. In doing so, they are free to draw on all its conceptual and historical resources. Thus, Kantians can, if they like, appeal to all of Kant's moral thought to show why justice as fairness should be accepted. They could do so by arguing, for instance, that Rawls's two principles really are instances of the categorical imperative and are binding on all rational beings. Catholic theologians could argue that Rawls's two principles guarantee that each individual will have the social bases of the dignity to which he or she is entitled as a creature made in God's image and likeness. Religious and philosophical arguments in favor of justice as fairness need not be deductive; indeed, it should not be expected that many moral and religious views entail justice as fairness. Instead, these arguments may show that justice as fairness would realize the political values of a given religious or philosophical tradition better than any other conceptions of justice so far developed.[38] This might require interpreting the history of a religious tradition to show that the basic intuitive ideas or the values they express have played a hitherto unappreciated role in that tradition. Or it might require, to take a different example, connecting the interpretation of political freedom provided by a philosophical view with the interpretation implicit in the ideal of the well-ordered society. These tasks will be undertaken by moral philosophers who endorse Kantianism or utilitarianism as comprehensive moral doctrines, as well as by theologians who are trying to work out the political implications of their religious views.[39]

There is no guarantee that an overlapping consensus on justice as fairness can be achieved. That is why Rawls's political theory is, as I said earlier, an act of faith. Some religions might well be without a developed tradition of political thought; it may seem unlikely, therefore that grounds for justice as fairness can be found within them. In that case, faith that adherents can participate in an overlapping consensus rests on the hope that they can accept justice as fairness because of what political beliefs they hold independent of their religion.

Other religions may initially seem hostile to liberal democracy. Rawls conjectured that long experience of social cooperation with those of other religions eroded hostility between Catholics and Protestants and removed the barriers to moral acceptance of the principle of toleration.[40] Similarly, we might conjecture that religious and philosophical traditions that have long persisted and flourished in a democratic culture will come to incorporate the basic intuitive ideas and political values on which justice as fairness is founded. These basic ideas and values might not be prominent in the traditions in question. But presentation of justice as fairness can draw attention to neglected values like equality and fairness latent in a body of religious or philosophical thought. And it can elicit moral interest in building a liberal democracy by showing how liberal theory specifies and combines those values in the way I discussed earlier. Political theory can therefore be educative, teaching us about new political possibilities and about neglected aspects of our own comprehensive views.

3. When philosophers and theologians working for consensus are called upon to justify their work, they need not appeal only to their interest in securing peace and stability as Hampton suggests. These may well be among their motives. But they can also claim that the moral ideals of persons with the two moral powers and of a Rawlsian well-ordered society realize the political values implicit in their tradition.[41] They can number among their motives the belief that their society is an unjust one that would be made far more just by its adoption of justice as fairness. They are, they might conclude, trying to persuade other utilitarians, Kantians, or Christians of what they themselves are already convinced is right. Their position will therefore be much like that of the theologians who built a religious consensus on the principle of toleration because they thought intolerance morally wrong.

To understand how an overlapping consensus on justice as fairness or some other political conception is secured, then, it is important to appreciate the division of labor I mentioned earlier. One task is that of articulating a reasonable and workable conception of justice on which members of political society will overlap in their consent. The other task in the establishment of an overlapping consensus is that of convincing adherents of diverse religious and philosophical views that they should consent to justice as fairness as the appropriate moral basis for a democratic society. I have used the term "political theory" for the first of these tasks and "comprehensive public philosophy" to designate the second.[42]

Political theory is a limited enterprise but it is to this enterprise that Rawls restricts himself. What further justification can be provided for justice as fairness, what further work must be done to secure an overlapping consensus, is the task of comprehensive public philosophy. The work falls here because the strong moral interest Rawls supposes we can take in the ideals of citizenship and the well-ordered society is either derivative from or must be reconciled with our interest in our comprehensive moral views. Displaying the derivation or effecting the reconciliation is the task of comprehensive public philosophy, for it requires taking as premises substantive moral claims drawn from those views. This is an important point about the development of an overlapping consensus that both Rorty and Hampton miss.

IV

I have discussed how an overlapping consensus on justice as fairness might be secured. But what will be the character of a society in which such a consensus obtains?

Philosophy and theology will not, to be sure, have a place in the public justification of the Rawlsian society's public policies—in the justification offered by judges in their opinions or by other occupants of public office in their official capacities. Policies and judicial decisions will be justified by pointing to their promotion of the political values justice as fairness articulates, including the value of conformity with Rawls's two principles. Justice as fairness itself will be publicly justified only by pointing to its reasonability for a society that is heir to the democratic tradition and accepts its fundamental political values. Public reliance on any further philosophical or religious justification would be divisive.

Rorty thinks that the prevalence of this public conception of justification will lead citizens to forswear the need for any deeper foundations, that philosophy and religion will wither under pressure from the public culture of a liberal society. A liberal society will, he says, be one that "encourages the 'end of ideology,'" one "accustomed to the thought that social policy needs no more authority than successful accommodation among individuals" and one in which "the need for [more] legitimation may gradually cease to be felt." Its citizens will inhabit what he calls a "disenchanted" world.[43]

These are sociological forecasts that resist a priori refutation. But Rawls's well-ordered society need not provide the encouragement or apply the pressure that Rorty thinks it will. To see this, consider first how the transition to a society well ordered by justice as fairness might be effected in the United States. Religion obviously looms large in American national politics. This suggests that adherents of various religious positions would demand religious or philosophical arguments for the acceptability of justice as fairness before agreeing to it as the public conception of justice for the United States. Arguments drawn from comprehensive public philosophy therefore would be necessary to move this country toward the ideal Rawlsian society. Comprehensive public philosophy would not, of course, be sufficient to effect the transition to a well-ordered society; but it would be necessary in the United States under current political conditions.

The habits of religious and philosophical thought about politics—vital and necessary during the transitional stages to a well-ordered society—could continue even after an overlapping consensus on justice as fairness has been attained. Acceptance of Rawls's principles of justice leaves open questions about what policies best implement them. And while religion and philosophy would play no role in the public justification of policies, policy questions could provide the subject matter for religious and philosophical debate even in a society well ordered by justice as fairness. The situation would then be analogous to that which now obtains with respect to religious tolerance: Catholics and Protestants overlap on the principle, but Catholic and Protestant groups engage in vigorous internal debate about what tolerance requires.

But if transition to a Rawlsian well-ordered society requires comprehensive public philosophy and if policy questions would provide comprehensive public philosophy its subject matter even in a well-ordered society, what reasons does Rorty have for thinking that it would gradually disappear? What reasons has he for thinking that the sort of justification available in the public culture would gradually come to seem justification enough?

Perhaps Rorty thinks that the felt need for the philosophical justification of public policy would be extinguished in a Rawlsian society much as he thinks the need for religious justification has already disappeared in extant liberal democracies. Indeed, there are places where he suggests as much.[44] But Rorty's empirical claims about the demise of religious belief and about religion's political marginalization are demonstrably false, at least of the United States.[45] His conjecture that the public culture of a liberal society would extinguish the metaphysical urge therefore cannot be supported by appealing to the observed impact of liberal institutions on religious belief or political vitality.

Alternatively, Rorty might suppose that religion and philosophy would die out in a truly liberal society because, good Deweyan that he is, he believes that a well-ordered society would educate its children in public schools whose curricula encouraged pragmatism and discouraged religion and metaphysics. But surely, whether schools in a well-ordered society would be public and not, for example, sectarian with the support of a voucher system, is a question of public policy. It may be that a system of secular public education would win out in policy debates. Rorty cannot assume, however, that it would and hence cannot assume that a Deweyan education would lead to "the end of ideology" in a liberal society. Of course, Rorty could assume that secular public education would win out if he could safely assume that no citizens of the well-ordered society had sufficient religious interest to care whether their children had a religious education. But since the question at issue is whether citizens of the well-ordered society would retain their philosophical and religious interests, the latter assumption is one Rorty cannot make without begging the question.

The alleged decline and political marginalization of religion do not support Rorty's claim that the public culture of Rawlsian society would eliminate comprehensive public philosophy and the metaphysical impulses that give rise to it. Neither do claims about the character of such a society's educational system. Rorty has therefore provided us no reason to think that a liberal political culture would have the impact he suggests it would.

A society in which an overlapping consensus on justice as fairness has been achieved is one in which religious and philosophical views converge on and support the conception of justice that well orders that society. Its public culture can therefore encourage citizens who want assurance that the principles by which the basic structure of their society is assessed are true to "an independent metaphysical and moral order."[46] Instead of encouraging the end of ideology, it can encourage them to seek such assurance from the comprehensive public philosophers of their tradition.

Those who retain the need for such assurance will not privately "despise most of their fellow citizens" for not sharing their moral views, as Rorty intimates. Nor will they cooperate with them only "for pragmatic, rather than moral reasons."[47] In a Rawlsian liberal society, religion and philosophy give their adherents moral and not just pragmatic reasons to be good citizens. Moreover, comprehensive moral views in a Rawlsian liberal society will overlap on basic political values and ideals. This overlap provides citizens some moral common ground, and thus some reason not to "despise" one another. The citizens of such a society will not share all moral views, but they can regard one another as cooperating in the pursuit of the same basic political values.

Rorty professes a concern with the "sort of culture [that] might lie at the end of the road we liberal intellectuals have been travelling since the Enlightenment."[48] That culture, he thinks, would be one publicly disenchanted with religion, metaphysics, and ideology. It would also be one in which the few citizens who retain the metaphysical urge suffer a powerful tension between their public and their private lives,[49] between publicly cooperating with and privately despising their fellow citizens. Rorty hails Rawls's recent work because he thinks he finds there a sketch of the largely disenchanted culture that lies at the journey's end. But Rorty's interpretation is, I believe, mistaken. Rawls would lead us down another fork to a another destination. He would have us part company with Rorty, for he holds out the possibility of ending our journey at a very different liberal culture than Rorty envisions.

V

What, then, are we to make of Hampton's charge that Rawls has made political philosophy into practical politics? And what are we to make of Rorty's hope that Rawls has accorded democracy priority over philosophy? To make anything at all of them, we must appreciate the division of political philosophy into political theory and comprehensive public philosophy.[50]

Comprehensive public philosophy may be political in some respects. Those who engage in it may do so for political reasons, trying to build an overlapping consensus on justice as fairness because they think it will make society more peaceful and stable. But the motives for engaging in comprehensive public philosophy need not be entirely political, as I have argued. A philosopher or theologian may try to convince others in his or her tradition to accept justice as fairness because she or he is convinced that Rawls's principles are just, given his or her own commitment to democratic values and ideals. He or she might believe that the society in which he or she lives would be more just were justice as fairness widely accepted.

The comprehensive public philosopher's motives, therefore, need not be entirely or at all political.

Neither need his or her arguments be political. The philosopher can work within moral and religious traditions, appealing to their views of human nature, the value of human life, human equality, the nature of moral obligation, and the importance of justice. She or he can appeal to them by trying to find a moral basis for justice as fairness within a tradition or by trying to bring the two into reflective equilibrium. If the comprehensive public philosopher is a Kantian or a utilitarian, the arguments will be straightforwardly philosophical. If he or she is a moral theologian, they may not fall squarely within the bounds of philosophical argument as it is usually conceived. But some of the theological arguments will concern philosophical problems: the purposes of political authority and the demands of distributive justice, for example. And Rorty, who shows no reluctance to assimilate theology to philosophy,[51] would reckon them philosophical, or at least "ideological," rather than political.

Now consider political theory. Political theory as Rawls practices it is a subject that combines philosophy with politics, as well as with political history and political sociology. Note first that the very decision to engage in political theory is in large part a political decision.

"The aims of political philosophy," Rawls writes in a much-noted and -quoted passage, "depend on the society it addresses."[52] A political philosopher's choice of aims depends upon his or her political judgment about the needs and shortcomings of the society for which he or she intends the work.

Some political thinkers judge their society to be primarily in need of social criticism. They write political philosophy accordingly; here utopian thought, beginning with More, comes most readily to mind. Others may judge that the greatest service a political philosopher can render is the recovery or revitalization of some aspect of the history of political thought.[53] Still others, like Locke, will judge their society in greatest need of a theory of political legitimacy and justified rebellion.

The decision to perfect the conception of justice inherited from the contract tradition is a similarly political judgment. Rawls judged that the society he addressed stood in need of "an alternative systematic account of justice that is superior . . . to the dominant utilitarianism of the tradition."[54] And, we might add, to the dominant utilitarianism of economic thought and of judicial and bureaucratic practice. He judged such an account necessary to provide a more adequate moral basis for political consensus than utilitarian or natural rights views. And he judged such a consensus necessary to overcome long-standing political controversies generated by the conflicting claims of liberty and equality.[55] Rawls's desire to achieve a morally based consensus, and thus to engage in political theory, was in part a political motive.

But Rawls's political theory is also a historical and sociological enterprise. It draws on texts, like those of Locke, Rousseau, and Kant, and ideas, like that of the social contract, central to the tradition of liberal thought. It derives its reasonability in part from its explicitly locating itself in that intellectual and political tradition. Practicing political theory demands recognition of the myriad ways in which these ideas and texts have shaped liberal political culture, the self-conceptions of citizens in liberal democracies, and the terms of political debate. Historical and sociological sensitivity is needed to isolate the basic ideas and values around which consensus can coalesce once they are further specified and combined.

Finally, Rawls says that what he calls "philosophical inclination" is an "essential" motive for doing moral theory. If moral theory is left to social theorists or psychologists, who are "not prompted by philosophical inclination to pursue moral theory," then, he says, "the inquiry will have the wrong focus."[56] What holds of moral theory generally presumably holds of political theory: political theory would have the wrong focus if not motivated in part by philosophical inclination. Political theory is, therefore, a properly philosophical task, for it requires an inclination to pursue traditionally philosophical questions. To see this, recall that one of the questions definitive of political philosophy, at least since Rousseau, is that of what a democratic regime would be like under realistically favorable circumstances.[57] Rawls, in specifying a conception of justice for such a society, provides part of the answer to Rousseau's question. His interest in providing such a conception is therefore itself a philosophical inclination.

Moreover, Rawls's attempt is focused differently than would be a social theorist's or a psychologist's attempt to provide a conception of justice. Rawls's attempt is not focused, for example, on providing a conception that would be judged most stable in light of the findings of psychology, equilibrium theory, or theories of social choice. He is interested, rather, in the question: what conception of justice is the most appropriate moral conception for a liberal democracy? Questions of psychology and social theory are taken up, but only insofar as they help to answer that question. And while the decision to develop a moral conception of justice may have been in large part a political one, that decision, once made, required Rawls to address fundamental philosophical problems about the relationship between the right and the good and about the reconciliation of liberty and equality.

Politics thus stands in a quite complicated relationship to political theory. It stands in a similarly complicated relationship to comprehensive public philosophy. The relationship between politics and political philosophy as Rawls conceives it is even more complex, for political philosophy includes both political theory and comprehensive public philosophy. The complicated nature of these relationships leads me to suggest that the question of whether Rawls has unduly politicized political philosophy is wrongly posed and should be rejected. It is a question premised on sharp but misbegotten distinctions between politics and philosophy, and between political argument and philosophical argument.

In the past two decades, historians of political thought have become increasingly suspicious of these sharp distinctions, arguing that an attempt to impose them on great political philosophers of the past is systematically misleading. Richard Ashcraft, for example, has shown how much we can learn about John Locke's political philosophy by studying its actual and foreseen political impact and by examining the political decisions Locke made in resolving to write and publish the Treatises. Detailed study of this kind shows how difficult it is to distinguish the political from the philosophical in his work. It also shows how much of Locke's thought we would misunderstand if our primary interest were in sorting his works into preconceived categories.[58]

It is similarly misleading to approach Rawls's work with such interests and categories in mind. Surely he is not just engaged in practical politics. But neither is it helpful to read him as attempting to answer timeless questions about the nature of justice. He is a philosopher whose philosophical project was shaped by political, historical, and sociological judgments about the society he addresses. His own work in political theory leaves ample room, and, indeed, assumes the subsequent metaphysical and theological arguments of others. Political theory as Rawls practices it may be done without metaphysics, but political philosophy as he conceives it need not be.

I have tried to show that Rawls has not unduly politicized political philosophy, any more than did Hobbes, Locke, and Mill; he has merely divided its labor. I have tried to show, too, that we understand better the work of individual thinkers such as Rawls and the enterprise of political philosophy generally if we attend to the intellectual and political tasks that political philosophers set for themselves.

Notes

Thanks to Elizabeth Anderson, Daniel Brudney, Barbara Herman, and Greg Kavka for comments on an early draft of this paper, and to Joshua Cohen, Neil Delaney, Alasdair MacIntyre, David O'Connor, and Richard Rorty for comments on a recent one.

1. John Rawls, "Justice as Fairness: Political Not Metaphysical," *Philosophy and Public Affairs*, 14 (1985): 223–51.
2. John Rawls, *A Theory of Justice* (Harvard University Press, 1971), 16.
3. Rawls, "Political Not Metaphysical," 225.

4. Joseph Raz, "Facing Diversity: The Case for Epistemic Abstinence," *Philosophy and Public Affairs*, 19 (1990): 8.
5. Rawls, "Political Not Metaphysical," 230.
6. Ibid., 230: "That is, [justice as fairness] presents itself not as a conception of justice that is true, but as one that can serve as a basis of informed and willing political agreement between citizens viewed as free and equal persons."
7. Ibid.
8. John Rawls, "The Idea of an Overlapping Consensus," *Oxford Journal of Legal Studies*, 7 (1987): 7–8.
9. Rawls, "The Idea of an Overlapping Consensus," 9–10.
10. Jean Hampton, "Should Political Philosophy Be Done without Metaphysics?" Ethics, 99 (1989), 791–814, 799ff. [Reprinted as the eighth essay in this collection.]
11. Richard Rorty, "The Priority of Democracy to Philosophy," in *The Virginia Statute for Religious Freedom*, eds. Peterson and Vaughan (Cambridge University Press, 1988), 260.
12. Hampton, "Should Political Philosophy Be Done without Metaphysics?," 807.
13. Patrick Neal, "Justice as Fairness: Political or Metaphysical?" *Political Theory*, 18 (1990): 46.
14. Rorty, "The Priority of Democracy to Philosophy," 260.
15. Cf. Ibid., 271ff.
16. Kurt Baier, "Justice and the Aims of Political Philosophy," *Ethics*, 99 (1989): 784.
17. Raz, "Facing Diversity: The Case for Epistemic Abstinence," 15.
18. Baier, "Justice and the Aims of Political Philosophy," 780–81; Hampton, "Should Political Philosophy Be Done without Metaphysics?," 812ff.
19. For criticism of Rorty's distinction, see Richard J. Bernstein, "One Step Forward, Two Steps Backward: Richard Rorty on Liberal Democracy and Philosophy," *Political Theory*, 15 (1987): 538–63.
20. John Rawls, "The Independence of Moral Theory," *Proceedings and Addresses of the American Philosophical Association*, 48 (1975): 5. Rawls's distinction between moral theory and moral philosophy has its origins in the division of moral philosophy Rawls found in Sidgwick. On the distinction in Sidgwick and Rawls's modifications of it, see John Rawls, "Kantian Constructivism in Moral Theory," *Journal of Philosophy*, 77 (1980): 554–56. Implicit in my argument is that Rawls's own attempts to secure but limited justification of justice as fairness and his refusal to assert its truth are natural consequences of the views expressed in "The Independence of Moral Theory." That paper was published just four years after *A Theory of Justice*. This suggests that Rawls's recent views are not the startling departure from earlier work that many have thought. I will not try, however, to substantiate this suggestion here.
21. Rawls, "The Independence of Moral Theory," 22: "All the moral conceptions in the tradition of moral philosophy must be continually renewed

. . . In this endeavor the aim of those most attracted to a particular view should not be to confute but to perfect."
22. Rawls, "Political Not Metaphysical," 226ff.
23. Rawls, *Theory*, viii.
24. Rawls, *Theory*, 20. My thoughts about political values and political guidance have been much advanced by Joshua Cohen's meticulous paper, "Democratic Equality," *Ethics*, 99 (1989): 727–51. I am grateful to Prof. Cohen for making available to me the paper's longer unpublished version.
25. Note that in "Political Not Metaphysical," 236, note 19, Rawls calls justice as fairness an "ideal-based view." I intend the discussion of moral ideals as specifications of basic ideas to help explain this remark.
26. Rawls, *Theory*, 477.
27. Rawls, "The Idea of an Overlapping Consensus," 25.
28. Rawls, "The Independence of Moral Theory," 7: "Since the history of moral philosophy shows that the notion of moral truth is problematical, we can suspend consideration of it until we have a deeper understanding of moral conceptions. But one thing is certain: people profess and appear to be influenced by moral conceptions. These conceptions themselves can be made the focus of study; so provisionally we may bracket the problem of moral truth and turn to moral theory."
29. Rorty, "The Priority of Democracy to Philosophy," 270.
30. Rawls, "The Independence of Moral Theory," 9–10.
31. Hampton, "Should Political Philosophy Be Done without Metaphysics?," 798.
32. Hampton, "Should Political Philosophy Be Done without Metaphysics?," 806-7.
33. Rawls, "The Idea of an Overlapping Consensus," 13. The term "comprehensive moral view" is used in deference to Rawls's distinction between moral views framed for a particular subject, like the basic structure of society, and those of more comprehensive scope that specify what is valuable in human life, ideals of character, etc.; see Ibid., 3, note 4.
34. Ibid., 11, 18.
35. John Courtney Murray, S.J., "The Problem of State Religion," *Theological Studies*, 12 (1952): 155–78; see 165 for a concise statement.
36. John Courtney Murray, S.J. "Freedom of Religion: I. The Ethical Problem," *Theological Studies*, 6 (1945): 229–86, 241.
37. Ibid., 239–41.
38. Rawls, "The Idea of an Overlapping Consensus," 19.
39. See, for example, Harlan Beckley, "A Christian Affirmation of Rawls' Idea of Justice as Fairness," *Journal of Religious Ethics*, 13 (1985): 210–42; 14 (1986): 229–46.
40. Rawls, "The Idea of an Overlapping Consensus," 23.
41. Consider a theological example. In their pastoral letter "Economic Justice for All" (USCC, 1986), the U.S. Roman Catholic bishops wrote that "Distributive justice requires that the allocation of income, wealth and power in society be evaluated in light of its effects on persons whose basic material

needs are unmet" (paragraph 70), and that "the investment of wealth, talent and energy should be specially directed to benefit those who are poor or economically insecure" (paragraph 92). These norms, the bishops claim, are part of Catholic moral tradition. They are said to be implicit in the Bible's injunctions to be just toward the poor (paragraph 68) and in official church documents (paragraph 70).

A society the basic structure of which conformed to the Difference Principle would, I presume, satisfy these two norms. A theologian trying to secure Catholic acceptance of justice as fairness could point this out. She could cite her commitment to the bishops' moral teaching, rather than her interest in peace and stability, as her motive for trying to build a consensus on justice as fairness.

42. Admittedly, the phrase "comprehensive public philosophy" is somewhat unfamiliar. And other terms may seem better to fit the enterprise in which, for example, utilitarian political thinkers have traditionally been engaged. The phrase does have two advantages, however. First, the adjective "comprehensive" marks the fact that those who take as theirs this second task are working within and avail themselves of the resources of comprehensive moral conceptions. Second, the phrase "public philosophy," which it modifies, resonates with the term "public theology," a label that some moral theologians have applied to the project of drawing out the political implications of their theology. This resonance serves to remind us that theologians, as well as philosophers, will have to perform the second task if an overlapping consensus on justice as fairness is to be secured. The phrase "public philosophy" was originally Walter Lippman's. See his *The Public Philosophy* (Little, Brown, 1955). For this use of the phrase "public theology", see Richard McBrien, *Caesar's Coin* (Macmillan, 1987), 238, note 34.

43. All references in this paragraph are to Rorty, "The Priority of Democracy to Philosophy," 264.

44. Richard Rorty, *Contingency, Irony and Solidarity* (Cambridge University Press, 1989), 85–87. Rorty's conjecture about the demise of philosophy under the pressure of a liberal culture is reminiscent of Thomas Jefferson's prediction about the demise of religion: "I trust there is not a young man now living in the United States who will not die a Unitarian." Jefferson made this prediction in 1822; subsequent events have, of course, shown him wrong. Jefferson's remark is quoted by Stephen Macedo in *Liberal Virtues* (Oxford University Press, 1990), 73.

45. For an accessible and convincing treatment, see Garry Wills, *Under God* (Simon and Schuster, 1990).

46. Rawls, "Political Not Metaphysical," 230.

47. Rorty, "The Priority of Democracy to Philosophy," 270.

48. Richard Rorty, "Thugs and Theorists: A Reply to Bernstein," *Political Theory*, 15 (1987): 578, note 25.

49. Rorty, *Contingency, Irony and Solidarity*, 120.

50. After completing this essay, I came upon Stephen Macedo, "The Politics of Justification," *Political Theory*, 18 (1990), 280–304. Macedo, too, notes

that Rawls divides the labor of justification (see 290ff). He criticizes Rawls's conception of justification as unrealistic, saying "[a] more realistic model of justification would allow, in effect, that participants' personal moral convictions are engaged as each feature of the political view is constructed" (290). Macedo's arguments require far more attention than I can give them here; I mention only one point in response. Successfully arguing that a conception of justification is unrealistic requires successful criticism of the moral epistemology that underlies it. Rawls's moral epistemology is Kantian. Kant thought that moral interest in the categorical imperative is best elicited by conceiving both of agents realizing their autonomy by acting from it and of the imperative as supremely regulative of a realm of autonomous citizens. Rawls thinks that moral interest in his two principles is best elicited by conceiving both of citizens whose sense of justice is informed by the principles and of the principles as supremely regulative of a well-ordered society of just citizens. But eliciting an interest in the principles in this way requires laying out the political construction as a whole rather than presenting it to citizens piece by piece. To sustain his thesis that Rawlsian justification is unrealistic, Macedo must provide some argument against Rawls's Kantian views about how best to elicit moral interest in principles of justice.

51. Rorty, "Priority of Democracy," 264.

52. Rawls, "The Idea of an Overlapping Consensus," 1.

53. Consider Quentin Skinner's work on the civic republican tradition; Richard Ashcraft's recent work on Mill is similarly motivated. For the practical import of the history of political thought, see Ashcraft, "Whose Problem? Whose Ideology? A Reply to My Critics," *Journal of Politics*, 42 (1980): 716–21, 720. For Ashcraft's work on Mill, see "Class Conflict and Constitutionalism in J. S. Mill's Thought," in *Liberalism and the Moral Life*, ed. Nancy Rosenblum (Harvard University Press, 1989), 105-26.

54. Rawls, *Theory*, 8.

55. Cf. Rawls, "Political Not Metaphysical," 226ff.

56. References in this sentence and the last are to Rawls, "The Independence of Moral Theory," 22.

57. I owe this point to John Rawls.

58. For Ashcraft's work on Locke, see his *Revolutionary Politics and Locke's "Two Treatises of Government"* (Princeton, N.J.: Princeton University Press, 1986). For his methodological arguments, see Ibid., Introduction. For his criticism of a misguided attempt to separate Locke's works into the philosophical and the nonphilosophical, see his "Political Theory and the Problem of Ideology," *Journal of Politics*, 42 (1980): 687–705, especially 693, note 23.

10

A Hobbesian Foundation for Welfare Rights

Sheldon Wein

Hobbes was a conservative and Hobbes's political theory, Hobbesian contractarianism, has most frequently been endorsed by political conservatives. However, in recent years, Hobbes's approach to political philosophy has been used to defend key elements of liberalism. This essay reviews the attempts to "liberalize" the Hobbesian approach and continues the project by developing a Hobbesian argument for one key part of liberalism, the commitment to welfare rights.

Liberalism, in the sense I will be using the term, is a political position that consists of four key elements. At the theoretical level, liberals hold that reasons for action are not limited to those based on self-interest and that governments must respect the neutrality principle, according to which government programs should be chosen in a way that does not favor particular conceptions of the good life.[1] At the practical level, contemporary liberals have a strong commitment to civil rights and, on the issue of distributive justice, contemporary liberals are firmly committed to the welfare state.[2]

Utilitarianism of some form or other has long seemed the best hope for defending the four key elements of liberalism. However, utilitarianism faces well-known problems and, consequently, some philosophers have turned to contractarian thought as a possible philosophic foundation for liberalism. And, in John Rawls's *A Theory of Justice*, a work which takes the contractarian insights of Rousseau and Kant and develops them in the tradition of American pragmatism, those liberals who seek a political philosophy to order and defend their views have an attractive contractarian alternative to utilitarianism.[3]

But the other major type of contractarianism, Hobbesian contractarianism, seems to have little to offer the liberal. In part, this is due to the fact that Hobbes, who rejects all four of the elements constitutive of liberalism, so eagerly embraces conservatism. Hobbes argues for an egoistic conception of rationality, according to which all our reasons are necessarily self-interested reasons. And Hobbes rejects the notion that governments should be neutral between various conceptions of the good life, arguing instead that governments ought to act in ways that best preserve public stability and safety, even when so doing conflicts with other values. In pursuing public stability and safety, governments need make no effort to recognize, let alone to promote and protect, any of the civil rights liberals cherish so deeply. Finally, Hobbes does not even give the idea of welfare rights serious enough consideration to bother rejecting them. Such liberal foolishness never occurs to him.

But, of course, it does not follow from the fact that Hobbes was no liberal that Hobbesian political thought does not have liberal elements. And, as recent scholarship has shown, Hobbesian political theory can be employed to support and defend positions much more liberal than those accepted by Hobbes.[4] While Hobbesian contractarianism cannot easily be used to defend the idea that rational individuals should take some interest in the interests of others, it can be used to support a version of the neutrality principle and some of the civil rights liberals recognize.[5] But it is widely thought that Hobbesian contractarianism cannot be used to defend the liberal economic program because Hobbesian theory argues for a state where the role of government is limited to far less in the way of egalitarian redistribution than the welfare measures liberals wish to endorse. Thus, the leading contemporary advocates of Hobbesian contractarianism, David Gauthier and Jan Narveson, both reject the idea that welfare rights follow from Hobbesian starting points.[6]

The Logical Structure of Hobbesian Contractarianism

All contractarian theories hold that the basic principles of justice are those principles that, when adhered to by all, lead to each person's being better off than he or she would be without the acceptance of those principles. To aid in the formulation of the principles which have this property, the contract, or bargaining game, is employed. An initial choice situation, often referred to as the "state of nature," is postulated, in which rational individuals, each of whom seeks to maximize his or her own utility and, in so doing, recognizes no social rules that might constrain that pursuit, are asked what set of principles each will accept, providing that others accept those principles also. The agreed-upon principles are the basic principles of justice. Thus, every contractarian theory consists of two parts. First, there is the specification of the initial choice situation, the description of the state of nature, from which the basic principles governing social interaction are to be chosen. Second, there is the defense and employment of particular decision-theoretic principles of rational choice to derive principles acceptable to rational maximizers bargaining from the initial choice situation.[7]

The Hobbesian contractarian holds that the great strength of contractarianism is that it offers the potential of uniting rationality with morality—it offers us the hope of producing amoral reasons for convincing individuals to become moral persons. This is because, by stipulation, the principles agreed upon in the precontract situation are in the individual amoral interest of each and, therefore, it is rational for each to accept them. Since the accepted principles are moral principles, contractarianism shows that it is (amorally) rational to be, or become, moral. Thus, the Hobbesian contractarian holds that the hope of uniting morality with rationality in this rigorous way is lost if one imports moral considerations into the solution to the specification problem. Thus, he or she rejects the social contractarianism of Rawls, who uses moral considerations—fairness—as a guide in specifying the initial choice situation.[8] The Hobbesian claim is that if morality is to be truly grounded on rationality, one cannot slip moral considerations into the precontract situation and then, from this "morally tainted" state of nature, use rationality to derive principles of justice.

But if moral considerations are not to guide the Hobbesian contractarian in specifying the initial choice situation, how is he or she to determine which precontract situation is the one from which to begin in deriving the basic principles of justice? The Hobbesian answer is that rationality alone must be used to determine the proper description of the state of nature. I said above that all contractarian theories hold that the principles of justice are those that it is rational for each to accept in some precontract situation. What is distinctive about Hobbesian contractarianism is that it holds that rationality must be used not only to derive principles of justice once the initial choice situation has been properly characterized, but also to guide one in specifying the position from which the principles of justice are to be derived. It must be rational to contract *into* civil society from the state of nature; and the state of nature must be specified so that it is rational to begin bargaining *from* that position.

Rawls holds that if we are to be fair, the initial choice situation must be specified in a manner such that natural attributes do not influence the outcome of the bargaining. To ensure fairness, Rawls adopts an initial choice situation—which he refers to as the original position—that has a veil of ignorance preventing the contractors from knowing their natural attributes. The original position may represent the contractors in a way that is fair to each. But fairness is nothing to the Hobbesian; for him or her, rationality is all that counts. And it would be irrational for those well endowed with natural attributes to begin bargaining from a position like Rawls's original position. It would be irrational for the strong to agree to begin bargaining from any position that deprived them of the full use of their biggest bargaining chip—their natural attributes. Rationality, therefore, requires that the Hobbesian represent the contractors as having all their natural attributes in the initial choice situation. And, of course, this is just what Hobbes does. His solution to the specification problem represents the contractors (with their natural attributes) just as they are. Hobbesian contractarianism, then, holds that rationality requires that each contractor be represented as accurately as possible, and, indeed, that the world's nonhuman resources be represented as accurately as possible. Thus, a Hobbesian argument for welfare rights must begin by representing the contractors, together with their natural attributes, in a way that accurately reflects the extent of those attributes.

Natural attributes are of many sorts, but here I want to focus on two kinds of natural attributes, which I will call productive talents and destructive talents. Productive talents enable one to produce utilities for oneself and/or others, and destructive talents enable one to produce disutility. Obviously, it is to each contractor's advantage to have greater talents of both types when he or she bargains with his or her fellows. Productive talents give their owners advantages because others will be more willing to make contractual concessions in order to have someone with such talents be a member of their civil society.[9] Destructive talents also give their owner a bargaining advantage because it is not rational for someone with great destructive powers to forego those powers before the bargaining begins. Rather, he or she will want to use the threat of those powers to obtain the best possible contract. Furthermore, the fact of universal threat motivates the contractors to agree to abandon the state of nature and contract into civil society. As Hobbes noted, in the state of nature, even the weakest can kill the strongest and it is this threat that ensures that everyone has a reason to abandon the anarchy of the state of nature and accept the moral and political constraints of civil society.

For our purposes, a Hobbesian theory will count as liberal just to the extent that the contract agreed upon by the Hobbesian rational maximizers in the Hobbesian state of nature captures key elements of liberalism. We count Hobbes as a conservative because the contract his contractors agreed to was, in its content, extremely conservative. In this paper, I am concerned only to derive a Hobbesian contract that includes one part of the liberal political program, welfare rights. My task then is to describe an initial choice situation that is Hobbesian in character and to show that, from that initial choice situation, Hobbesian rational agents would choose principles of justice that, when implemented in contemporary society, require governments to adopt the standard liberal catalogue of welfare measures.

Hobbes's Contractarian Theory

Hobbes's state of nature has the following characteristics:

1. There are no social rules, no morality, no government, and no laws.
2. Each individual is a rational maximizer concerned only to further his or her own interests.
3. Each individual has ordinary rational beliefs about his or her own and other people's aspirations, abilities, and situation. The individuals in the state of nature do not suffer from a Rawlsian veil of ignorance, which fogs their vision. Nor is their vision artificially clarified so that they become ideal observers.
4. The conditions of justice obtain. That is, the contractors know that substantial utilities can be gained if and only if they are able to engage in cooperative interaction.[10]
5. Individuals are in a prisoner's dilemma with respect to each other: noncooperation dominates cooperation for each contractor.[11]
6. Productive talents are distributed unevenly, that is, roughly as they are in the world today. Some are better than others at producing utilities for themselves and others.
7. Destructive talents are also distributed unevenly. However, everyone has destructive talents sufficient for the weakest to kill even the strongest.
8. The level of technology available is roughly that of seventeenth-century Europe.
9. Each individual has an overriding desire to preserve his or her

own life and, consequently, favors rational decision rules—such as Rawls's maximin rule or Gregory Kavka's disaster avoidance principle—which reflect his or her adversity to risk.[12]

10. Consequently, in Hobbes's evocative phrases, the state of nature is a war of all against all and life is solitary, poor, nasty, brutish, and short.

Hobbes argues that from such an initial choice situation, the contractors will agree to extremely authoritarian and conservative political arrangements. I cannot here enter into the debate about the extent to which Hobbes's political positions follow from the state of nature he describes.[13]

An Alternative Hobbesian State of Nature

It is important to note that the first five characteristics are the only ones essential to the Hobbesian contractarian theory; points six through nine are empirical claims. These empirical claims have a substantial effect on the content of the contract it is rational to agree upon. The following thought experiment makes this perfectly clear.

Suppose that we alter conditions seven and eight in the following way. Instead of supposing that destructive powers are limited in the way Hobbes says they are, suppose that each individual has an unalienable power to kill everyone. Suppose further that this power is one that it is quite easy to exercise, in the sense that it does not take one who wishes to put it to work much planning or effort to carry out mass destruction. Now, let us also alter condition nine so that the contractors in this new Hobbesian state of nature are not as risk averse as Hobbes's contractors are. Indeed, let us suppose that they are risk neutral and employ the maximize expected utility principle as their rational decision rule.[14] As we will see, altering condition nine in this way makes it more difficult to develop a Hobbesian argument for welfare rights. Consequently, if the argument goes through for risk neutral, rational individuals, the argument will also apply to those who are risk averse.

The revised state of nature outlined above shares the essential characteristics of Hobbes's initial choice situation. The significant alteration is that in this choice situation, the level of technology available to the contractors has changed: for Hobbes's "even the weakest can kill the strongest" I have substituted "even the weakest can kill all." Since the level of technology available at any given time and how vulnerable it makes each contractor is clearly a contingent matter, altering that feature of the initial choice situation does not change the essential Hobbesian character of the state of nature. I now turn to the question of what principles of justice Hobbesian contractors would agree to when bargaining from this altered state of nature. I will not argue that Hobbesian contractors in the twentieth century should bargain from my state of nature. I only want to show that if they did, they would adopt principles of justice much more liberal than those favored by Hobbes. Showing that much will establish that Hobbesian contractarianism is not essentially opposed to liberalism. I will later address the question of the extent to which our circumstances mimic those I have outlined, as opposed to those Hobbes favored.

A Hobbesian Derivation of Welfare Rights

Hobbesian contractors in the initial choice situation specified above would, I believe, choose very liberal principles of distributive justice. Indeed, they would choose as their principle of distributive justice something very much like Rawls's second principle of justice, the difference principle. Rawls's difference principle holds that society is to adopt those institutional arrangements that will distribute goods and services equally unless it can develop and maintain arrangements that are Pareto superior to an egalitarian distribution.[15] Put another way, a society may justly adopt institutional arrangements that allow for inequalities in the distribution of wealth if such inequalities are beneficial to the worst-off group. A society that adopts the difference principle as its principle of distributive justice will implement the economic program advocated by contemporary liberals. That is to say, they will arrange society's economic activities so that there is a free market coupled with a redistributive tax system, which funds various welfare programs for those whose talents and abilities are not rewarded by market arrangements. They will, in short, be welfare-state liberals, for the simple reason that no alternative set of economic arrangements has been developed that in practice come as close to fulfilling the requirements of the difference principle. Thus, if I am able to show that Hobbesian contractors will choose the difference principle as their principle of distributive justice, I will have succeeded in showing that they will be welfare-state liberals.

When Rawls argues that rational maximizers in his initial choice situation, the original position, would choose the difference principle as their principle of distributive justice, he is able to use individual choice theory to argue that his principles of justice are the most rational choice. However, Hobbesian contractors, unlike Rawls's, are not confronted with a problem in individual rational choice theory. Rather, they are confronted with a problem of strategic rationality and hence must use game theory to solve their problem.

I begin with some general considerations that suggest that Hobbesian contractors in the state of nature outlined above would gravitate toward the difference principle as their principle of distributive justice and I then argue that the difference principle is preferable to other initially attractive alternatives. First, the state of nature outlined above has the effect of granting those who expect that they will be among the worst off in civil society a veto on which principles of justice are adopted.[16] Since they know that they will do better under the difference principles than under other principles of distributive justice, it would be rational for them to propose the difference principle when bargaining for principles of distributive justice. Given the vast destructive powers we have granted individuals in the state of nature, everyone realizes that the social contract that is eventually adopted must be universally accepted. No one can be left out of the contract, no obstinate contractors can be told simply to rot in the state of nature while the others go on to form their civil society, for, by hypothesis, life is barely worth living in the state of nature and anyone who finds it not worth living has the power to kill everyone. All the contractors—both those who are well endowed with natural attributes and those who are likely to be among the worst-off group in any civil society—realize this and, consequently, the threat held by the worst off becomes very important.

In addition, those who can reasonably expect to do well in civil society (and hence will do well in a civil society governed by the difference principle) will lose much more than others if the contracting fails to produce the principles of justice needed to ensure sufficient cooperation for them to be able to utilize efficiently their productive talents in a civil society. In the Hobbesian way of looking at things, failure to agree on principles of justice results in remaining in the state of nature. Those who will do well in a society of moral cooperators realize that only cooperative efforts can lead to a change from the miserable conditions of the state of nature to circumstances in which the many delights available to talented individuals in a liberal society are at their disposal. The civil get all the efforts and cooperative artifices of civil society acting effectively in its massive way to amplify their work and to help them achieve their ends. Civilization and moral order are effective machines for the exponential increase in their happiness. They have much to lose and, consequently, will be willing to bend quite far to obtain the benefits that they can get only if some contract is found agreeable to all.

Furthermore, those contractors who are uncertain about where they will end up (and it is not easy to tell in advance how well one will do in a society with advanced technology) will be tempted to accept the difference principle on the basis of Rawls's arguments about the rationality of playing it safe when making decisions under conditions of great uncertainty.[17]

Finally, the difference principle will be attractive to the contractors because, once they have left the state of nature and formed a civil society, the principle provides a particularly powerful argument to encourage the worst off to continue supporting their cooperative venture rather than wrecking it (as we are supposing they could). The argument is simply that on no other principle of justice will the worst off group do any better. Thus, it will be clear even to those who fare relatively badly in civil society that everything that can be done for them is being done. The worst off can then view social arrangements as the best available attempt to secure their continued cooperation. That more is not done for them is not out of any failure to realize that justice requires structuring society to benefit the worst-off group, but simply from the fact that nothing more can be done. With the adoption of the difference principle, society chooses to view the worst off as unfortunate persons for whom we should do everything possible, rather than as unworthy individuals who do not deserve more. Thus, the worst off have no basis for complaint against other members of society.[18]

Not only do the considerations above argue for adoption of the difference principle, but the difference principle is a more rational choice for our Hobbesian contractors than are alternative principles of justice. Let us begin with utilitarianism. I will assume that the contractors would prefer some form of average utilitarianism to any form of classical utilitarianism. This is because the contractors, being rational maximizers, have no interest in simply increasing the total amount of happiness in the universe. Rather, each is interested solely in increasing his or her own happiness. Since each realizes that accepting classical utilitarianism could lead to the adoption of policies that would increase the total utility while lowering the average (and, hence, increasing the probability that he or she would be worse off), each prefers average to classical utilitarianism. But is average utilitarianism a more or a less rational choice than the difference principle? The argument for average utilitarianism is that, unless one is likely to be among the worst off, one will likely do better under average utilitarianism (or so it would seem) than under the difference principle. After all, the expected utility of a randomly selected contractor will be greater under average utilitarianism than under any other principle. This is a strong argument for average utilitarianism.

However, the fact that utilitarianism and the difference principle will both recommend similar policies in civil society reveals another important reason for selecting the difference principle. If each contractor has the power to destroy all, then it is in the interest of every contractor to ensure that no one ever has an expected utility level below zero. The rational thing to do when one's expected utility falls below zero with little prospect of it rising is to commit suicide. In the case we are discussing, a suicidal person just might do this by killing everyone. So, a utilitarian society will adopt policies that ensure that the expected utility level of each remains above this minimum level. Of course, the utilitarian society, realizing that particular political programs do not always have their intended effect, will allow for a substantial margin of error to ensure that no one's expected utility level falls to the point where disaster results. In the circumstances we are considering, utilitarianism dictates that a great deal of effort be made to ensure that the worst off are fairly well off. The difference principle makes the worst off as well off as possible, which, in these circumstances is just what is wanted.

Since the contractors realize this, they will opt for the difference principle on the following grounds. Both the difference principle and utilitarianism recommend that society take special steps to ensure that those worst off are taken care of. The difference principle recommends this straight out. But average utilitarianism recommends this only on the basis of an intermediate argument that must be made and accepted within the politics of civil society. Error about the argument or its force might occur and, if so, disaster would ensue. Better to choose the difference principle now (while we are all rational) than leave it to later for the politicians in civil society to discover that utilitarianism demands that in practice we follow the difference principle. Consequently, the contractors will prefer the difference principle to utilitarianism.

The difference principle will also be preferable to any conception of equality of welfare—that is, to any conception that holds that goods and services should be distributed so that, so far as is practicable, the welfare of each member of society is equal. Under the difference principle, each person, even the worst off, is as well off as, or better off than, he or she would be under equality of welfare.

I conclude that contractors in my Hobbesian state of nature will prefer the difference principle to other popular liberal or egalitarian principles of distributive justice. I turn now to the question of whether they would choose the difference principle rather than more standard Hobbesian principles of distributive justice. So as not to have my argument rest on any controversial economic assumptions, I will assume, *arguendo*, that, in theory, laissez-faire capitalism provides for Pareto optimal outcomes and that, in practice, laissez-faire economic policies result in stronger economies producing more overall wealth than any other social arrangement.

Still, I hold that the contractors, each being a rational maximizer of his or her own utility, will each prefer welfare-state liberalism to laissez-faire capitalism. The reasoning here is analogous to that which led the contractors to select the difference principle over average utilitarianism. Each contractor recognizes that every other contractor has sufficient power to wreck the entire cooperative enterprise we call civil society. He or she thus realizes that it is vital that each person, regardless of what value the laissez-faire capitalist market puts on him or her, must be granted sufficient resources to ensure that he or she is able to lead a life that, from the point of view of the person living that life, is rich and rewarding. The difference principle and the welfare-state liberalism it leads to, do this in a way that is far superior to any other system yet discovered. Thus, any rational individual who is concerned, as he or she must be, with the survival of civil society will choose that alternative. I conclude, then, that rational contractors in the Hobbesian state of nature outlined above would choose the difference principle as their principle of distributive justice. Since the difference principle recommends the standard liberal program of welfare rights, I have shown that Hobbesian contractarianism supports liberal economic policies in the special circumstances outlined above.

Relevance of the Hobbesian Defense of Liberalism

We have seen that there are circumstances under which a Hobbesian should adopt a liberal position of distributive justice, cases where the Hobbesian should be a welfare-state liberal. But, it hardly follows from the fact that particular liberal programs are the rational choice for a Hobbesian in certain imaginary—and somewhat far-fetched—circumstances that a contemporary Hobbesian ought to embrace contemporary liberal attitudes toward welfare rights. Just as the Hobbesian rejects Rawls's argument for the difference principle because it is based on a "morally tainted" original choice position, he or she might reject my argument for the difference principle because it is based on a "science-fiction tainted" state of nature. And, he or she would be right to do this. But, as I observed above, the Hobbesian is committed to using rationality to determine the initial bargaining position.

And I certainly grant that the circumstances of those of us living today are not those used to frame the state of nature outlined above, nor are our circumstances like those that Hobbes uses to frame his state of nature. A lot has changed in the interval between the publication of the *Leviathan* and the arrival of the last decade in the nineteen hundreds. And one of the most striking changes has been the great technological advances, advances that show all signs of continuing.

The logical structure of Hobbesian political philosophy dictates that the Hobbesian must alter his or her account of the original choice situation to accommodate changes in the world. And, as those changes move us toward the circumstances I outlined above, to that same extent the contemporary Hobbesian must move toward a liberal position on welfare rights.[19] Insofar as the Hobbesian sees that technological advances have made constant and continuing cooperation necessary for the successful operation of civil society, to that same extent philosophic consistency dictates that he or she abandon the conservatism of Hobbes for the liberalism that characterizes today's most successful civil societies.[20]

Notes

1. For an account of liberalism that ties it to the neutrality principle, see Ronald Dworkin, "Liberalism," in *A Matter of Principle* (Cambridge: Harvard University Press, 1985), and Joseph Raz, *The Morality of Freedom* (Oxford: Oxford University Press, 1986). For an argument that liberalism is not committed to the neutrality principle but to a partial conception of the good, see James Sterba, "Liberalism and a Non-Question-Begging Conception of the Good," in this volume.

2. For an account of welfare-state liberalism, see James Sterba, *How to Make People Just: A Practical Reconciliation of Alternative Conceptions of Justice* (Totowa, N.J.: Rowman & Littlefield, 1988), Chapter 4.

3. John Rawls, *A Theory of Justice* (Cambridge: Harvard University Press, 1971). For an account of the extent to which Rawls succeeds in merging contractarianism with pragmatism, see, C. F. Delaney, "Rawlsian Constructivism: A Version of Liberalism," in this volume.

4. Works that attempt to uncover the logical structure of Hobbes's political thought and argue that, given that structure, Hobbes should have been less antagonistic toward liberalism include David Gauthier, *The Logic of the Leviathan: The Moral and Political Theory of Thomas Hobbes* (Oxford: Ox-

ford University Press, 1969); Jean Hampton, *Hobbes and the Social Contract Tradition* (Cambridge: Cambridge University Press, 1989); and Gregory S. Kavka, *Hobbesian Moral and Political Theory* (Princeton, N.J.: Princeton University Press, 1986).

5. David Gauthier's argument that Hobbesian rational maximizers should become constrained maximizers goes some way toward showing that Hobbesian moral theory can employ a liberal conception of rationality. Gauthier's *Morals by Agreement* (New York: Oxford University Press, 1986) includes this argument, as well as a Hobbesian account of the neutrality principle and a Hobbesian defense of civil rights. For a comprehensive analysis of Gauthier's arguments, see Duncan MacIntosh, "Libertarian Agency and Rational Morality: Action-Theoretic Objections to Gauthier's Dispositional Solution of the Compliance Problem," *The Southern Journal of Philosophy*, 26, no. 4 (1988): 499–525.

6. The leading contemporary Hobbesian contractarian works are Gauthier's *Morals by Agreement* and Jan Narveson's *The Libertarian Idea* (Philadelphia: Temple University Press, 1988). Narveson holds that Gauthier's contemporary Hobbesian theory can be put to good use to defend the substantive political positions found in Robert Nozick's *Anarchy, State, and Utopia* (Oxford: Basil Blackwell, 1974).

7. See Rawls, *A Theory of Justice*, 15, 121.

8. For similar reasons, Hobbesians reject the approach used by Locke and Nozick, the postulation of precontractual moral rights. Narveson, in *The Libertarian Idea*, argues for a Hobbesian approach and then, having adopted a Hobbesian approach, derives principles of justice similar to those advocated by Nozick in the leading neo-Lockean contemporary work, *Anarchy, State, and Utopia*. But Narveson and Gauthier are adamant in their rejection of Nozick's method of postulating natural rights to liberty.

9. Imagine a group of individuals, none of whom is very good at growing food—to the point where even given their best cooperative efforts all will be near starvation—contracting with someone who can easily grow bountiful amounts of varied and delicious food for all. Might he or she not reasonably demand, and get, some concessions? Suppose all the grower asks for is an exemption from society's parking regulations. Would it not be reasonable to grant that?

10. On the conditions of justice, see David Hume, *A Treatise of Human Nature*, Book 3, part 2, section 2, and *An Inquiry Concerning the Principles of Morals*, section 3, part 1. Regarding cooperation, see David Gauthier, "Rational Cooperation" *Noûs*, no. 1 (March 1974), and "Reason and Maximization," *Canadian Journal of Philosophy*, 4, no. 3 (March 1975).

11. *Paradoxes of Rationality and Cooperation: Prisoner's Dilemma and Newcomb's Problem* (Vancouver: University of British Columbia Press, 1985) edited by Richmond Campbell and Lanning Sowden, is an excellent collection of essays on the prisoner's dilemma.

12. On the maximin rule, see Rawls, *A Theory of Justice*, 152–157. On the disaster avoidance principle, see Kavka, 142–44.

13. On this issue, see Hampton, *Hobbes and the Social Contract Tradition*, and Kavka, *Hobbesian Moral and Political Theory*.

14. The maximize-expected-utility principle tells an agent to act on the alternative that has the highest expected utility where the expected utility of an alternative is the sum of the utility of each possible outcome given that alternative times the probability of that outcome given that alternative. Since nothing in the subsequent argument depends on how we assign probabilities to outcomes given alternatives, I won't address the issue here.

15. For a full statement of the principle, see Rawls, *A Theory of Justice*, section 13.

16. On the role of the veto in Rawls's theory, see Ronald Dworkin, "Justice and Rights," in *Taking Rights Seriously* (London: Duckworth, 1978).

17. Rawls, *A Theory of Justice*, section 26.

18. I am grateful to C. F. Delaney for suggesting this line of argument.

19. Pierre E. Trudeau points out that even when we merely anticipate that the next generation of those worst off will have the technology to wreck civil society, we now have reason to help the worst off. See "Prime Minister's Address to the House of Commons on Canadian Foreign Policy," Ottawa, June 15, 1981 (esp. p. 4).

20. An earlier version of this paper was presented to the North American Society for Social Philosophy Conference at the University of Vermont in Burlington, during August 1990. I thank C. F. Delaney and James Sterba for helpful comments. My research was supported by a grant from the Saint Mary's University Senate Research Fund.

11

Liberalism and a Non-Question-Begging Conception of the Good

James P. Sterba

In his inaugural lecture for the McMahon-Hank Chair of Philosophy at the University of Notre Dame, entitled "The Privatization of Good," Alasdair MacIntyre argues that virtually all forms of liberalism attempt to separate rules defining right action from conceptions of the human good.[1] On this account, MacIntyre contends, these forms of liberalism not only fail but have to fail because the rules defining right action cannot be adequately grounded apart from a conception of the good.

Responding to this type of criticism, some liberals have openly conceded that their view is not grounded independently of some conception of the good.[2] John Rawls, for example, has recently made it very clear that the form of liberalism he defends requires a conception of the political good, although not a comprehensive conception of the good.[3] Unfortunately, this defense of liberalism, although helpful, is still inadequate in the light of an even more serious criticism that can be brought against the view. This criticism is that defenders of liberalism cannot give a non-question-begging defense of the particular conception of the good they do endorse. Moreover, this criticism applies both to defenders and critics of liberalism alike because neither has provided a non-question-begging defense of the particular conception of the good they happen to endorse.

Earlier versions of this chapter were presented at the Meeting of the International Society for Philosophy of Law and Social Philosophy, American Section, held in Salt Lake City on October 17–19, 1990 and to the philosophy department of the University of Notre Dame with Alasdair MacIntyre commenting on February 21, 1991.

In this paper, I will sketch a defense of liberalism against this more fundamental criticism. As I see it, there are four necessary elements to an adequate defense of liberalism. First, liberals need to provide a non-question-begging argument for a moral rather than a self-interested conception of the good.[4] Unfortunately, most liberals have not even attempted this task,[5] and it is just where critics of liberalism, such as MacIntyre, have pressed their attack.[6] Second, since most liberals do not limit themselves simply to endorsing negative rights of noninterference but also endorse positive rights (such as a right to welfare and a right to equal opportunity), these liberals need to provide a non-question-begging argument for a conception of the good that includes positive rights as well as negative rights. More specifically, these liberals need to provide a non-question-begging defense of positive rights against libertarians who claim that only negative rights are required. Unfortunately, although many liberals have attempted to defend their view in this regard, most have simply begged the question against the libertarian view.[7] Third, liberals need to provide a non-question-begging argument specifying the economic structure of the society required by the rights they endorse. Specifically, would it be capitalist or socialist and what sort of equality would prevail? Now while liberals have had much to say on this topic, rarely have they based their considerations on premises that are acceptable to both defenders of capitalism and socialism.[8] Fourth, liberals need to provide a non-question-begging argument for enforcing a partial rather than a complete conception of the good. Here, in contrast to the other required elements of an adequate defense of liberalism, liberals have presented an essentially successful non-question-begging defense of their views, but the confusing terminology they have employed has made it difficult for others to appreciate the force of their defense.[9] Accordingly, here I propose simply to eliminate the confusing terminology and recast the underlying defense.

Of course, the defense of liberalism that I propose to provide, like any defense, is embedded in a tradition with its presuppositions.[10] Nevertheless, the basic presupposition of this defense, namely, that views that can be supported with non-question-begging arguments are rationally preferable, is hardly open to challenge.

A Moral Conception of the Good

There is little doubt that providing liberals with a non-question-begging defense of their commitment to a moral rather than a self-interested conception of the good is the most difficult part of defending liberalism. But to see how such a defense is possible, let us begin by imagining that we are as members of a society deliberating over what sort of principles governing action we should accept. Let us assume that each of us is capable of entertaining and acting upon both self-interested and moral reasons and that the question we are seeking to answer is what sort of principles governing action it would be rational for us to accept.[11] This question is not about what sort of principles we should publicly affirm, since people will sometimes publicly affirm principles that are quite different from those they are prepared to act upon, but rather it is a question of what principles it would be rational for us to accept at the deepest level—in our heart of hearts.

Of course, there are people who are incapable of acting upon moral reasons. For such people, there is no question about their being required to act morally or altruistically. But the interesting philosophical question is not about such people, but about people, like ourselves, who are capable of acting self-interestedly or morally and are seeking a rational justification for following one course of action over the others.

Obviously, from a self-interested perspective, the only principles we should accept are those that can be derived from the following general principle of egoism: Each person ought to do what best serves his or her overall self-interest. But we can no more defend egoism by simply denying the relevance of moral reasons to rational choice than we can, by simply denying the relevance of self-interested reasons to rational choice, defend the view of pure altruism that the principles we should accept are those that can be derived from the following general principle of altruism: Each person ought to do what best serves the overall interest of others. Consequently, in order not to beg the question against either egoism or altruism, we seem to have no other alternative but to grant the *prima facie* relevance of both self-interested and moral reasons to rational choice and then try to determine which reasons we would be rationally required to act upon, all things considered.

In this regard, two kinds of cases must be considered. First, there are cases in which there is a conflict between the relevant self-interested and moral reasons.[12] Second, there are cases in which there is no such conflict.

Now, it seems obvious that where there is no conflict, and both reasons are conclusive reasons of their kind, both reasons should be acted upon. In such contexts, we should do what is favored both by morality and by self-interest. Of course, defenders of rational egoism cannot but be disconcerted with this result since it shows that actions that accord with rational egoism are contrary to reason at least when there are two equally good ways of pursuing one's self-interest, only one of which does not conflict with the basic requirements of morality. Notice also that in cases where there are two equally good ways of fulfilling the basic requirements of morality, only one of which does not conflict with what is in a person's overall self-interest, it is not at all disconcerting for defenders of morality to admit that we are rationally required to choose the way that does not conflict with what is in our overall self-interest. Nevertheless, exposing this defect in rational egoism for cases where moral reasons and self-interested reasons do not conflict would be but a small victory for defenders of morality if it were not also possible to show that in cases where such reasons do conflict, moral reasons would have priority over self-interested reasons.

When we rationally assess the relevant reasons in such conflict cases, it is best to cast the conflict not as a conflict between self-interested reasons and moral reasons but instead as a conflict between self-interested reasons and altruistic reasons.[13] Viewed in this way, three solutions are possible. First, we could say that self-interested reasons always have priority over conflicting altruistic reasons. Second, we could say, just the opposite, that altruistic reasons always have priority over conflicting self-interested reasons. Third, we could say that some kind of a compromise is rationally required. In this compromise, sometimes self-interested reasons would have priority over altruistic reasons and sometimes altruistic reasons would have priority over self-interested reasons.

Once the conflict is described in this manner, the third solution can be seen to be the one that is rationally required. This is because the first and second solutions give exclusive priority to one class of relevant reasons over the other, and only a completely question-begging justification can be given for such an exclusive priority. Only the third solution, by sometimes giving priority to self-interested reasons and sometimes giving priority to altruistic reasons, can provide a non-question-begging resolution.[14]

Notice also that this standard of rationality would not support just any compromise between the relevant self-interested and altruistic reasons. The compromise must be a nonarbitrary one, for otherwise it would beg the question with respect to the opposing egoistic and altruistic views. Such a compromise would have to respect the rankings of self-interested and altruistic reasons imposed by the egoist and altruistic views, respectively. Since for each individual there is a separate ranking of that individual's relevant self-interested and altruistic reasons, we can represent these rankings from the most important reasons to the least important reasons as follows:

Individual A		Individual B	
Self-interested reasons	Altruistic reasons	Self-interested reasons	Altruistic reasons
1	1	1	1
2	2	2	2
3	3	3	3
.	.	.	.
.	.	.	.
.	.	.	.
N	N	N	N

Accordingly, any nonarbitrary compromise among such reasons in seeking not to beg the question against egoism or altruism will have to give priority to those reasons that rank highest in each category. Failure to give priority to the highest-ranking altruistic or self-interested reasons would be, other things being equal, contrary to reason.

Of course, there will be cases in which the only way to avoid being required to do what is contrary to your highest-ranking reasons is by requiring someone else to do what is contrary to his or her highest-ranking reasons. Such cases are sometimes called "lifeboat cases." But while such cases are surely difficult to resolve (maybe only a chance mechanism can offer a reasonable resolution), they surely do not reflect the typical conflict between the relevant self-interested and altruistic reasons that we are or were able to acquire. Typically, one or the other of the conflicting reasons will rank higher on its respective scale, thus permitting a clear resolution.

It is important to see how morality can be viewed as just such a nonarbitrary compromise between self-interested and altruistic reasons. First of all, a certain amount of self-regard is morally required or at least morally acceptable. Where this is the case, high-ranking, self-interested reasons have priority over the low-ranking altruistic reasons. Second, morality obviously places limits on the extent to which people should pursue their own self-interest. Where this is the case, high-ranking altruistic reasons have priority over low-ranking, self-interested reasons. In this way, morality can be seen to be a nonarbitrary compromise between self-interested and altruistic reasons, and the "moral reasons" that constitute that compromise can be seen as having an absolute priority over the self-interested or altruistic reasons that conflict with them. In this way, therefore, liberals can provide a non-question-begging defense of their commitment to a moral rather than a self-interested conception of the good.

A Conception of the Good with Positive Rights

Assuming that we have a non-question-begging defense for endorsing a moral rather than a self-interested conception of the good, the next step in the defense of liberalism is to provide a non-question-begging defense of a moral conception of the good that incorporates positive as well as negative rights. Specifically, we need to address the view of libertarians who contend that only a conception of the good that incorporates negative rights is required. To counter the libertarian view, we need to focus on a typical conflict situation between the rich and the poor. In this conflict situation, the rich have more than enough resources to satisfy their basic needs. By contrast, the poor lack the resources to meet their most basic needs even though they have tried all the means available to them that libertarians regard as legitimate for acquiring such resources. Under circumstances like these, libertarians usually maintain that the rich should have the liberty to use their resources to satisfy their luxury needs if they so wish. Libertarians recognize that this liberty might well be enjoyed at the expense of the satisfaction of the most basic needs of the poor; they just think that liberty always has priority over other political ideals, and since they assume that the liberty of the poor is not at stake in such conflict situations, it is easy for them to conclude that the rich should not be required to sacrifice their liberty so that the basic needs of the poor may be met.

Of course, libertarians would allow that it would be nice of the rich to share their surplus resources with the poor. Nevertheless, according to libertarians, such acts of charity are not required because the liberty of the poor is not thought to be at stake in such conflict situations.

In fact, however, the liberty of the poor is at stake in such conflict situations. What is at stake is the liberty of the poor to take from the surplus possessions of the rich what is necessary to satisfy their basic needs. When libertarians are brought to see that this is the case, they are genuinely surprised, one might even say rudely awakened, for they had not previously seen the conflict between the rich and the poor as a conflict of liberties.

Now, when the conflict between the rich and the poor is viewed as a conflict of liberties, we can either say that the rich should have the liberty to use their surplus resources for luxury purposes, or we can say that the poor should have the liberty to take from the rich what they require to meet their basic needs. If we choose one liberty, we must reject the other. What needs to be determined, therefore, is which liberty is morally preferable: the liberty of the rich or the liberty of the poor.

I submit that the liberty of the poor, which is the liberty to take from the surplus resources of others what is required to meet one's basic needs, is morally preferable to the liberty of the rich, which is the liberty to use one's surplus resources for luxury purposes. To see that this is the case, we need only appeal to one of the most fundamental principles of morality, one that is common to all moral conceptions of the good, namely, the "ought" implies "can" principle. According to this principle, people are not morally required to do what they lack the power to do or what would involve so great a sacrifice that it would be unreasonable to ask them to perform such an action, and/or in the case of severe conflicts of interest, unreasonable to require them to perform such an action.[15]

For example, suppose I promised to attend a departmental meeting on Friday, but on Thursday I am involved in a serious car accident that puts me into a coma. Surely it is no longer the case that I ought to attend the meeting now that I lack the power to do so. Or suppose instead that on Thursday I develop a severe case of pneumonia for which I am hospitalized. Surely I could legitimately claim that I no longer ought to attend the meeting on the grounds that the risk to my health involved in attending is a sacrifice that it would be unreasonable to ask me to bear. Or suppose the risk to my health from having pneumonia is not so serious that it would be unreasonable to ask me to attend the meeting (a supererogatory request); it might still be serious enough to be unreasonable to require my attendance at the meeting (a demand that is backed up by blame or coercion).

What is distinctive about the formulation of the "ought" implies "can" principle is that it claims that the requirements of morality cannot, all things considered, be unreasonable to ask, and/or in cases of severe conflict of interest, unreasonable to require people to abide by. The principle claims that reason and morality must be linked in an appropriate way, especially if we are going to be able to justifiably use blame or coercion to get people to abide by the requirements of morality. It should be noted, however, that while major figures in the history of philosophy, and most philosophers today, including virtually all libertarian philosophers, accept this linkage between reason and morality, this linkage is not usually conceived to be part of the "ought" implies "can" principle. Nevertheless, I claim that there are good reasons for associating this linkage between reason and morality with the "ought" implies "can" principle. These are our use of the word "can" (I can't come to the meeting) as in the examples just given, and the natural progression from logical, physical, and psychological possibility found in the traditional "ought" implies "can" principle to the notion of moral possibility found in this formulation of the "ought" implies "can" principle. In any case, the acceptability of this formulation of the "ought" implies "can" principle is determined by the virtual universal acceptance of its components and not by the manner in which I have proposed to join those components together.

Applying the "ought" implies "can" principle to the case at hand, it seems clear that the poor have it within their power willingly to relinquish such an important liberty as the liberty to take from the rich what they require to meet their basic needs. Nevertheless, it would be unreasonable to ask or require them to make so great a sacrifice. In the extreme case, it would involve asking or requiring the poor to sit back and starve to death. Of course, the poor may have no real alternative to relinquishing this liberty. To do anything else may involve worse consequences for themselves and their loved ones and may invite a painful death. Accordingly, we may expect that the poor would acquiesce, albeit unwillingly, to a political system that denied them the right to welfare supported by such a liberty, at the same time that we recognize that such a system imposed an unreasonable sacrifice upon the poor—a sacrifice that we could not morally blame the poor for trying to evade. Analogously, we might expect that a woman whose life was threatened would submit to a rapist's demands, at the same time that we recognize the utter unreasonableness of those demands.

By contrast, it would not be unreasonable to ask and require the rich to sacrifice the liberty to meet some of their luxury needs so that the poor could have the liberty to meet their basic needs.[16] Naturally, we might expect that the rich, for reasons of self-interest and past contribution, might be disinclined to make such a sacrifice. We might even suppose that the past contribution of the rich provides a good reason for not sacrificing their liberty to use their surplus for luxury purposes. Yet, unlike the poor, the rich could not claim that relinquishing such a liberty involved so great a sacrifice that it would be unreasonable to ask and require them to make it; unlike the poor, the

Liberalism and a Non-Question-Begging Conception of the Good 235

rich could be morally blameworthy for failing to make such a sacrifice.

Consequently, if we assume that, however else we specify a moral conception of the good, it cannot violate the "ought" implies "can" principle, it follows that, despite what libertarians claim, the right to liberty endorsed by them actually favors the liberty of the poor over the liberty of the rich.

Yet couldn't libertarians object to this conclusion, claiming that it would be unreasonable to require the rich to sacrifice the liberty to meet some of their luxury needs so that the poor could have the liberty to meet their basic needs? As I have pointed out, libertarians don't usually see the situation as a conflict of liberties, but suppose they did. How plausible would such an objection be? Not very plausible at all, I think.

For consider: what are libertarians going to say about the poor? Isn't it clearly unreasonable to require the poor to sacrifice the liberty to meet their basic needs so that the rich can have the liberty to meet their luxury needs? Isn't it clearly unreasonable to require the poor to sit back and starve to death? If it is, then there is no resolution of this conflict that would be reasonable to require both the rich and the poor to accept. But that would mean that the libertarian ideal of liberty cannot be a moral conception of the good, for a moral conception of the good resolves conflicts of interest in ways that it would be reasonable to require everyone affected to accept. Therefore, as long as libertarians think of themselves as putting forth a moral conception of the good, they cannot allow that it would be unreasonable *both* to require the rich to sacrifice the liberty to meet some of their luxury needs in order to benefit the poor and to require the poor to sacrifice the liberty to meet their basic needs in order to benefit the rich. But I submit that if one of these requirements is to be judged reasonable, then, by any neutral assessment, it must be the requirement that the rich sacrifice the liberty to meet some of their luxury needs so that the poor can have the liberty to meet their basic needs; there is no other plausible resolution, if libertarians intend to be putting forth a moral conception of the good.

It might be objected that the rights that this argument establishes against the libertarian are not the same as the rights endorsed by most liberals. This is correct. We could mark this difference by referring to the rights that this argument establishes against the libertarian as "negative welfare rights" and by referring to the rights endorsed by most liberals as "positive welfare rights." The significance of this difference is that a person's negative welfare rights can be violated only when other people through acts of commission interfere with the exercise of those rights, whereas a person's positive welfare rights can be violated by such acts of commission as well as by acts of omission. Nonetheless, this difference will have little practical import, for once libertarians come to recognize the legitimacy of the negative welfare rights I've defended, then in order not to be subject to the discretion of rightholders in choosing when and how to exercise these rights, libertarians will tend to favor the only morally legitimate way of preventing the exercise of such rights: they will institute adequate positive welfare rights that will then take precedence over the exercise of negative welfare rights. Accordingly, if libertarians adopt this morally legitimate way of preventing the exercise of such rights, they will end up endorsing the same sort of welfare institutions favored by most liberals.

In brief, I have argued that a libertarian conception of the good can be seen to support a right to welfare through an application of the "ought" implies "can" principle to conflicts between the rich and the poor. In the interpretation that I have used, the "ought" implies "can" principle supports such rights by favoring the liberty of the poor over the liberty of the rich. In another interpretation (developed elsewhere), the principle supports such rights by favoring a conditional right to property over an unconditional right to property.[17] In either interpretation, what is crucial to the derivation of these rights is the claim that it would be unreasonable to require the poor to deny their basic needs and accept anything less than these rights as the condition for their willing cooperation.

A Conception of the Good Requiring Socialist Equality

Assuming that we have a non-question-begging defense of a moral conception of the good that incorporates positive as well as negative rights, the next step in the defense of liberalism is to provide a non-question-begging argument specifying the economic institutions required by this conception. In particular, would the conception allow the inequality that is characteristic of capitalism or require the equality that is characteristic of socialism? What I propose to show is that it is the equality that is characteristic of socialism that is required. To keep my argument non-question-begging, I will continue to argue from premises that are acceptable to libertarians.

In view of the argument of the previous section, libertarians would have to accept a right to welfare but they would still want to deny that this would lead to anything like the equality of a socialist state. At most, libertarians would concede that the argument of the previous section shows that a non-question-begging moral conception of the good supports a welfare state but not a socialist state. They would claim that this is because, at least in an affluent society, a right to welfare could be fully secured while inequalities of wealth and privilege incompatible with the socialist ideal of equality remain.

I now hope to show why this is not the case. To begin with, it should be clear that, as libertarians see it, the fundamental rights recognized by them are universal rights; that is, they are rights that are possessed by all people, not just those who live in certain places or at certain times. To claim that these rights are universal rights does not mean that they are universally recognized. Obviously, the fundamental rights that flow from a libertarian conception of the good have not been universally recognized. Rather, to claim that they are universal rights, despite their spotty recognition, implies only that they ought to be recognized because people at all times and places have or could have had good reasons to recognize these rights, not that they actually did or do so.

Nor need these universal rights be unconditional. This is particularly true in the case of the right to welfare, which, I argued in Section 2, flows from a libertarian conception of the good. For this right is conditional upon people doing all that they legitimately can do to provide for themselves and conditional upon there being sufficient resources available so that everyone's welfare needs can be met. Where people do not do all that they can to provide for themselves or where there are not sufficient resources available, people simply do not have a right to welfare.

Yet even though libertarians have claimed that the rights they defend are universal rights in the manner I have just explained, it may be that they are simply mistaken in this regard. Even when universal rights are stripped of any claim to being universally recognized or unconditional, still it might be argued that there are no such rights, that is, that there are no rights that all people ought to recognize.

But how would one argue for such a view? One couldn't argue from the failure of people to recognize such rights because we have already said that such recognition is not necessary. Nor could one argue that not everyone ought to recognize such rights because some lack the capacity or opportunity to do so. This is because "ought" implies "can" here, so that the obligation to recognize certain rights only applies to those who actually have or have had at some point the capacity and opportunity to do so. Thus, the existence of universal rights is not ruled out by the existence of individuals who have never had the capacity and opportunity to recognize such rights. However, it would be ruled out by the existence of individuals who could recognize these rights but for whom it would be correct to say that, all things considered, they ought not to do so. But we have just seen that even a minimal libertarian conception of the good supports a universal right to welfare. And, as I have argued in Section 1, when "ought" is understood self-interestedly rather than morally, a non-question-begging conception of rationality favors a moral conception of the good over a self-interested conception. So for those capable of recognizing universal rights, it simply is not possible to argue that, all things considered, they ought not to do so.

Still, it might be granted that there are universal rights, even a right to welfare, that can be supported by a libertarian conception of the good but still denied that such rights lead to a socialist rather than a welfare state. But to see why this is not the case, consider what would be required to recognize a universal right to welfare.

At present, there is probably a sufficient worldwide supply of goods and resources to meet the normal costs of satisfying the basic nutritional needs of all existing persons. According to former U.S. Secretary of Agriculture Bob Bergland, "For the past 20 years, if the available world food supply had been evenly divided and distributed, each person would have received more than the minimum of calories."[18] Other authorities have made similar assessments of the available world food supply.

Needless to say, the adoption of a policy of supporting a right to welfare for all existing persons would necessitate significant changes, especially in developed societies. For example, the large percentage of the U.S. population whose food consumption clearly exceeds even an adequately adjusted poverty index would have to substantially alter their eating habits. In particular, they would have to reduce their consumption of beef and pork so as to make more grain available for direct human consumption. (Presently the amount of grain fed to American livestock is as much as all the people of China and India eat in a year.) Thus, at least the satisfaction of some of the nonbasic needs of the more advantaged in developed societies would have to be foregone, leading to greater equality, so that the basic nutritional needs of all existing persons in developing and underdeveloped societies could be met. Of course, in order to meet the long-term basic nutritional needs of all existing persons in developing and underdeveloped societies, other kinds of aid involving appropriate technology and training and the removal of trading barriers favoring developed societies would be required.[19] Moreover, once the basic nutritional needs of future generations are also taken into account, then the satisfaction of the nonbasic needs of the more advantaged in developed societies would have to be further restricted in order to preserve the fertility of cropland and other food-related natural resources for the use of future generations. And once basic needs other than nutritional needs are taken into account as well, still further restrictions would be required. For example, it has been estimated that presently a North American uses fifty times more resources than an Indian. This means that in terms of resource consumption the North American continent's population is the equivalent of 12.5 billion Indians.[20]

So unless we assume that basic resources, such as arable land, iron, coal, oil, and such are in illimitable supply, then this unequal consumption would have to be radically altered if the basic needs of distant peoples and future generations are to be met.[21] In effect, recognizing a universal right to welfare applicable both distant peoples and future generations would lead to an equal sharing of resources over place and time. In short, socialist equality is a consequence of recognizing a universal libertarian right to welfare.[22]

It might be objected that this argument falls victim to its own success. If a universal right to welfare requires an equal sharing of resources, wouldn't talented people simply lack the incentive to produce according to their ability when such a right is enforced? But what sort of incentive is needed? Surely, there would be moral incentive for the talented to make the necessary sacrifices if even a libertarian conception of the good requires a right to welfare.[23] Yet, except for those who closely identify with such moral incentives, there would not be sufficient self-interested incentive to accept the equality of resources required by a universal right to welfare. Even so, in light of the argument of Section 1 that a moral conception of the good has priority over a self-interested conception, there is no question of what ought to be done.

A Partial Rather Than a Complete Conception of the Good

Assuming that we have a non-question-begging defense of a moral conception of the good that incorporates positive rights and the equality of resources that is characteristic of a socialist state, the next step in the defense of liberalism is to provide a non-question-begging argument for enforcing a partial rather than a complete conception of the good. Now it is important to note that this is not how the contrast between liberals and their communitarian critics is usually formulated. Instead, liberals are usually said to defend the view that society should be neutral with respect to conceptions of the good, while communitarians are usually said to defend the view that society should enforce a particular conception of the good. For example, according to Ronald Dworkin, "[L]iberalism takes, as its constitutive political morality, that theory of equality [which holds that] political decisions must be, so far as possible, independent of any particular conception of the good life, or of what gives value to life."[24] In contrast, MacIntyre contends that, "Any political society . . . which possesses a shared stock of adequately determinate and rationally defensible moral rules, publicly recognized to be the rules to which characteristically and generally unproblematic appeals may be made, will therefore, implicitly or explicitly, be committed to an adequately determinate and rationally justifiable conception of the human good."[25]

But this way of putting the contrast—liberals favoring neutrality with respect to conceptions of the good, and communitarians favoring commitment to a particular conception of the good—has bred only confusion. What it suggests is that liberals are attempting to be value neutral when they clearly are not. Liberals, like their communitarian critics, are committed to a substantive conception of the good. For example, the political conception of the good that Rawls endorses rules out any complete or comprehensive conception of the good that conflicts with it.[26] It also rules out, without much argument, a libertarian conception of the good.[27] So clearly, in this respect, Rawls makes no claim to being neutral with respect to conceptions of the good.

Rawls further contends that his political conception of the good marks the limits of enforceability. To enforce anything more, Rawls claims, would require "the oppressive use of state power."[28] So for Rawls, as for liberals generally, only a partial conception of the good can be justifiably enforced. This permits the adoption of any complete or comprehensive conception of the good that is compatible with the substantive, yet partial, conception of the good that liberals endorse. And it is only in this limited respect that liberals can be said to be neutral in regard to conceptions of the good. Accordingly, it seems far better to avoid this terminology altogether and simply to describe the liberal view as requiring the enforcement of a partial rather than a compete conception of the good.[29]

But is there any non-question-begging defense of this liberal commitment to enforcing a partial rather than a complete conception of the good? There is, and the defense is fairly straightforward once it is recognized that a complete conception of the good is not monolithic. For part of such a conception can be maintained, and even caused to flourish without any enforcement whatsoever. With respect to this part of a conception of the good, therefore, there would be no moral justification for enforcement. Another part of a complete conception of the good is counterproductive to enforce. So here too there would be no moral justification for enforcement.[30] Still another part of a complete conception of the good cannot be reasonably established as good to those against whom it would be enforced. So here too it would seem there would be insufficient moral grounds for enforcing this part of a complete conception of the good. How could we be morally justified in enforcing a conception of the good upon those who could reasonably object to it?[31] Consequently, at least with respect to these three parts of a complete conception of the good—the part that can be maintained and even caused to flourish without any enforcement whatsoever, the part that is counterproductive to enforce, and the part that cannot be reasonably established as good to those against whom it would be enforced—enforcement is not morally justified. On this account, only a partial conception of the good can be justifiably enforced.

Nor is there anything in the above argument that begs the question against the communitarian view because there is no reason why communitarians should be committed to enforcing a complete conception of the good. In fact, I have just given three very good reasons why communitarians should not be committed to enforcing a complete conception of the good.

Yet, even if one accepts the view that society should enforce a partial rather than a complete conception of the good, this still leaves open the question of what sort of partial conception should be enforced, and here obviously liberals and communitarians might still disagree. Of course, if the arguments of Sections 1, 2, and 3 of this paper are correct, and liberalism can be provided with a non-question-begging defense of a moral rather than a self-interested conception of the good, a conception that incorporates positive rights and the equality of resources that is characteristic of a socialist state, then the domain over which reasonable debate can still take place is considerably narrower in scope than most philosophers today have yet to realize.

Notes

1. *Review of Politics*, 52, no. 3 (Summer, 1990): 344–61.
2. See Carlos Nino, "The Communitarian Challenge to Liberal Rights," *Law and Philosophy* (1989): 37–52; Allan Buchanan, "Assessing the Communitarian Critique of Liberalism," *Ethics* (1989), 852–83; Gerald Doppelt, "Is Rawls's Kantian Liberalism Coherent and Defensible?," *Ethics* (1989): 815–51, and my own work *How to Make People Just* (Lanham, Md.: Rowman & Littlefield, 1988), esp. 58–59 and "Recent Work in Liberal Justice," *Philosophy and Law Newsletter* (1984): 3–11.
3. John Rawls, "The Priority of Right and Ideas of the Good," *Philosophy and Public Affairs* (1988): 251–76.
4. Of course, there are (Aristotelian) ways to understand self-interest so that it includes the moral. In such views, the contrast I am referring to reappears as a contrast between the priorities given different (possible) interests of the self.
5. Rawls, for example, simply assumes egoism away. See John Rawls, *A Theory of Justice*, (Cambridge: Harvard University Press, 1971), 132–36. Other liberals, such as Kurt Baier, Alan Gewirth, and Stephen Darwall, have attempted a defense of this sort, but there are weaknesses in their defenses that need to be overcome. For a survey of such attempts, see my "Justifying Morality: The Right and the Wrong Ways," in James P. Sterba, *Contemporary Ethics* (Englewood Cliffs, N.J.: Prentice Hall, 1989), 138–54.
6. MacIntyre, "The Privatization of Good" and *After Virtue* (Notre Dame: University of Notre Dame Press, 1981), especially chapters 2, 4–5, 17, and the Postscript to the second edition of *After Virtue* (1984).
7. As I did in "Neo-Libertarianism," *American Philosophical Quarterly*, (1978), but see its expanded version in my *Justice: Alternative Political Perspectives*, (Wadsworth, 1979). For a similar mistake, see Allan Buchanan, "Deriving Welfare Rights from Libertarian Rights," in *Income Support: Conceptual and Policy Issues*. ed. Peter Brown, Conrad Johnson, and Paul Venier (Lanham, Md.: Rowman & Littlefield, 1981).
8. See, for example, Ronald Dworkin, "Liberalism," in *Public and Private Morality*, ed. Stuart Hampshire (New York: Cambridge University Press, 1978), 113–43.
9. See John Rawls, "The Idea of an Overlapping Consensus," *Oxford Journal of Legal Studies* (1987), 1–25 and Dworkin, op. cit. Of course, the classical defense of liberalism on this point is John Stuart Mill, *On Liberty* (1859).
10. I take this to be one of the central points of MacIntyre's *Whose Justice? Which Rationality?* (Notre Dame: University of Notre Dame Press, 1988), but what MacIntyre has not yet acknowledged in this book or elsewhere, and what I hope to establish, is that there exists sufficient "common ground" among the presuppositions of various traditions to provide a defense of liberalism.
11. "Ought" presupposes "can" here. Unless the members of the society have the capacity to entertain and follow both self-interested and moral rea-

sons for acting, it does not make any sense asking whether they ought or ought not to do so.

12. For an account of what counts as *relevant* self-interested or moral reasons, see my *How to Make People Just*, 165–66.

13. This is because, as I shall argue, morality itself already represents a compromise between egoism and altruism. So, to ask that moral reasons be weighed against self-interested reasons is, in effect, to count self-interested reasons twice—once in the compromise between egoism and altruism and then again when moral reasons are weighed against self-interested reasons. But to count self-interested reasons twice is clearly objectionable.

14. For a slight qualification, see my "How to Make People Moral" (forthcoming).

15. I first appealed to this interpretation of the "ought" implies "can" principle to bring libertarians around to the practical requirements of welfare liberalism in an expanded version of an article entitled "Neo-Libertarianism," which appeared in the fall of 1979. In 1982, T. M. Scanlon in "Contractualism and Utilitarianism," (in *Utilitarianism and Beyond*, edited by Sen Amartya (London: Cambridge University Press, 1982) appealed to much the same standard to arbitrate the debate between contractarians and utilitarians. In my judgment, however, this standard embedded in the "ought" implies "can" principle can be more effectively used in the debate with libertarians than in the debate with utilitarians, because sacrifices libertarians standardly seek to impose on the less advantaged are more outrageous and, hence, more easily shown to be contrary to reason.

16. By the liberty of the rich to meet their luxury needs I continue to mean the liberty of the rich not to be interfered with when using their surplus possessions for luxury purposes. Similarly, by the liberty of the poor to meet their basic needs I continue to mean the liberty of the poor not to be interfered with when taking what they require to meet their basic needs from the surplus possessions of the rich.

17. See *How to Make People Just*, pp. 92–97.

18. Bob Bergland, "Attacking the Problem of World Hunger," *The National Forum* 69, no. 2 (1979): 4.

19. See Henry Shue, *Basic Rights* (Princeton, N.J.: Princeton University Press, 1980), Chapter 7.

20. Janet Besecker and Phil Elder, "Lifeboat Ethics: A Reply to Hardin," in *Readings in Ecology, Energy and Human Society: Contemporary Perspectives*, ed. William R. Burdi, Jr. (1977), 229.

21. Currently, the United States, which constitutes 6 percent of the world's population, consumes 30 percent of the world's natural resources. There is no way that the resource consumption of the United States can be matched by developing and underdeveloped countries, and, even if it could be matched, doing so would clearly lead to ecological disaster. See *Planet under Stress*, ed. Constance Mungall and Digby McLaren (Oxford: Oxford University Press, 1990) and *World Hunger: Twelve Myths* by Frances Lappe and Joseph Collins (New York: Grove Press, 1986).

22. Of course, a society characterized by socialist equality may not have all the legal trappings of a socialist state. For example, it may not have full communal ownership of the basic means of production. However, in order to guarantee socialist equality, the private ownership of the basic means of production would be so severely restricted by democratic controls that there would be little practical difference between a society with socialist equality and a society with full communal ownership of the basic means of production.

23. One might think that the objection from incentive is that it would prove impossible to motivate people to work for others. But people work for others once they support any kind of a welfare system, and at least in developed societies, the existence of welfare systems are nowhere threatened. Nor, it seems to me, do the recent events in Eastern Europe and the Soviet Union signal a rejection of welfare or even socialist equality. Five months of travelling and lecturing in the Soviet Union and Eastern Europe in 1989 and visits to the Soviet Union in 1990 and 1991 have convinced me that what has been rejected in Eastern Europe and is being rejected in the Soviet Union is widespread corruption and authoritarian control over *everything* by local bureaucrats and ultimately by Moscow.

24. Op. cit., p. 127.

25. MacIntyre, "The Privatization of Good."

26. "The Priority of Right and Ideas of the Good," 264–76.

27. There is some argument for the rejection of libertarianism in "The Basic Structure as Subject," in *Values and Morals*, ed. A. Goldman and J. Kim (Boston: D. Reidel, 1978), 47–71, but what the argument ignores is that in the libertarian view, *fairness* cannot be interpreted as choice from behind an imaginary veil of ignorance.

28. "The Idea of an Overlapping Consensus," 4.

29. Nor do I think that the most defensible form of liberalism is appropriately characterized as a view in which "the right is prior to the good" because when this claim is correctly unpacked, it only asserts that a certain partial conception of the good has priority over any complete conception of the good that conflicts with it. However, what the claim incorrectly suggests is that the right has primacy and independence over both partial and complete conceptions of the good. On this point, see also Will Kymlicka, *Liberalism, Community, and Culture* (New York: Oxford University Press, 1989), Chapter 3.

30. Rawls appears to be endorsing a justification of this sort in "The Idea of an Overlapping Consensus."

31. This line of argument obviously appeals again to the "ought" imples "can" principle.

Index

Ackerman, Bruce, 130
Anscombe, Elizabeth, 55n30
Aquinas, Thomas, 1–2, 8–10, 13–17
Aristotle, 1–2, 8–10, 15–17, 41, 141, 154
Ashcraft, Richard, 207
Augustine, 13

Baier, Kurt, 161
Bakunin, Michael, 107
Barber, Benjamin, 105, 117, 120–27, 131, 135n57
Barry, Brian, 49
Benn, Stanley, 86n5
Bentham, Jeremy, 40
Bergson, Henri, 28
Berlin, Isaiah, 49, 55n22
Berry, Wendell, 16
Borges, Jorge, 16
Broad, C. D., 40
Brook Farm, 60, 71, 79
"burdens of reason," 176, 183

capitalism, 96, 99, 223, 236
Carlyle, Thomas, 63
Channing, William, 79
Chrysostom, John, 13
collectivism, 92–93
community, ix, 8, 12, 30–31, 57–65, 70–71, 74–75, 78, 86n3–5, 94, 113–15, 132, 148–50, 152–54, 186n12

"comprehensive public philosophy," 191, 203–6, 210n42
"comprehensive view," 148–50, 157, 174–80, 197
consensus, 5–6, 10, 39–41, 43, 48, 148–50, 152, 157–58, 161, 165–80, 189–207
consequentialism, 40–41
Constant, Benjamin, 13
constitution, 127–31
constructivism, 137–50
Cover, Robert, 127

democracy, 58–59, 64–65, 67–70, 78, 80–85, 115–27, 139–40, 144, 156–59, 162, 169–76, 178–79, 181, 189–90, 195, 204
deontology, 40
de Paulo, Bella, 7
Devlin, Patrick, 44–45, 51, 55n18
Dewey, John, 190, 202–3
difference principle, 111, 209n41, 219–23
dilemmas, moral, 9
"disintegration thesis," 42–51
Dostoyevsky, Fyodor, 16
Durkheim, Émile, 44–45, 51
Dworkin, Ronald, 4, 53, 240

Economic Justice For All (Bishops' letter), 209n41
elitism, 117–20, 125–27

Ely, John, 105, 128–29
Emerson, Ralph, 62–63, 79
equality, vii, 20, 110, 122–24, 157, 179, 181–84, 193, 195, 222, 236–40

feminism, 33–35
Ferguson, Kathy, 97
Fishkin, James, 49
Fourier, Charles, 75, 77
freedom, vii, 20–22, 47, 95–96, 109–10, 178–84, 193, 195, 223
Friedman, Marilyn, 94
Frost, Robert, 164

Gauthier, David, 225n4–6
Gilligan, Carol, 33–35
good, the, 1–17, 144, 159, 166, 227–41

Hampton, Jean, 190–91, 196–97, 200–201, 204
Hart, H. L. A., 45–48
Hawthorne, Nathaniel, 57–86
Hegel, G. W. F., 153–54
Heidegger, Martin, 28
Held, Virginia, 4
Hobbes, Thomas, 155, 160–63, 168, 170, 185n9, 190, 207, 213–24
Hume, David, 17
Husserl, Edmund, 28

"individual sovereignty," 19–30
individualism, viii, 31, 58, 91–95, 98, 100, 160
intuitionism, 141–42

James, Henry, 63, 65, 74, 78, 84
Jefferson, Thomas, 209n44
Jerome, Saint, 14
justice, 13, 36n9, 104, 108–12, 122–24, 137–40, 143–46, 151–85, 189–207, 213–15, 219

Kant, Immanuel, 17, 21–22, 25–28, 30, 92, 141, 144, 152–53, 183–84, 189, 192, 195, 197, 199, 205, 213
Kanter, R. M., 58
Kekes, John, 42–51
Kropotkin, Peter, 92–93
Kymlicka, Will, 114

Lawrence, D. H., 63, 76, 83
Leibnitz, Gottfried, 141
Leo XIII, 1
libertarianism, 232–36, 243n15
Locke, John, 49, 94, 192, 195, 205, 207
lying, 6–8, 13–14
Lytle, Andrew, 16

Macedo, Stephen, 210n50
MacIntyre, Alasdair, vii, 52, 55n30, 113, 153, 160, 173, 227–28, 240, 242n10
marginalization, 103, 132–33
Marx, Karl, 23, 32–34, 35n1, 37n22–23, 92–93, 97, 99, 107, 128
Melville, Herman, 84
metaphysics, 151–85, 189–90, 196
"method of avoidance," 159, 189
Mill, J. S., 13, 17, 21–22, 49, 53–54, 98, 166, 173, 207
Miller, David, 100
Miller, Perry, 64
modus vivendi, 149–50, 161, 163–68
Moore, G. E., 40–41, 141
moral requirements, 23–27, 34–35
Murray, John Courtney, 197–98

Nagel, Thomas, 27
Narvenson, Jan, 225n6, 8
Nietzsche, Friedrich, 24, 29, 146
Noyes, John, 57, 60, 75, 77

Index

Nozick, Robert, vii, 50, 225n6, 8

objectivity, 146–48, 176
Oneida, 57
original position, 108–9, 145–46, 151

paradox of liberalism, 163–64
Peabody, Elizabeth, 64
Peirce, C. S., 148
perfectionism, 71–73, 82, 192
Pinkard, Terry, 92, 97
Plato, 41, 141, 170
pluralism, 39–54, 140–41, 155–59, 162, 165–66, 168
Pooge, Thomas, 112
Powell, Lewis, 127
Price, Richard, 141

rationality, 5, 8, 11–12, 16, 215
Rawls, John, vii, 4, 50, 104–5, 107–13, 127, 132, 137–50, 151–85, 189–211, 213, 219–23, 227, 240
Raz, Joseph, 189
realism, 143–44, 148
reasonableness, 146, 176–83
Rehnquist, William, 130
respect, 25
rights–theorists, vii–ix
romanticism, 58, 62–65, 72–78, 82, 84
Rorty, Richard, 173, 190–91, 196–97, 201–5, 210n44
Ross, W. D., 40–41, 141
Rousseau, Henri, 98, 192, 195, 205–6, 213
rules, moral, 1–8, 12, 40

Sandel, Michael, vii, 104–5, 107, 113–15, 127, 131, 134n21, 153, 160, 173
Santayana, George, 65
Scanlon, Thomas, 183, 243n15
Schumpeter, Joseph, 105, 117–21, 125–27
Sidgwick, Henry, 141, 208n20
socialism, 236–41, 244n22
Socrates, 169–76
Sterba, James, 91
Stout, Jeffrey, 5–6, 8
subjugation, 23–25
Sunstein, Cass, 130–31

Taylor, Charles, vii, 59
Thoreau, Henry, 60, 62–63, 79
toleration, vii, 48, 150, 162, 164–67, 170–72, 184, 197–99
Trilling, Lionel, 65–67
truth, 14, 142–44, 147–48, 169, 174

utilitarianism, vii, 40–41, 158, 186n17, 192, 199, 213, 221–22

virtue, viii, 13–14

Walzer, Michael, 94, 99
welfare rights, 218–24
Whitman, Walt, 62–63, 83
Williams, Bernard, 48–49, 74
Wolff, Christian, 141
Wolff, Robert Paul, 86n4
Wollstonecraft, Mary, 34, 37n26

Young, Iris, 124

About the Contributors

C. F. Delaney	Professor of Philosophy, University of Notre Dame
Richard F. Galvin	Associate Professor of Philosophy, Texas Christian University
Jean Hampton	Professor of Philosophy, University of Arizona
Alasdair MacIntyre	McMahon-Hank Professor of Philosophy, University of Notre Dame
Thomas Moody	Associate Professor of Philosophy, California State University, San Bernardino
Jeffrey Reiman	William Frazer McDowell Professor of Philosophy, The American University
Nancy L. Rosenblum	Professor of Political Science, Brown University
Thomas W. Simon	Professor of Philosophy, Illinois State University
James P. Sterba	Professor of Philosophy, University of Notre Dame
Sheldon Wein	Associate Professor of Philosophy, St. Mary's University, Halifax, Nova Scotia
Paul Weithman	Assistant Professor of Philosophy, University of Notre Dame